Learning, Through First Hand Experience, Out Of Doors

The contribution which outdoor education can make to children's learning, as part of the National Curriculum

A compendium of articles written over time

PW Keighley

1998

D0896216

Published by National Association for Outdoor Education

Printed by Sheffield Hallam University Print Department

ISBN 1 898555 03 6

Photographs

Simonside Hills: Northumberland
(by kind permission of Northumberland National Parks)

Cat Bells: Cumbria
by the Author

Derwentwater: Cumbria
(by kind permission of Gary Burn)

Stanley Head: Staffordshire
by the Author

Acknowledgements

I should like to acknowledge with a deep sense of gratitude profound thanks to Shirley Payne, Ken Ogilvie, Susan Lamb and Fran Belbin for all their inspiration, help, support and advice throughout the compilation and publication of this book. Without their editorial skills I have no doubt that the ideas contained in these pages might never have been transformed into a typed script. I should also like to thank the many children, friends and other outdoor professional colleagues with whom I have shared many varied and wonderful experiences, all of which to some degree, have both inspired and influenced me in shaping my philosophy of "learning out of doors".

Text and diagrams

Patrick William Keighley: Northumberland

Author's Foreword

This book is a collection of papers and articles, written over a period of time, to support teachers on initial training and 'In Service' courses. It is dedicated to my wife Jenny and my children Hannah and Jonathan, who have been my companions during many of my experiences out of doors. I am grateful for the way they have put up with all the moments of anxiety and frustration during the book's compilation.

It is also written as a tribute to my father, Dr Robert Keighley, who nurtured within me both an inspiration and a love of the great outdoors from a very early age.

Mountain Summit

> Looking down from this mountain top view
> Ripples sweeping across a tarn way below
> Before me 'the edge' - all rocky, bumpy and steep
> Rolling hills to the East all velvet and smooth
> Fields in the distance like a patchwork quilt
> Everything before me is peaceful and still.

> *Hannah Rachel (aged 10)*
> *June 1989*

Perspectives

I have learned to look on nature, not as in the hour of thoughtless youth, but hearing oft times the still, sad, music of humanity; nor harsh, nor grating though of ample power to chase and subdue. And I have felt a presence that disturbs me with a joy of elevated thoughts, a sense sublime, of something far more deeply interfused, whose dwelling is the light of setting suns and the round ocean and the living air and the blue sky ... and in the mind of man.

William Wordsworth - 1807

In these days of indoor and mechanised life, man is beginning to realise that he is in danger of being ensnared by his mode of living and by the power and prodigity of his inventions. He longs for contrast, longs to escape from the artificial to the natural order of things; longs to free himself from mass suggestion and mass hypnotism, from narrow die-hard religious, social and political creeds and dogmas and rejuvenate himself; to seek the purer airs amid the grandeurs and beauties of nature, a physical well being, a mental solace and a spiritual expansion.

The appreciation of natural beauty is an inevitable development. It is part of man's progress. There have always been those who have found joy in the beauty and grandeur of the hills, and a power which comes in the struggle with difficulty and danger. For these reasons the mountains have the power of drawing out the very best that is within us; in them we are given a full measure of perfect contentment.

Frank Smythe - 1946

Those who contemplate the beauty of the earth find reserves of strength that will endure as long as life lasts. There is symbolic as well as actual beauty in the migration of birds, the ebb and flow of the tides, the folded bud ready for spring. There is something infinitely healing in the repeated refrains of nature - the assurance that dawn comes after night and spring after winter.

Rachel Carson - 1961

Contents

SECTION ONE - SETTING THE SCENE

SECTION TWO - OUTDOOR AND ADVENTUROUS ACTIVITIES

SECTION THREE - OUTDOOR ENVIRONMENTAL STUDIES

SECTION FOUR - RESIDENTIAL EDUCATION

SECTION FIVE - RELATED ISSUES AND TOPICS

Preface

I have come to believe that peace, happiness, contentment and fulfilment lie in the appreciation of nature - particularly the natural beauty of the outdoor environment. In my journeys through the natural world, on open water and river, in cave and on rock, in woodland, moor and mountain, I have learned that each environment has a unique capacity for welding into an harmonious whole, an individual's physical, mental and spiritual potential for human development. Each environment has the power to reveal a most fundamental and simple truth - in contrast to the welter of things that are less important, yet often loom so large in our everyday experience.

The enormous benefit and value of developing an intimate appreciation of the outdoor environment, is that people of all ages are able to learn about and discover, beauty, truth and contentment, in many diverse ways. I have benefited beyond words from journeying out of doors and in particular when interacting with nature. All my experiences have provided me not only with healthy exercise and mental stimulation, but also with a challenge and an adventure, often in the most beautiful of surroundings - giving me memories that I know will last a lifetime.

Those who are in tune with nature will never cease to hear her song; be it the song of the high, wild, lonely places, or the song of the might and majesty of the sea; the song of the mystery of the forest glade or the early songs of the open plain and moorland dell. The beauty and rhythm of nature are always on the borderline of consciousness; for beauty lives eternally in the memory - once seen, once known, once experienced ... it is immutable, never to be forgotten.

Beauty and truth are part of the very essence of nature. Such characteristics are largely nurtured and developed in the individual, not just through knowledge and understanding, but more especially through an interaction with nature, often leading to a deep personal relationship with all facets of the natural world. The sensitive mountain traveller does not seek merely to reach the highest summit, so much as to simply be amongst and be part of the natural landscape; the ocean voyager does not seek merely to exploit the power of the wind to accomplish the safe completion of a journey, so much as to experience and become part of the sea's dynamic. The cave explorer does not seek to conquer yet another aspect of the labyrinth of passages, but to be at one with and interact with all the mysteries of the subterranean world.

The sea, the earth, the hills and the sky all stand out as fundamental and basic elements of nature. All are subject to evolutionary changes, but in very different ways from those that order the progress of the human race. To seek inspiration and a solace for our often self-made muddles, amidst the simplicity and quietude of nature; to abide peacefully and harmoniously with those forces of creation which we know to be present, but which we cannot always understand - is one way of finding beauty and truth. To have attained this level of consciousness with the natural world, will not only affect the quality of our lives and those of our children, it will give life a true richness. It may even be that we become more content in our faith and re-affirm a belief in 'the creator'. This is my hope, this is my conviction and the reasons why I do believe young people should be introduced and encouraged to learn in and about the natural world, through first hand experience.

Inspired by the writings of Frank Smythe (1935)

P.W. Keighley

December 1997

Introduction

Events in recent times have demonstrated very clearly that the world in which we live is undergoing the most dramatic changes yet experienced this century. Continuing inflation, high unemployment, advanced technology, political and social unrest, turmoil and confusion in all areas of the public sector highlight some of the complexities facing society at large at the present time. Within the State system of education continuing changes and pressures are constantly being experienced, in terms of central funding, demographic trends, pre- and post-16 education, and in all forms of educational management and administration. These pressures when measured against the relative calm and complacency of the 1960's and 70's have sharply brought into focus the need for a re-appraisal of many of the policies and strategies forced upon local authorities during the past decade. Despite attempts to create legislation for many areas of State Education there is still an urgent need for educationalists to re-examine and consider alternative approaches to the curriculum of schools in order that young people may be sufficiently equipped with the necessary skills which they will require to adapt to the emerging and changing employment patterns of the future.

During the 1980's, largely as a result of political debate, the then Department of Education and Science published a report entitled *Better Schools*. In essence this report highlighted that there was much agreement about the purposes of education. In particular, that pupils should develop lively, enquiring minds, acquire understanding, knowledge and skills relevant to adult life and employment and develop personal and moral values. To serve these purposes the government of the time believed that introducing a National Curriculum for all pupils would ensure that each child would receive a broad, balanced, relevant and differentiated curriculum. It was considered that a curriculum based upon these four principles would serve to develop the potential of every pupil, whether in mainstream or special education, so equipping them for the responsibilities of citizenship and for the challenges of a working life.

The report advocated that the best schools would strive to provide a broad curriculum in which pupils of all abilities would reach high standards. Good schools would turn out young people with self-confidence, self-respect, respect for others, who would be enterprising, adaptable, eager and well-equipped to face the adult world.

At a similar point in time, the Institute of Personnel Management also published a report entitled *Schools and the World of Work*. Great emphasis was again laid upon the importance of education and training in preparing young people for the world of work. The report highlighted the need for schools to prepare its young people with appropriate social, technical and coping skills, having a knowledge of their own strengths and weaknesses and an understanding of the social and economic environment.

In 1989 the National Curriculum was launched as a mandatory requirement for all State maintained schools in England and Wales, to be taught to all pupils between the ages of 4 and 16. Science, mathematics and English were to form the 'core' subjects and history, geography, technology, modern foreign languages, art, PE and music as 'foundation' subjects and also religious education.

Since the introduction of the National Curriculum as many words have been written against as in support of its achievements, in helping to raise educational standards. One thing is certain. The National Curriculum which is now delivered in all schools is anything but broad, balanced, relevant and differentiated. In a climate where prescriptive programmes of study have been identified for each subject, with descriptors for assessment and testing at regular intervals for all pupils throughout both the primary and secondary phases, it is indeed questionable whether any of the original objectives of the *Better Schools* report have, or ever will be, achieved. Many would contend that the National Curriculum has in fact developed into a dinosaur, and that its prescription has not only contributed to inflexibility but sterility. Somewhere between the rhetoric and reality there has been a mismatch; between on the one hand the establishment of a curriculum which was ostensibly about breadth and balance, and on the other which has become narrow and imbalanced.

By contrast in the decade immediately prior to the implementation of National Curriculum many exciting and valuable curriculum initiatives were being developed throughout all phases of education. Experienced-based learning out of doors was not only extremely relevant in meeting the needs of young people, but was generally used to good effect, both in the primary and secondary sectors of education in providing breadth and balance to the curriculum.

The imposition of a National Curriculum, while laudable in some respects as a concept, has been hampered from its inception by bureaucracy, autocracy and political dogma. It has shaken the confidence of teachers and in many instances undermined their professional flair, imagination, creativity and autonomy. Stress levels are at an all time high with many experienced teachers simply looking for a way of escape from the whole plethora of curriculum imposition. People are tired of the weight of documentation now required, they are exhausted by constant external pressures, they are frustrated that there is no longer room for inspirational thinking, for divergent planning; they fear the consequences of taking risks and instituting impromptu curriculum projects which are outside the framework of the "requirements".

It is a great sadness, that many teachers now grappling with the demands of the National Curriculum have had to reassess those educational experiences and opportunities which they used to provide for children within a constant climate of so much pressure and restraint.   Some teachers who have hitherto tentatively subscribed both to the benefits and value of exposing pupils to first hand experiences out of doors, have become disillusioned, and abandoned their beliefs, largely due to the straitjacket of the National Curriculum. Some have sought to find alternative ways of developing teaching and learning strategies which are more manageable within the context of school.   There is substantial evidence that many teachers are now using an increased number of secondary sources in preference to providing first hand experience-based learning opportunities for pupils.

Bearing all these difficulties in mind has given me both the motivation and inspiration to compile this compendium of materials. This book has been written in the fervent hope that the ideas contained within it, may not only be of some value to overburdened teachers in the planning of their work, but demonstrate how experienced based learning out of doors, is one way to reinstate breadth and balance in the curriculum.   More especially, it has been written to enable teachers to have the confidence to engage children in alternative approaches to first hand learning which are perhaps more relevant and meaningful to their needs, and prepare them more appropriately for adult life.

The book is divided into 5 sections. Section 1 outlines the origins of experience-based learning and offers a rationale and framework for outdoor education within the National Curriculum.

Sections 2, 3 and 4 provide examples of curriculum opportunities in outdoor adventurous activities; in outdoor environmental studies; in residential experience at primary and secondary levels.

Section 5 is a collection of articles which highlight a range of issues and strategies associated with teaching and learning in this area of the curriculum.

Section 1

Setting the Scene

Chapter 1

Origins of Experience-based Learning Out of Doors

INTRODUCTION

Experienced based learning is not a new phenomenon in education. As an approach to teaching and learning, the concept of learning by doing has been used by many educators and can be traced back to a number of early exponents of educational theory and practice. Plato and Aristotle believed that knowledge and understanding were best developed in children through first hand experiences. Dewey believed that learning often largely comes about through quality experiences, particularly when interaction takes place between the learner and the environment. Piaget, on the other hand, believed that intellectual and social development are often best achieved through relevant first hand experiences. Good learning also takes place when the learner is not only self-motivated but when the environment provides a focus for interest and stimulation. Much of Rousseau's philosophy of learning stemmed from a conviction that children often progress best when they are encouraged to interact with their natural surroundings and when experiences are not only relevant but first hand.

Experienced based learning, using the outdoor environment clearly has its roots in early educational philosophy. More recently its value and impact upon children's learning and development has been articulated by Hahn. He strongly criticised his native education system, by suggesting that the curriculum bore little or no relation to the age and stages of children's development; that it was neither relevant nor in keeping with their interests. It seems that even in his day, most of the educational reforms were considered to be superficial and inappropriate. One of his constant beliefs was the need for pupils to be educated in a stimulating and attractive environment in order to ensure that learning took place. He considered that "challenge, interaction, awe and a sense of wonder ... of the natural environment" often promoted good learning.

The origins of outdoor environmental studies

The first mention of the potential value and relevance of the outdoor environment for experience-based learning in English educational reform was articulated in the *Haddow Report* of 1927. This report considered the outdoor environment essential for the first hand study of geographical relationships and urged the importance of 'Outdoor Studies' in science, geography, history and nature study. It seems that 'Nature Study' remained as a title for a large range of subjects, projects and excursions, arranged from schools, up to and including the war period. Gradually the term was replaced by 'Rural Studies' and more recently by 'Environmental Studies'.

The *Norwood Report* of 1943 stated that, "it is essential to bring boys and girls in touch with sea and mountain and other open areas". The establishment of the Field Studies Council in 1945, despite being an independent organisation, was to play a significant part in the development of 'environmental education'. A number of specialist field centres were established during the post war period, and many children from education authorities began attending courses in field biology and geography during this time.

During the late 1940s two important parliamentary acts outside Education were to have an effect upon the growth of environmental studies in schools. These were the *Town and Country Planning Act* of 1947 and the *National Park and Access to the Countryside Act* of 1949. The emergence of 'Environmental Education' in schools paved the way for a dynamic approach to the environment by the Nuffield Foundation. Junior science projects were established in schools and the Environmental Studies Development Council was set up, to make recommendations for the use of the environment by schools.

There is evidence that by the early 1960's many primary schools in England and Wales were beginning to make use of the natural environment for projects and topic work generally (Plowden Report). Field studies also began to emerge as an important part of the secondary school system.

The *Newsom Report* of 1963 emphasised the value of residential experience for all children and supported a variety of approaches to the environment, both through Environmental Studies and Outdoor Activities. Contained within the report was the recommendation, that *"by introducing boys and girls to fresh surroundings and by either helping them to acquire new knowledge or try their hand at fresh experience and skills, such an approach to the countryside can provide a general educational stimulus"*.

These recommendations were echoed in the *Plowden Report* of 1966 which stated that *"nearly all children are interested in living forms, whether they be animal or plant. Some physical acquaintance with them is an essential part of being educated"*. *The report went on to suggest that* "an effective way of integrating the curriculum is to relate it through the use of the environment to the boundless curiosity which children have for the world around them". The report also suggested the advisability of involving urban children in an exploration of the countryside by providing residential centres. By 1970 a number of education authorities had acquired premises for 'Residential Education' in the countryside. From many of these 'Field Centres', both environmental studies and outdoor activities began to be undertaken.

The origins of outdoor adventurous activities

In contrast to the Environmental Studies tradition, Outdoor Adventurous Activities embraces all the physical demands made upon the individual within the environment, through a variety of challenging activities, to achieve a notion of self-reliance, co-operation and understanding. The earliest reference made to Outdoor Adventurous Activities by the Board of Education was in 1920, twelve years after the foundation of the Boy Scouts Movement. The Board produced a document entitled *Camping in Education*. This publication expressed the view that campcraft was valued as part of the education process.

Th*e Norwood Report* of 1943 encouraged a wider approach to physical education and stated that, "there should be such other wholesome Outdoor Activities as circumstances of the school allowed". The Report also recognised that other organisations, for example, the Youth Hostels Association, formed in 1920, and the Boy Scout's Association were playing a significant role in bringing boys and girls in touch with the environment; building up moral strength, courage and physical endurance.

The 1944 Education Act was to be the most significant factor in the development of experience-based learning, Outdoor Activities and Residential Education in England and Wales after the war. The Act made it the duty of every local authority to ensure that provision in their locality included "adequate facilities for recreation", and that "organised cultural training and recreational experiences were to be provided". This, being a "recommendation" for all local authorities, led to the formation of educational policy with regard to the establishment of Outdoor Activities. Many local authorities were slow to act on these "recommendations", owing to the financial limitations of the immediate post-war period. Several authorities, however, were able to purchase and convert suitable properties to develop as Outdoor Activities Centres in areas of open country throughout England and Wales.

The establishment of the Outward Bound Schools by Kurt Hahn in 1946 provided schools with a model for the development for outdoor and adventurous activities. The Outward Bound Schools fostered the ideology of "challenge through direct contact with the environment", using a variety of activities which included mountaineering, canoeing, sailing, camping and conservation courses. Experienced based learning was further fostered by the development, in 1956, of the Duke of Edinburgh's Award Scheme, which was constructed to enhance self reliance, initiative and self confidence amongst young people throughout the nation.

The *Newsom Report* of 1963 accelerated the growth of Outdoor Activities in schools and the development of many Local Education Authority (LEA) Centres. The Report recommended the work of Outdoor Centres and suggested that "out of school activities have an advantage of introducing pupils to recreational interests which can be readily carried forward into adult life."

The *Plowden Report* of 1966 further encouraged Local Authorities to make provision of 'Residential Establishments' and emphasised the advisability of involving 'urban children' in countryside outdoor activities. Gradually with the growth in economic prosperity nation-wide, many LEAs acquired property to convert into Field Study and/or Outdoor Activity Centres.

The emergence of outdoor education

In 1975 the Department of Education and Science held a conference at Dartington to look explicitly at the whole field of Outdoor Education, "to examine, identify and explore the general principles and practices of the subject". This conference recognised the differences in the two traditions of first hand learning out of doors in education; between Environmental Studies and Outdoor Adventurous Activities which were increasingly being seen as a unified area of learning.

In the same year Her Majesty's Inspectorate of Schools published a report entitled *Outdoor Education 11 - 16* and concluded that learning out of doors or Outdoor Education, should be regarded as part of the formal intended curriculum for all children - and that residential experiences should also form an essential part of education for all.

A further report on Outdoor Education was published in 1980 by the Schools Council. In reviewing the whole area of outdoor learning, the Council made specific reference to the value of outdoor education within the curriculum, the role of the LEAs in respect of provision and opportunities, and to the beneficial impact of residential experiences for all children in primary and secondary education.

In 1983 *Learning Out of Doors* was published by Her Majesty's Inspectorate (HMI). This survey of the practice of outdoor education and short stay residential experience in education provided yet another stimulus for schools to make wider use of the outdoors in the curriculum for all pupils. This development in educational practice was further reinforced by the publication of the *Hunt Report* of 1989. By means of a 'study project' the Report identified the wide range of provision for outdoor education and the opportunities which existed in Britain for young people to participate in adventure. Almost all LEAs had by this time purchased their own residential and day activity centres, so that children could undertake first hand, experienced based learning, out of doors. However, no one would have believed that the situation would change so radically in the decade that was to follow.

A time of challenge and uncertainty

In 1994, the Sports Council undertook an audit of the provision of LEA centres in England and Wales and indicated that during the previous five to ten years, there had been a massive reduction of residential provision in the order of between 10 and 15 per cent. The reasons for this huge reduction in resources were largely to do with the partial and complete withdrawal of funding by LEAs for outdoor education centres. This action was largely due to the financial pressures faced by local councils in having to redistribute inadequate government funds to meet the requirements of the 1989 Education Act and delegate their centrally held budgets to schools. The results were devastating. One LEA, for example, had to close four of its residential outdoor education centres and thereby reduce the potential capacity for youngsters to experience residential outdoor learning from 19,500 places in 1989 to 4,200 in 1994. Such a pattern was mirrored in many parts of the country.

The marked reduction in LEA provision has been further exacerbated in the mid 1990's by schools making less time available for first hand experiences in the curriculum on a daily basis. For most schools this has been caused mainly by the pressures of delivering the National Curriculum, the difficulties of releasing staff, and costs of supply cover.

It is somewhat ironic, that at a time when the National Curriculum both encourages and supports the notion of young people learning from direct experience, that the provision and relevant resources to engage children in first hand learning have been so savagely reduced. Schools will now have to examine very carefully alternative ways in which young people may encounter experiences out of doors, in order that their learning may be both appropriate and relevant and have breadth and balance. It is hoped that the ideas outlined in this book may foster and encourage many teachers to experiment and explore the potential of using the outdoor environment to engage pupils in first hand learning.

Chapter Two

Outdoor Education: a vehicle for curriculum development

INTRODUCTION

Outdoor Education is an integral part of the whole curriculum and makes a significant contribution to the *National Curriculum*. It is widely accepted as an approach to learning which crosses subject boundaries. Through first hand experiences it encourages greater understanding of relationships between ourselves, others, and the environment in which we live, and provides opportunities for pupils to develop new interests, skills, and cognitive learning. Application and practice give meaning to facts, theory and knowledge, when they are used in the context of human relationships and development.

Apart from opportunities for personal fulfilment and the development of leisure interests, outdoor education stimulates the development of awareness, understanding, self-reliance, self discipline, judgement, responsibility, relationships and the capacity for sustained practical endeavour.

Outdoor Education embraces three interlinked areas of experiential learning: outdoor adventurous activities, outdoor environmental studies and the residential experience. Through *outdoor adventurous activities* young people develop a skill in one or more activity; they develop personally and socially, and develop leisure time interests. *Outdoor environmental studies* promote academic development, an understanding of the natural world, aesthetic awareness and sensitivity towards the total environment. Through *Residential Experience* young people acquire personal and social awareness leading to a range of interpersonal skills *(see Figure 2.1)*.

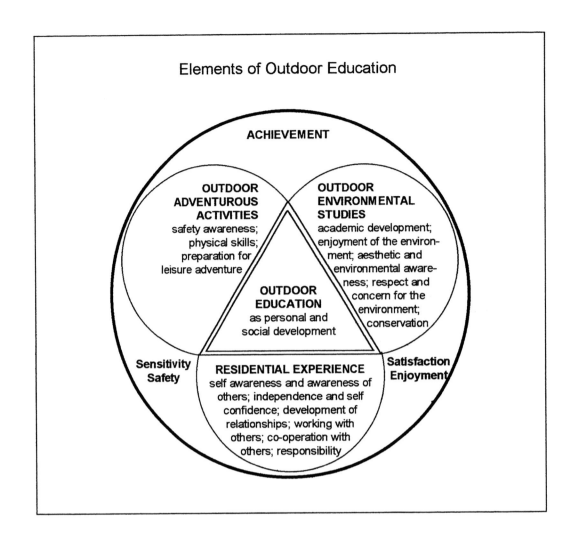

Figure 2.1

Outdoor education appeals to children's curiosity, their sense of adventure and the urge to explore. It is immediate and exciting. Pupils are faced with decisions which have tangible consequences. Shared experiences in the outdoors, especially when linked with a residential experience, encourage positive attitudes and a better understanding of the pupils themselves and with each other. The learning situation is often a concentrated and sharply focused experience.

Bridging the gap between experience and learning is vital to all three elements of outdoor education. Young people should be encouraged at all levels and in all activities to plan, do and review their work. By imaginative and creative follow-up, leaders should ensure that the experiences of the learner are reinforced *(Figure2. 2)*.

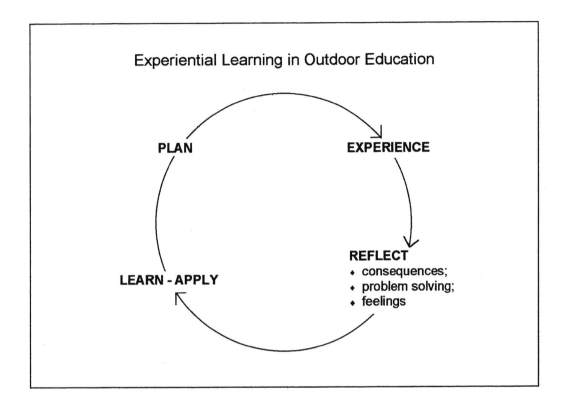

Figure 2.2

Outdoor education within the National curriculum should commence in the Primary School, develop in the Secondary School and continue through to adulthood. Approaches must be relevant for young people of all ages, backgrounds and abilities, including the handicapped. Outdoor education experiences must be progressive, flexible and workable throughout all phases of education. *(Figures 2.3 and 2.4)*

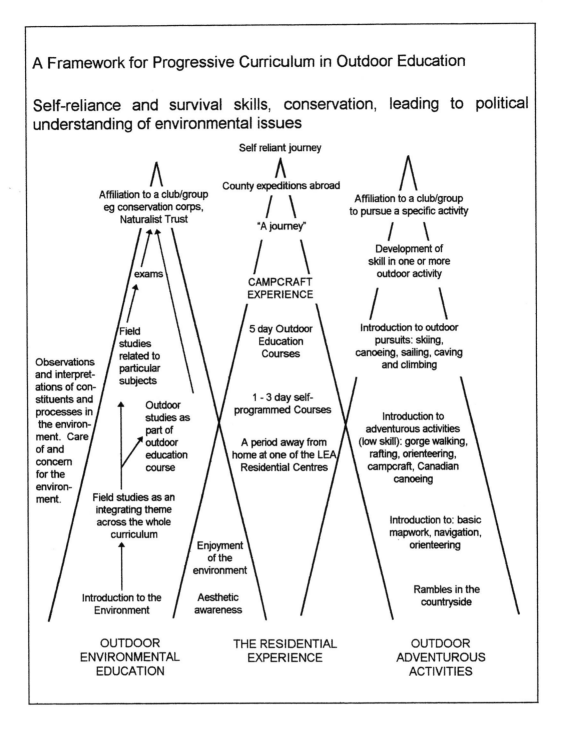

A Framework for Progressive Curriculum in Outdoor Education

Self-reliance and survival skills, conservation, leading to political understanding of environmental issues

Self reliant journey

County expeditions abroad

Affiliation to a club/group eg conservation corps, Naturalist Trust

"A journey"

Affiliation to a club/group to pursue a specific activity

exams

CAMPCRAFT EXPERIENCE

Development of skill in one or more outdoor activity

Field studies related to particular subjects

5 day Outdoor Education Courses

Introduction to outdoor pursuits: skiing, canoeing, sailing, caving and climbing

Observations and interpretations of constituents and processes in the environment. Care of and concern for the environment.

Outdoor studies as part of outdoor education course

1 - 3 day self-programmed Courses

A period away from home at one of the LEA Residential Centres

Introduction to adventurous activities (low skill): gorge walking, rafting, orienteering, campcraft, Canadian canoeing

Field studies as an integrating theme across the whole curriculum

Introduction to: basic mapwork, navigation, orienteering

Enjoyment of the environment

Introduction to the Environment

Aesthetic awareness

Rambles in the countryside

OUTDOOR ENVIRONMENTAL EDUCATION

THE RESIDENTIAL EXPERIENCE

OUTDOOR ADVENTUROUS ACTIVITIES

Figure 2.3

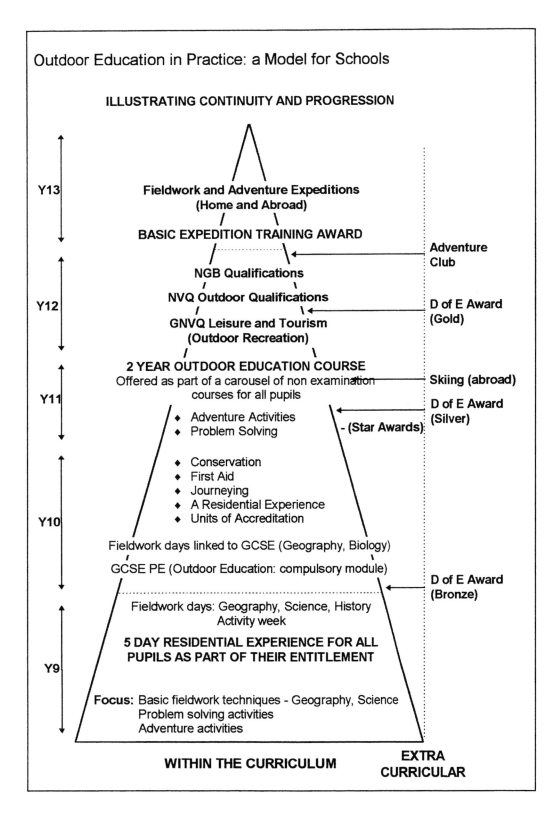

Outdoor Education in Practice: a Model for Schools

ILLUSTRATING CONTINUITY AND PROGRESSION

Y13

**Fieldwork and Adventure Expeditions
(Home and Abroad)**

BASIC EXPEDITION TRAINING AWARD

**Adventure
Club**

NGB Qualifications

NVQ Outdoor Qualifications

Y12

**D of E Award
(Gold)**

**GNVQ Leisure and Tourism
(Outdoor Recreation)**

2 YEAR OUTDOOR EDUCATION COURSE
Offered as part of a carousel of non examination
courses for all pupils

Skiing (abroad)

Y11

**D of E Award
(Silver)**

♦ Adventure Activities
♦ Problem Solving

- (Star Awards)

♦ Conservation
♦ First Aid
♦ Journeying
♦ A Residential Experience
♦ Units of Accreditation

Fieldwork days linked to GCSE (Geography, Biology)

GCSE PE (Outdoor Education: compulsory module)

Y10

**D of E Award
(Bronze)**

Fieldwork days: Geography, Science, History
Activity week

**5 DAY RESIDENTIAL EXPERIENCE FOR ALL
PUPILS AS PART OF THEIR ENTITLEMENT**

Y9

Focus: Basic fieldwork techniques - Geography, Science
Problem solving activities
Adventure activities

WITHIN THE CURRICULUM

**EXTRA
CURRICULAR**

Figure 2.4

27

Outdoor education: its contribution to the National Curriculum

Relevant, direct, first-hand experience is of benefit to all areas of study. Outdoor education enhances all foundation and core subject areas by providing a practical approach to learning in stimulating surroundings. It is in its potential for the development of cross curricular themes, dimensions and skills that outdoor education is able to make a valuable contribution to the whole of the National Curriculum.

One of the main aims of the whole curriculum is to prepare pupils for the opportunities and experiences of adult life. The trust ensuing from a shared experience, perhaps in a strange, challenging or even hostile environment encourages the exploration of personal beliefs, attitudes and values. Working in small groups that are engaged in a collective enterprise encourages the use of all the faculties of each individual as well as the development of group skills.

Education in the outdoor environment is often concerned with discovery, learning processes and outcomes which lead to the development of understanding. Safe movement through an unfamiliar environment develops the skills of questioning, interpretation, decision making, all of which necessitate communication. The ability to assess and respond to changing circumstances is developed by solving problems and reaching varied but appropriate conclusions.

Cross curricular skills of, oracy and numeracy acquire a new significance when they are the tools of planning, carrying out and reviewing a real venture. In this way outdoor education contributes directly to cross curricular themes such as: environmental awareness and responsibility; awareness of economic relationships in urban or rural environments and citizenship.

Outdoor education is cross curricular, as in:

- *dimensions* (personal and social education, multicultural education, equal opportunities);
- *skills* (oracy, numeracy, graphicacy, study, problem-solving);
- the relating of learning to the real world.

  It also contributes to:

- the broadening of the total educational experience;
- the development of a learning experience.

Outdoor education can also be subject based. For example, physical education and geography use approaches which use outdoor education. Outdoor education is used in the core subjects of mathematics, English, science and in foundation subjects such as history, geography, technology (including design) and art. Music and modern foreign languages are taught on occasions through outdoor education processes. Aspects of religious education can well be explored in outdoor education programmes.

Outdoor education can thus be an effective approach to learning and utilised at every stage and in every phase of the education process.

Outdoor education: delivering the National Curriculum and supporting the whole curriculum.

In general, outdoor education tends to be cross curricular. However, it can, where necessary and appropriate, be closely defined to achieve specific objectives. Six principal inter-related components can be identified. They are:

- Personal reaction to the environment itself, either through inspiration or sensory experiences which enhance the understanding of natural processes.

- Reaction and concern for the environment, through environmental awareness. Outdoor education gives opportunities for developing feeling, understanding and concern for the environment which leads to personal commitment to improve the environment. This contributes to the cross curricular theme of environmental education.

- The active use of the environment for physical education and recreation. Physical skills, such as those used in rock climbing and canoeing relate specifically to the foundation subject of physical education.

- The active use of the environment, whether rural or urban, wasteland or woods, geographical or biological as sources of objective study, through field studies. The knowledge, understanding and skills involved are directly related to core and foundation subjects.

- The residential experience is an element which can significantly enhance all the previous components and has additional educational benefits.

- The contribution outdoor education makes through all these elements, to develop pupils' spiritual, moral, cultural, personal and social education. Personal and social skills can be effectively developed through problem solving, decision making, teamwork and living together in the outdoors.

A few examples:

(a) Living and moving together in the outdoors encourages awareness of others. Guidelines for living and safety need to be accepted by all involved.

(b) A residential experience provides opportunities for pupils to be involved in wide ranging discussions. It may involve individuals in facing up to emotional and social issues, as well as problems, particularly when they are in small groups. Health and safety matters have to be learned. Hygiene, first aid, safe handling of themselves and equipment are all important and seen as relevant.

(c) Learning out of doors brings pupils up against real issues, for example: land uses, difficulties of access and environmental problems.

(d) Specific curriculum areas, for example mathematics, geography and history all make use of the outdoors in mapwork, through the compilation of statistics and calculations using information technology.

(e) The use of language is often stimulated when guide books are used, letters are written, research carried out; all giving real purpose to studies and experiences.

(f) The observation of scientific processes occur out of doors in meteorology, geology and biology.

(g) The design and making of equipment, clothing, use of measuring instruments, are all included in many outdoor programmes.

(h) Outdoor education can develop aesthetic awareness. Powerful experiences in a naturally beautiful setting can evoke a strong and moving response. The grandeur of nature is uplifting for the spirit and leads to speculation about the mysteries and meaning of life.

Some examples of curriculum approaches

(i) Infant and Junior Schools (Key Stages 1 and 2)

Outdoor education is of considerable value in Infant and Junior Schools and is often related to topics and themes. It may be combined with a residential experience. It is frequently approached:-

- as part of physical education;
- as an important part of a combined studies/humanities programme or topic;
- as part of the personal and social education programme;
- as part of spiritual, moral and cultural development.

(ii) Secondary Schools (Key Stages 3 and 4)

Outdoor education contributes to several areas of learning in the secondary school. For example it can be considered:

- as a discrete area on its own;
- as part of physical education;
- as a support for examination fieldwork and art/craft projects;
- as part of the personal and social education programme;
- as part of a residential experience.

It may also be approached either as a combination of any one or all of the above.

Examples of allocations of time for outdoor education within the curriculum

(i) Infant and Junior School Phase

Outdoor education is used:

- as a prominent element of environmental studies, or as part of a topic or project;
- as part of outdoor and adventurous activities in the PE curriculum;
- through a programme of day excursions to environments where features of scientific, historical or geographical interest are studied;
- through a programme of visits to an LEA or out of County centre on a day or residential basis.

(ii) Secondary School Phase

Outdoor education is used:

- as timetabled provision when resources, staff, and staffing expertise have been identified;

- as timetabled provision when resources, staff, and staffing expertise have been identified;

- as part of a programme of physical education which provides challenging experiences in a variety of outdoor environments;

- through day excursions which feature particularly worthwhile opportunities for study in a range of subject and cross curricular areas;

- through a programme of structured visits to an LEA centre on a day or residential basis within a programme of personal and social development or specifically as part of BTEC or GNVQ programmes;

- as part of a training programme connected to a Work Experience module.

(iii) All Phases of Education

Outdoor education is used:

- as part of a programme of foreign travel where language study is combined with the opportunity to extend knowledge of overseas environments and other cultures;

- as part of a flexible timetable which occasionally is suspended for a week to offer a whole range of different educational activities, some of which could be outdoor and residential opportunities;

- as part of the pastoral activities organised by a class or year tutor;

- as part of the extended curriculum (this will greatly depend upon both the goodwill of staff, the flexibility of the school's directed time and the presence and skills of Youth Service staff);

- as part of an after school activity to a rural or urban environment;

- as part of an organised venture offering camps, activities and journeys at weekends or in holidays, either in Britain or abroad.

Section 2

Outdoor and Adventurous Activities in the National Curriculum

Chapter 3

A conceptual framework for outdoor and adventurous activities in the National Curriculum.

INTRODUCTION

Traditionally, the term outdoor and adventurous activities applied to a wide range of potentially hazardous activities out of doors, which involved some degree of physical challenge and risk. Most often the focus was upon the acquisition of the physical skills of a particular activity and on developing a person's confidence to cope in a variety of environments. While such an approach still has its place in the National Curriculum, the concept has been widened to embrace the development of young peoples' personal, social and environmental awareness.

In the context of National Curriculum the aims of outdoor and adventurous activities should be:-

- To provide young people with the opportunity to participate in a series of outdoor adventurous activities carried out in a challenging progression.

- To develop aspects of their personal, social and environmental awareness.

- To provide opportunities to develop lasting leisure activities.

- To experience adventurous, mentally challenging and physically demanding situations within a framework of safety.

Personal Development

- To develop personal confidence through the mastery of physical skills and techniques developed in the outdoor environment.

◆ To develop personal awareness and sensitivity to others.

Social Development

◆ To stimulate awareness of group interdependence.

◆ To provide opportunities for developing leadership skills.

◆ To enhance staff/student relationships through shared experiences.

Environmental Development

◆ To develop awareness of the impact of outdoor adventurous activity upon the natural environment and a sensitivity to the implications of one's involvement within it.

A rationale for outdoor adventurous activity in the National Curriculum

Outdoor adventurous activities now feature as an entitlement for all pupils at Key Stages 2 - 4 within the Physical Education National Curriculum *(Figure 3.1)*.

At a time when social and life skills are viewed as an integral and valuable part of the school and college curriculum, outdoor adventurous activities are regarded as being of direct relevance and importance in providing young people with a stimulating and challenging environment and offering a quality and depth of experience which is entirely unique. Furthermore, the process of acquiring the varied and physical skills needed for participation in outdoor adventurous activity provides many valuable opportunities for personal development and fulfilment. Developing positive life-long leisure interests complement the learning planned by and within the organisation and can utilise the invaluable environmental resources which most schools have close at hand.

Outdoor and Adventurous Activities in the Context of the PE National Curriculum (Revised Orders 1995)

Programmes of Study for Key Stages 2 - 4

Key Stage 2

A   to perform outdoor and adventurous activities, e.g. *orienteering exercises*, in one or more different environments, e.g. *playground, school grounds, parks, woodland, seashore*;

B   challenges of a physical and problem solving nature, e.g. *negotiating obstacle courses*, using suitable equipment, e.g. *gymnastic or adventure playground apparatus, whilst working individually and with others*;

C   the skills necessary for the activities undertaken.

Key Stage 3

UNIT A	A	to perform at least one outdoor and adventurous activity, either on or off the school site;
	B	to apply the techniques and skills specific to the activity or activities undertaken;
	C	to plan and review the activity or activities undertaken
UNIT B	D	to perform at least one other outdoor and adventurous activity, including, where possible, off-site work in unfamiliar environments;
	E	a variety of roles in each activity, including leading, being led and sharing.

Key Stage 4

A   to prepare for and undertake a journey safely, encompassing one or more activities, e.g. *canoeing, rock climbing*, in an unfamiliar environment;

B   to develop their own ideas by creating challenges for others;

C   increasingly complex techniques and the safety procedures appropriate to the activity or activities undertaken;

D   the effects of nutrition and climatic conditions on the body, through the activity or activities undertaken, and be aware of and respond to changing environmental conditions.

Figure 3.1

A progressive programme of adventurous activities offers major physical and intellectual challenges in real life situations, where self-discipline and a sense of responsibility can reduce danger to safer levels. They encourage an outward looking attitude, develop curiosity, tenacity and resourcefulness through problem solving activities. The discovery of personal strengths and limitations in a challenging and sometimes hostile environment can lead to heightened self confidence and self respect. It also increases sensitivity and understanding of the strengths and weaknesses of others in the group, promoting valuable opportunities for developing skills of leadership, tolerance, co-operation and decision making. The development of close and personal relationships between adult and young person and the mutual respect and confidence thus established, can do much to extend the opportunities for personal and social development.

Whilst outdoor adventurous activities may justifiably be included in the curriculum simply for its own sake in terms of personal, social and physical fulfilment and achievement, it can additionally make a valuable contribution to some of the essential areas of experience identified in the National Curriculum. For example many outdoor activities require the acquisition of mathematical skills in their planning and execution, where the consequences of ignorance or error are more serious than a cross in an exercise book. Conversely, activities which require calculation, measurement, understanding of scale, estimation and a feeling for space and distance can help to give meaning to mathematical concepts. Respect for and understanding of scientific principles can be developed and natural phenomena observed, recorded, predicted and tested. Activities can provide stimuli for creative writing, art, drama, aesthetic appreciation and spiritual development as a result of the need to respond to new experiences and heightened sensitivities to the environment and the implications of one's involvement. Participation should also foster an appreciation and sensitivity to the responsibilities of one's own specific involvement, to the impact of activities in general on the natural environment and the problems of leisure, conservation, economic and human use.

The links thus forged between outdoor adventurous activity, in a variety of subject disciplines and other educational experiences gives rise to the production of lasting values and opportunities already outlined. Never before has the demand for active use of leisure been so important. Schools provide one of the most significant pathways of introduction to leisure activities. A wide variety of activities can be offered to stimulate interests which can be continued into adult life.

Outdoor adventurous activities offer the opportunity for young people to take part in open air experiences, providing situations of varied difficulty so that all may participate at their own level of ability.

38

Activities promote a healthy way of life and impart a sense of well being, overcoming lethargy and developing physical, mental and emotional stamina. Total personal involvement through endeavour, exploration, discovery and adventure is demanded in socially acceptable forms of physical expression.

Experiences should be frequent, sufficiently intense, planned in sequence and evaluated if such objectives are to be achieved. The establishment of a basic core of knowledge, understanding, awareness and skills should start to be laid down in the primary school, providing opportunities for growth and development throughout an individual's education and creating a foundation from which deeper studies and skill learning can take place. When combined with a residential experience and outdoor environmental studies, outdoor adventurous activities offer an integrated approach to learning and should be an integral part of every young person's educational experience.

Outdoor Adventurous Activity Within The Physical Education National Curriculum

The following guidelines illustrate those activities and approaches which may feature as part of the programmes of study at Key Stages 2 - 4 (Figure 3.2). Teachers should understand very clearly that personal and social education should feature as an integral aspect of all adventurous activities within the National Curriculum and not regard the acquisition of skills as an end in itself.

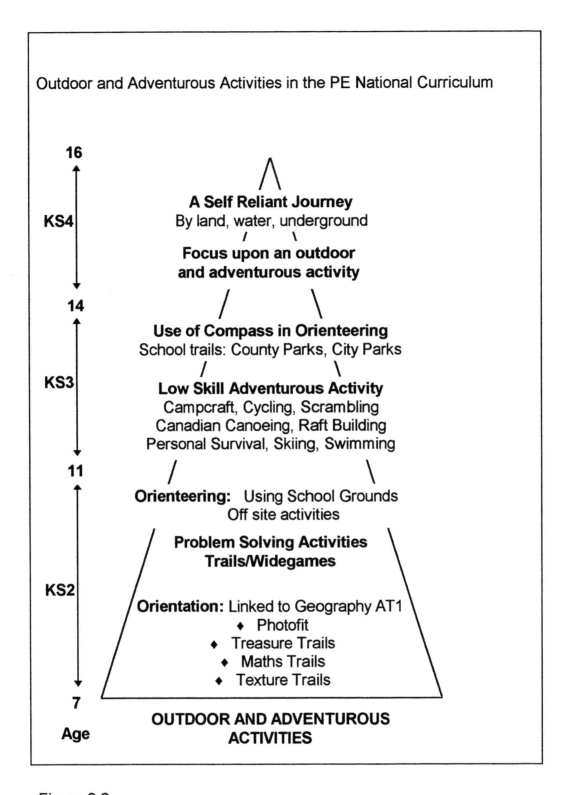

Outdoor and Adventurous Activities in the PE National Curriculum

16

KS4

A Self Reliant Journey
By land, water, underground

**Focus upon an outdoor
and adventurous activity**

14

Use of Compass in Orienteering
School trails: County Parks, City Parks

KS3

Low Skill Adventurous Activity
Campcraft, Cycling, Scrambling
Canadian Canoeing, Raft Building
Personal Survival, Skiing, Swimming

11

Orienteering: Using School Grounds
Off site activities

**Problem Solving Activities
Trails/Widegames**

KS2

Orientation: Linked to Geography AT1
♦ Photofit
♦ Treasure Trails
♦ Maths Trails
♦ Texture Trails

7

Age

**OUTDOOR AND ADVENTUROUS
ACTIVITIES**

Figure 3.2

Suggestions of how it can be implemented

a.   *Key Stage 2*

In the early years of a child's experience in the primary school, much of the adventurous activity should ideally be focused upon the immediate environment and those of the school grounds.

Activities may include:

♦   *Orientation:* involving the development from basic map reading skills which starts from interpreting classroom plans to school building plans; to 'site' plans to ordinance survey maps of the local area. Skills involved will be those associated with basic map reading to negotiate routes between several points identified by simple clear markers placed in the ground at strategic points.

♦   *Night-lines:* this is an adventurous activity which involves children negotiating their way blindfold along a rope laid between and around a number of objects on the playing field or on the school playground or within a local woodland.

♦   *Tracking, treasure hunts and other 'wide games'* provide unique opportunities for children to undertake a range of adventurous activities in a familiar environment.

♦   *Campcraft:* involving the basic skills of siting and tent pitching and in designing and constructing simple shelters.

In the latter years of Key Stage 2, activities can be more challenging and be undertaken on site or some distance away from school.

Activities may include:

♦   *Cycling activities:* which have a clear progression and are built into a planned sequence of journeys.

♦   *Walking in the countryside:* which develops children's skills of map reading and the introduction of the skills of first aid and personal survival within new and differing environments.

♦   *Basic scrambling* on outlying edges, coastal environments, boulders and on artificial surfaces.

♦   *Basic problem solving* activities in the context of an expedition, journey or role play scenario.

♦   *Skiing,* whether on artificial matting and/or on local fells, in Scotland or abroad, should also feature as an appropriate activity within the Physical Education Curriculum.

b.   Key Stage 3

At secondary school level most students, having experienced a foundation of outdoor and adventurous activities in the primary school, should be able to tackle at least two major adventurous activities. The level of provision and opportunity will largely depend upon *(a)* the availability of qualified expertise of the staff, *(b)* the resources available locally and *(c)* the equipment which the school may have on site, or nearby.

Low level skilled activities may include:

♦   *Orienteering:* at this level students should not only be able to navigate with some precision using maps and compasses, but they should be encouraged to embark upon competitive events. Activities should not only be confined to school grounds but also utilise unfamiliar environments.

♦   *Personal survival:* these activities should include some elements of personal survival, competence in map reading, packing a rucksack, camp craft, fitness, equipment, access and conservation.

♦   *Basic hill walking:* this activity should include some elements of personal survival, competence in map reading, packing a rucksack, camp craft, fitness, equipment, access and conservation.

♦   *Cycling:* provides many opportunities for students to undertake a self reliant journey which should involve awareness of safety considerations, knowledge of the highway code, fitness, stamina, accident procedure, navigation and technical knowledge of how to carry out basic repair and maintenance of cycles.

♦   *Campcraft:* although students embarking upon personal survival and hill walking activities may have touched upon elements of this activity the development of campcraft skills is an activity in itself. Elements should include the appreciation of sites, levels, drainage, knowledge and skills of cooking, materials, design and method of tent improvisation.

High level skilled activities:

The following activities will require staff to be experienced, qualified and validated. All the activities have equipment, staffing and resource implications.

Activities may include:

Canadian Canoeing
Kayaking
Caving
Rock Climbing
Mountaineering
Sailing
Skiing
Swimming
Wind Surfing

c. Key Stage 4

By the time secondary school students embark upon this level of the PE National Curriculum, they should have accumulated sufficient skills and expertise to be able to undertake a journey of a specific duration using a particular mode of transport with which they are fully conversant. At Key Stage 4, for those students opting for adventurous activities in the PE Curriculum, the adventurous journey should feature as the main focus of activity. While this may not appeal to all students, some may wish to continue to specialise in an activity at a high level. The execution of a 'journey' would satisfy all the demands of the PE Programme of Study. In judging the merits and suitability of all adventurous journeys, staff should ensure that the following criteria are met:

♦   To have the most beneficial effect and value, the journey should ideally last for at least a 36 hour period.

♦   Based upon the student's previous experience they should largely determine what mode of transport is used.

♦   Students should largely determine the nature, length and complexity of the journey, in collaboration and with the approval of their tutor.

♦   Group sizes should not be less than four or five people and no more than eight.

♦   Ideally, students should undertake their adventurous journey in unfamiliar territory, to include an overnight experience away from home, school and known environments.

♦   In devising their adventurous journeys students must observe both the country code, LEA safety guidelines and be aware of school policies.

♦   No journey should engage students in terrain or experiences with which they are familiar.

- Students should be completely self sufficient during the entire journey carrying their own equipment, food, clothing and shelter.

- Staff should supervise from a distance, giving students the feeling that they are self-reliant.

- Supervising staff should have some knowledge of the area and terrain being used for the journey.

- The whole experience should be evaluated to determine whether the objectives have been achieved.

Chapter 4

Orientation as part of Outdoor Adventurous Activities in the National Curriculum particularly at Key Stage 2.

INTRODUCTION

In the days before the implementation of the National Curriculum primary school teachers devised many excellent strategies for teaching children a wide range of skills and concepts using a 'topic based' approach. As a way of coping with the plethora of attainment targets and programmes of study demanded in the original 'orders' of the National Curriculum, much of this good practice remains, demonstrating the amazing enterprise and resourcefulness of teachers.

With the advent of the 'new orders' - 'post Dearing', little has changed. Many of the pressures still abound and teachers continue to look towards ways in which certain areas of learning can best be achieved through a cross curricular approach.

Orientation, both as a concept and as an area of learning, has been enormously successful during the period of the National Curriculum, because it has been used to deliver an important aspect of Outdoor and Adventurous Activity, and more importantly, because it has availed teachers of the opportunity of developing and reinforcing skills and concepts in Maths, English and Geography.

The purpose of this chapter is twofold. On the one hand it attempts to illustrate a range of activities which teachers can use to deliver outdoor and adventurous activities at Key Stage 2, but it also illustrates those cross curricular links with other subjects highlighting the range of possible learning outcomes achieved through orientation projects generally.

A Rationale

Orientation is an activity in which a 'base map' or 'ordnance survey map' is used to make decisions upon a route to a destination. The challenge for children is that of solving a 'route' problem efficiently and speedily, in order to reach the correct destination. The value of orientation activities are that they rapidly help youngsters to develop a whole range of skills, knowledge and understanding, to include map orientation, symbols, references, cardinal points, estimation, problem solving, co-ordinates, measuring, pacing and route finding. They can also be used to develop the skills of sharing ideas, describing events, observing... the list is endless! Many of these concepts feature as part of the programme of study in the 'new orders' of the National Curriculum, particularly in geography, PE, English and maths (see figure 4.1). However, more importantly, orientation activities are highly motivating and enjoyable. They help to develop young people's self esteem; their confidence, self reliance, co-operation, tolerance, sensitivity, leadership and teamwork skills. They foster decision making and problem solving skills, all so necessary in furthering pupils' personal and social development and in them helping become rounded and well adjusted individuals.

Geography

Geographical Skills

- Making plans/maps
- Scales
- Symbols/keys
- Co-ordinates
- Grid references
- Measuring distance/direction
- Following routes

Mathematics

- Use of diagrams/maps
- Searching for patterns
- Co-ordinates
- Solve problems
- Apply measuring skills
- Estimation of distance
- Use appropriates units of length/measurement

Orientation
in the Curriculum KS2

'Programmes of Study'

Physical Education

Outdoor and Adventurous Activities

- Orienteering exercises in differing environments
- Challenges of a problem solving nature
- Developing skills to participate in other activities

English

Speaking and Listening

- Sharing ideas
- Developing insight
- Describing events
- Observing situations
- Roles

Figure 4.1

46

Starting Out

Orientation as a concept and as an approach to teaching and learning should not be ignored throughout Key Stage 1. Writ large in the geography orders is the notion that pupils should:

Geography P.O.S. KS1

♦ Undertake fieldwork activities in the locality of the school, mapping the school and playground.

♦ Make maps and plans of real and imaginary places using pictures and symbols.

♦ Use plans and maps at a variety of scales ... and follow a route."

Orientation activities can be an extension to many of the programmes of study throughout Key Stage 1, in a number of subject areas. Tasks can be used to reinforce and develop skills, knowledge and understanding of maps, mapwork and in number and estimation, in a very practical way.

Foundations

Key Stage 1 - Activities

Despite the implementation of the National Curriculum, one cannot assume that pupils will always have undertaken work in this area at Key Stage 1, or that pupils will have been introduced to the notion of what a plan/map represents. For this reason a number of simple activities are suggested which could be used either to introduce, or to reinforce pupils' understanding of maps and plans.

Example 1 - Creating a table-top map/plan

Pupils use an A3 sheet of paper which is placed on the top of their own desk or table. Get them to place a number of items on the paper (for example, a ruler, pencil, rubber, book, cup, pencil case, yoghurt top). Suggest that pupils either draw round the objects, or attempt to draw them as far as they are able, to scale. On removal of the objects children begin to develop the idea of what a map is.

Example 2 - A classroom map/plan

By using either a trundle wheel or tape measure or indeed by just pacing the length and breadth of the classroom, pupils construct a basic plan of their own classroom. Follow this by suggesting that they locate all the desks and chairs and other large objects in the correct places, if possible to scale and using a key to provide information of the details.

Example 3 - Drawing an imaginary map

Lay down 'hula hula hoops' to delineate an area often outside the classroom. Pupils construct their own 'make-believe' maps. Give each child a large piece of paper (A3) on which a large circle is superimposed in bold felt tip pen. The children record what they see to scale as far as possible, using a key for symbols. Dividing the circle into quadrants will help pupils to draw their map to scale.

Example 4 - Constructing a map using co-ordinates

Some schools may have painted grids marked out on the playground. For those who do not, an area of paving slabs can be just as effective. The purpose of this activity is to create a grid 5 x 5 squares for pupils to map. Pupils place a variety of objects into the grid (for example a bench, a mat, books, pots etc). Pupils record what they see in the right place and to scale. Provide pupils with graph paper to make the task a little easier.

Example 5 - A plan of school (external area)

Pupils make a plan of the school. If the school is very large or complicated this is difficult. Provide tape measures, and/or trundle wheels, or encourage the use of "pace" to measure the length and breadth of the school building. Again, provide pupils with map paper.

Development

Key Stage 2

By the end of Key Stage 1 pupils should have developed some level of skill and knowledge in mapwork and in the construction of plans. They should be able to plan a route and follow directions. They should demonstrate some knowledge and understanding of plans - what they are, what they represent and have some idea of scale and symbols. With these foundations laid, pupils are now able to begin to develop their understanding of orientation - the ability to place a base map into the correct position and interpret the information to enable travel from one point to another efficiently.

Outlined in the following section are a number of activities and projects which may be used to develop pupils map work skills, knowledge and understanding. While all the activities closely relate to the programmes of study in several curriculum areas, the exercises specifically address key elements of the geography and PE (outdoor adventurous activities) programme of study (*figures 4.2 and 4.3*).

Geography

Key Stage 2 (POS)

◆ Make plans and maps at a variety of scales using symbols and keys.

◆ Use and interpret maps and plans at a variety of scales to include use of co-ordinates, four figure grid references, measuring direction and distance, and following routes.

Figure4. 2

Physical Education in the National Curriculum

Programme of Study

Outdoor and Adventurous Activities Key Stage 2

Pupils should be taught:

◆ to perform outdoor and adventurous activities, e.g. orienteering exercises in one or more different environments, e.g. playground, school grounds and where available parks, woodland or seashore;

◆ challenges of a physical and problem-solving nature, e.g. negotiating, obstacle courses using suitable equipment, e.g. gymnastic or adventurous play apparatus, plans, boxes or ropes whilst working individually and with others;

◆ the skills necessary for the activities undertaken.

Figure 4. 3

49

Learning outcomes

Using orientation several learning outcomes can be achieved. As a result of the activities suggested it is expected that pupils will make gains in map reading and observation skills. It is also likely that pupils will have gained sufficient knowledge and understanding to:

♦   plan a route;

♦   make quick decisions;

♦   respond to set tasks;

♦   orientate a map.

Some ideas for consideration: KS2

1.   Phototrail54

This activity involves pupils in recognising a number of photographs of the external features of their school building or unit. The object is for children to locate the relative position of each photograph onto a base map provided. Photographs can be taken of doors, windows, gutters, aerials, drain pipes, lights, bricks, skylights, notices and even graffiti. The purpose of the exercise is to use the activity to develop pupils' observational and locational skills. Teachers will need to brief the pupils well in advance; tour the outside of the building, stopping at intervals and getting pupils to orientate their base maps. Pupils should then be put into pairs. They should be given a photograph by the teacher and instructed to look carefully around the perimeter of the building to locate the item the photograph illustrates. On the back of the photograph is a number. Before returning to the teacher to obtain and exchange photographs, pupils will need to locate the exact position of the photograph on their base maps. Having pinpointed the correct location, the pupils are given another photographic detail to find by the teacher.

Resources

♦   Teacher will need to take 24 photos - developed into prints.

♦   Cover all photos with 'fablon' and number 1 - 24.

♦   Draw a simple base map of the school or unit.

♦   Photocopy base maps as required.

2. Texture Trail

This activity involves pupils working from a base map of either the school buildings or compound. On each base map there should be marked 16 or so points by the letters A-P. Pupils should ideally work in pairs. In addition to each pair having a base map they will also require a large piece of paper (A3 in size) which should be divided into 16 squares. At the top of each square should be marked a letter to correspond with points on the base map - outlining a 'clue'. The clue gives details of the texture children should look for at the specific location detailed on the map. Once children have arrived at a specific location, they look for the clue at the precise point and record what they see. They do this by presenting their sheet of A3 paper over the texture and by using a wax crayon rub gently over the surface to obtain an impression of the texture in the correct box (see below).

a A brick	b A windowledge	c Cement	d A drain
e A vent	f	g	h
i	j	k	l
m	n	o	p

Pupils then return to 'base' each time they record a texture impression so that the teacher can check their A3 record sheet. If the group is competent and demonstrates confidence in the task, the teacher may prefer that pupils exercise a little independence - only returning to base when the whole activity is completed. This exercise can be used in the similar way and developed as a 'Maths' trail.

Resources

♦ Teachers will need to develop a master map and clue sheet.

♦ Photocopy sufficient base maps for each child with locations clearly identified with letters A - P.

♦ Provide each pair with an A3 sheet to record their findings.

3. *Score orientation*

This activity is known as score orientation because the points on the base map can represent different 'score' values. For example if 16 locations were chosen, numbers 1-5 could be regarded as easier than the rest and carry a weighting of only 2 points per location. Locations 6-10 may be harder and thus be rated as being worth 4 points each. Those locations marked with numbers 11-16 by virtue of being the hardest, or furthest from base, may warrant high scores to the value of 6 points each. By setting score values to each location the orientation activity takes on an additional problem solving element. At the outset the class should be divided into several groups of 3 or 4 pupils. Emphasise that pupils must stick together in their groups. The object of the exercise is that within a specific time period each group has to visit a number of locations and note the letters on a 'score card'. As the task requires completion within a specified time period, groups have to decide which locations they are going to visit. They will need to develop a strategy either to find all the easiest locations, but gain only a few marks, or develop a plan to locate the difficult points and thereby gain lots of marks! Pupils should note that lateness will incur penalty points which will be deducted from their final score (see score sheet below).

SCORE SHEET		Time Out Time Back	
Location	**Letter**	**Points**	**TOTAL**
1	?	6	
2	?	6	
3	?	6	
4	?	4	
5	?	2	
6	?	2	

Resources

- ♦ Teachers will need to devise a course.

- ♦ Develop a base map, locate points and photocopy x pupils in the class.

- ♦ Prepare a score sheet outlining scores for each point and photocopy as required.

- ♦ Place lettered markers out in the grounds or paint letters on posts.

- ♦ Photocopy the base map as required.

4. *Point to Point*

This activity most closely resembles 'real' orienteering. The skills of route finding and route choice are developed, in addition to helping pupils develop an understanding of the relationship of maps to details on the ground. Base maps of the school grounds need to be prepared well in advance. These should outline those points (16 is considered appropriate) which the pupils are required to visit. At each of the points letter markers should be displayed. A score card will need to be devised so that pupils can record their findings. The class should then be divided up into small groups of between 3-5 pupils. In order to avoid all the groups simply following one another, the teacher will have to prepare a selection of different routes. For example group 'A' may need to begin at location number 5 and continue according to a pre-determined route set by the teacher. This is normally outlined on the 'score card'. Group B will have a totally different route, but use the same markers (see score sheet below).

SCORE CARD		Group A
Location	**Letter**	**Points**
5	?	
1	?	
6	?	
2	?	
3	?	
10	?	

Resources

The same resources will be required as for 'score orienteering'.

Teaching and Learning Styles

Orientation demands a somewhat different approach to teaching and learning compared with other more traditional class based activities. It is largely about teachers establishing clear aims, providing strong leadership and management, giving out clear explanations and information, having high expectations of pupils and giving them a high degree of space to exercise a large measure of responsibility for their own learning.

Teachers need to be very clear about what it is they want pupils to learn as a result of the activities. They need to provide strong leadership both in terms of the preparation and use of materials and in briefing the pupils by giving appropriate information to enable them to be successful. Teachers need to ensure that through effective management all pupils clearly understand the parameters of the task and of the expectations required of them. Teachers also need to provide time and space at the end of each activity for pupils to articulate their reactions to the tasks set and indicate what they have learned.

The key to good teaching of orientation lies principally in teachers knowing the right questions to ask of their pupils and in challenging their thinking. Figure 4.4 outlines some of the key questions which could be used by teachers to ensure pupils have a clear understanding of orientation. Other key factors include good class management, appropriate tasks and good intervention strategies.

Good learning takes place when organisation is effective and when planning and preparation is thorough and when expectations of pupils are high. Pupils often learn best when briefings are of a high order and when opportunities are provided, not only to challenge their thinking, but when quality time is set aside to enable pupils to reflect upon their experiences, and articulate what they know and understand.

Teachers' intending to develop orientation further with their pupils, would be well advised to obtain a copy of 'Orienteering in the National Curriculum' from their local library. It is quite excellent and provides countless ideas with some very helpful illustrations.

Orientation: Key Stage 2

Key questions to ask children when teaching orientation

Orientation

Is the map the right way round?
Does the map match the ground?
How can you use landmarks to set the map?

Route Choice

Where are you now?
Can you find this point on the map?
Where are you going?
Which way can you go?
Are there any other possible routes?
Are there obstacles or difficulties on your route?
Which route is shortest?
Which route is quickest?
Which route is easiest?
Which route is best?
How far is it?
How long will it take?
In which direction will you set off?

Staying on Route

How do you know you are still on route?
What will you notice and check off on your route?
How will you know when you're near your destination?
How can you keep a check on your position?
What skills do you need to do all this well?

On Completion

Did your plan work out in action?
Did you find the destination precisely?
Was the route a good one?
Did you meet unexpected problems?
Could your route have been simpler or quicker?
Were you hesitant or confident?
Did you need to keep checking the map?
Did you map read accurately?
Did you take note of the distance?
How long did it take?
How pleased were you with your performance?

Figure 4.4

In developing any of the activities suggested in this chapter teachers should take plenty of time in briefing pupils. Time spent in explanation and demonstration at the commencement of any activity will ensure enormous dividends. Pupils will be clear about tasks and confident to exercise responsibility. In short they will be encouraged to achieve good success. Conversely poor introductions and hasty briefings will almost certainly result in lesson chaos and failure.

As a general rule, for most orientation activities, it is advisable for teachers to walk the boundaries or perimeter of the area with youngsters at the start of the lesson. Use these sessions to encourage children to work in pairs and make use of the 'base maps' to determine their exact position. In this way map setting and orientation techniques are reinforced, boundaries are set and safety considerations are highlighted. It is also always advisable to tell and show the youngsters where you can be located throughout the exercise, and more importantly what to do in the event of difficulty. Pupils should be clear about how much time is being given for the task and which areas are 'out of bounds'.

Class management and organisation is always an important consideration for all teachers and never more so than when working out of doors. If details are attended to well in advance of the lesson, it will almost guarantee that everything else falls into place, and events run smoothly.

The teaching and learning of orientation cannot be separated from the assessment which is an important and inter-related part of the process. It should not be regarded as an add-on activity. Assessment has two essential purposes. First it tells the teacher about pupils individual progress and second it should, by its very nature, assist the teacher in evaluating the activities, providing the basis for forward planning. There is a third element to assessment which involves communicating the results to pupils, parents and others. Assessment needs to be a continuous process and woven into part of the teaching activities. It should be concerned with what a child knows and can do, in the context of 'end of key stage' descriptors.

Conclusion

Whatever level of experience individual teachers may have in the delivery of outdoor and adventurous activities, it is hoped that this chapter will inspire and prompt teachers to 'have a go' at this wonderful and stimulating activity. Seeing children grow in self confidence and awareness has convinced me that through orientation activities, young people quickly develop their knowledge and understanding of difficult concepts. More importantly, they develop valuable aspects of personal and social behaviour.

Chapter 5

Problem solving as a feature of outdoor and adventurous activities at Key Stage 2

INTRODUCTION

For many teachers the implementation of outdoor and adventurous activities as a compulsory element of the physical education curriculum has been a very difficult and demanding task. This has been largely due to a combination of poor guidance information about this area of learning and also the result of too few INSET courses which are available to specifically address teachers' needs in outdoor and adventurous activities.

The purpose of this chapter is twofold. Firstly, it attempts to highlight the benefits and value of engaging pupils at Key Stage 2 in practical problem solving tasks and, secondly, it suggests a range of activities, with a range of possible learning outcomes, which teachers may feel able to implement within their school grounds.

A Rationale

Outdoor and adventurous activities are very different to other forms of physical education. Activities are primarily not just to do with the development of physical skills. More importantly, they provide unique opportunities for the personal and social development of pupils. At Key Stage 2 the programme of study makes specific reference to 'problem solving' as an appropriate activity (*Figure5.1*).

Problem solving activities provide opportunities for pupils to discover new roles and responsibilities; to work through possible conflict of ideas and understand the need for co-operation and interaction. Moreover young people are able to learn together; to solve problems which individually they would find quite difficult; they learn to cope with personal and group setbacks; they learn how to plan - do - and evaluate their work and as a result ... learn from their achievements.

Physical Education in the National Curriculum

Programme of Study

Outdoor and adventurous activities Key Stage 2

Pupils should be taught:

A   to perform outdoor and adventurous activities e.g. orienteering exercises in one or more different environments, e.g. playground, school grounds and where available parks, woodland or seashore;

B   challenges of a physical and problem-solving nature, e.g. negotiating obstacle courses using suitable equipment, e.g. gymnastic or adventurous play apparatus, planks, boxes or ropes whilst working individually and with others;

C   the skills necessary for the activities undertaken.

Figure 5.1

Problem solving activities are close to the realities of life. 'Tasks' can release energy, offer opportunities for creativity, divergent thinking, spontaneity and initiative ... those very qualities which are considered important in encouraging pupils' personal and social development. Problem solving activities are viewed as being valuable in providing pupils with relevant and purposeful learning opportunities. Tasks involve students in 'active learning' and should not be used purely as an activity for its own sake. Teachers will need to develop strategies which not only involve pupils in planning and doing tasks but provide time and space and the opportunities for them to reflect upon their experiences in order that they may learn and develop.

Teaching and Learning Styles

There are four major and integral considerations involved in the planning, delivery and evaluation of problem solving activities. Teachers need to:

- ◆ Establish clear aims
- ◆ Select the appropriate task(s)
- ◆ Manage the session
- ◆ Facilitate reflection opportunities

Establishing clear aims is common to all areas of teaching not least in developing problem solving activities. Teachers need to think about what characteristics they are trying to develop. It may be teamwork, or

what characteristics they are trying to develop. It may be teamwork, or communication skills; it may be leadership and organisational skills; it may be trust, dependence or simply co-ordination and agility. Whatever the focus, teachers need to be clear in their own minds and select the most appropriate task to suit that purpose.

Selection of the task will require the teacher to consider the gathering together of resources, the location of the activity, organisational strategies and safety. Much of the equipment which already exists in schools will be appropriate for many of the tasks outlined. Some however may need to be found elsewhere! Tasks can be undertaken on hard play areas, but for some activities a grassed area is preferable. It is not practical to have the whole class either doing the same activity or in groups all embarked upon a range of tasks in sight of one another. Problem solving is best achieved in small groups (5 - 7 per group) by offering a wide range of tasks situated in different parts of a compound. The most successful sessions are those where the teacher organises a 'carousel' of activities - and moves from group to group throughout the session.

Managing the session is crucial to the success of the activity. Leaders need to think about what additional support staff are required, the ways in which groups are constructed, supervised, and informed of the various tasks. Often it is best to display the specific 'instructions' on cards outlining precise times for planning and doing. In this way groups remain well focused and 'on task'. There will be a temptation at times for teachers to intervene and offer suggestions. This should be resisted. Teachers should only intervene if pupils' safety becomes at risk. Pupils need to have the space to explore, experiment and modify without feeling that staff are always 'on hand' if the need arises.

Facilitating reflection opportunities is where effective teaching strategies tend to fall down. This is often due to the constraints of time, but more especially when there is a reluctance on the part of teachers to engage pupils in evaluation exercises, after what invariably has been an enjoyable session. Reviewing activities may take on a variety of different forms, for example, in pairs or in groups; through the use of drama activities; writing, drawing, painting and the use of video. Questioning pupils' perceptions of their achievements are crucial to the process (*Figure 5.2*).

Key Questions in Reviewing

How did the group get started on the task?
How did the group work?
Did a leader emerge - how effective was he/she?
Did members listen to one another?
What behaviour prevented the objective being achieved?
What strengths did each member bring to the project?
What weakness did you recognise in yourselves?
Which qualities/skills did each of you lack?
How did each of you feel during the exercise?
What have you all learned about yourselves?
Would you approach the exercise the same way if you did it again?

Figure 5.2

Some ideas for consideration

All of the activities included in this chapter offer a number of possible teaching aims/learning outcomes for each task. Teachers need to be clear about what it is they want to achieve as a result of encouraging pupils to embark upon each activity. The choice of 'aims' will largely determine the focus of activity and perhaps the style of review. Some tasks naturally lend themselves to a creative, pictorial review, while others are more productive if dealt with through discussion - first with a partner and then with the whole group.

1. Quicksand

Aim: to develop teamwork and co-operation skills.

Equipment: 3 oil drums/milk crates, 2 planks

Time allowed: 20 minutes

Task: To move the whole team across a delineated area of imaginary 'quicksand' without touching the ground. All equipment has to be taken to the finishing line and if the ground is touched the group must start again.

2.   *High rise*

Aim: to develop creative thinking, imagination, divergent thinking.

Equipment: 4 short poles, a plank, 6 short ropes.

Time allowed: 20 minutes

Task: Using the equipment provided, the whole group is to create a structure and stand on it half a metre above the ground for 60 seconds.

3.   *Radioactive container*

Aim: to develop decision making skills, divergent thinking

Equipment: mark a circle on the ground. An oil drum and a small hoop should be placed inside the circle. 2 ropes and a cycle tube should be placed outside the circle.

Time allowed: 20 minutes

Task: Place the radioactive container (oil drum) into the sterile bin (hoop) with the equipment provided. No person may enter the radioactive zone (marked by a circle).

4.   *The knotted rope*

Aim: to develop teamwork and co-operation

Equipment: 30 metres of rope and picture of a reef knot

Time allowed: 5 minutes of planning, 5 for doing

Task: The group have super glue on their hands! They must take hold of the rope with both hands. Once they have hold of the rope they cannot let go or change grip. Keeping to their grip the group are to tie a 'reef knot'.

5.   *Electric fence*

Aim: to encourage co-operation, working together.

Equipment: Two netball posts, a rope, a plank.

Time allowed: 20 minutes.

Task: The two netball posts, the rope, the vertical plane below the rope and the vertical planes to the side of the posts are all electrified. The whole group plus the plank must pass from one side of the electrified area to the other. Should any part of the body, or plank, touch the rope, posts, or break the vertical plane then this will result in electrocution. In this event the team must begin again.

6. *Blindfold soccer*

    Aim: to develop pupils' communication skills. To develop speaking and listening skills.

    Equipment: Football posts, (mini) football

    Time allowed: 5 minutes to plan, 10 minutes to play the game.

    Task: Two sets of goals are laid out and the normal rules of soccer apply. All but two of the team are blindfolded. The remaining two are the Coaches/Trainers. They can shout instructions from the sidelines.

7. *Sheep and shepherds*

    Aim: to develop communication skills. To develop speaking and listening.

    Equipment: one whistle, 20 feet of rope, blindfolds for all the group except one member.

    Time allowed: 5 minutes to plan, 10 minutes to get all the sheep into the pen.

    Task: The shepherd, who may not move, must herd the sheep into the fold (a circle formed by the rope) using only the whistle for communication. The sheep are blindfolded and placed in various parts of the field by the teacher. The rope (fold) is placed after the sheep have been blindfolded. The shepherd is also placed in position after the sheep have been blindfolded and must stay in that position until all the sheep are in the fold.

8. *Trolley*

Aim: to develop co-operation, teamwork skills, co-ordination.

Equipment: Two planks, four bits of rope. Two ropes to delineate area.

Time allowed: Ten minutes

Task: The area between the ropes is shark infested custard. The group must cross the area using only the four ropes and the planks provided. If any group member falls or puts a hand or foot into the custard, the group must start again.

9. *Blindline*

Aims:

1. to provide an opportunity for pupils to explore his/her own physical confidence, agility, co-ordination and concentration when blindfolded;

2. to encourage reliance on the senses of hearing, touch and smell;

3. to encourage awareness of the environment: sounds made by the surroundings and other game players; smell and touch of the ground and obstacles, by the earth and trees or tarmac and steel;

4. to encourage awareness of other people, co-operation, dependence, responsibility, trust (particularly when two people are tied together).

Equipment: a sixty metre length of rope laid out along the ground, between objects, over objects. Blindfolds for all the team.

Time allowed: 20 minutes to complete the route.

Task: Pupils are blindfolded and given instructions to follow a long guideline which has been laid over/under/through obstacles. Objects can be tied onto the guideline and pupils are asked to identify these at the end. Pupils can be set off individually or be tied together. An adult must be in a position to supervise closely those taking part.

A suitable area for the blindline could either be a wood with bushes, ditches and hedgerows or the urban environment using metal barriers, steps, park benches and similar objects.

10. *Bomb around the obstacle/assault course*

Aim: to develop problem solving skills, group organisation and initiative.

Equipment: obstacle course, ten gallon drum.

Time allowed: Ten minutes to complete the task.

Task: Set up a suitable obstacle course or use an existing assault course. The bomb, which consists of a suitable container (e.g. eight gallon container half-filled with water), has to be carried around the course. If the bomb is dropped or banged it will explode and all will be killed. The group may consist of 4/5 pupils.

Variations:

1. Use a bucket of water which is to finish the course as full as possible

2. Use a large log

3. Carry an egg each

11. *Pitching a tent blindfolded*

Aim: to develop communication and teamwork skills.

Equipment: One tent, blindfolds.

Time allowed: Ten minutes to complete the task.

Task: In groups of 4-6 the pupils are asked to erect a tent. All are blindfolded except one member who has the task of directing the rest of the team.

12. *Traffic jam*

Aim: to develop creative/divergent thinking, group co-operation.

66

Equipment: Seven beer crates.

Time allowed: Five minutes for planning, ten minutes to complete the task.

Task:

To begin, one group stands on the places to the left of the middle square, the other group stands to the right. Both groups face the middle unoccupied square.

Using the approved moves, people on the left side must end up in the places on the right side, and vice versa.

Illegal moves

1. Any move backwards

2. Any move around someone facing the same way you are, i.e. you are looking at their back

3. Any move which involves two people moving at once.

Legal moves

1. A person may move into an empty space in front of him/her

2. A person may move around a person who is facing him/her into an empty space.

Conclusion

Problem solving activities provide a huge potential for pupils to be fully engaged in their own learning. The key to the success of problem solving as a realistic component of the PE, outdoor and adventurous activity syllabus, is the extent to which pupils have a quality experience. Success is largely determined by good quality teaching. Poor teaching will result in problem solving tasks being no more than an activity in themselves. Good teaching will employ all the methods outlined in this chapter and enable pupils to plan and evaluate their work. By so doing, pupils will learn practical skills and develop new insights and interpersonal skills.

Chapter 6

Using the potential of outdoor and adventurous activities as a vehicle for integrated learning

INTRODUCTION

Through experiences in the outdoors, and particularly through adventurous activities, young people can be introduced to a wide variety of themes which may either introduce or reinforce other areas of the curriculum. Outdoor activities provide unique opportunities for integrated learning and for personal and social development. Being inter-disciplinary in nature, cutting across the entire curriculum, it has many implications for a host of learning areas such as the sciences, the humanities, social studies, languages, the arts, for health, physical education, music, mathematics and many others. Some activities and projects require calculation, measurement, or an understanding of scale which give real meaning to mathematical concepts. Similarly, respect for and an understanding of safety principles can be developed and natural phenomena observed, recorded, predicted and tested. Adventurous activities and projects can provide stimuli for creative writing, art, drama, aesthetic appreciation and spiritual development. As a direct result of new experiences, sensitivities to the natural environment are heightened and so too the implications of one's involvement.

Vehicles for integrated learning

Before deciding on a specific activity or project with a group of young people, the staff, who are involved in the planning of programmes, should know exactly what it is they intend to draw out of the activity. Several questions will need to be resolved. For example, what are the specific objectives? What learning will take place? Will the experience reinforce learning already introduced? By answering these questions the activity or project then becomes the 'tool' to enable several objectives either personal, social, or educational to be accomplished and used to reinforce specific learning skills rather than the activity being undertaken in isolation. Outlined over the page are a range of traditional outdoor activities which can be used to develop learning and enrichment in a host of other curriculum areas.

Mountain walking

This activity helps young people to become acquainted with landscapes and the forces which have shaped them, the study of wildlife, farming methods, settlement patterns, and livelihoods. Issues to do with conservation and respect for the natural environment can be introduced as well as scope for ecology studies of the flora and fauna of different areas. The activity develops the skill of navigation in unfamiliar terrain and provides a unique vehicle for the reinforcement of numerical concepts. Through expeditioning, young people develop a social responsibility to one another, group cohesion is reinforced and opportunities abound for problems to be solved and decisions to be taken. Leadership, tolerance, sharing and compromise are important learning skills which develop as a result of this activity.

Camping and bivvying

Camping provides unique opportunities for young people to develop personally and socially. Experiences of this nature enable individuals to really get to know one another; it develops group cohesion, initiative, provides problem solving situations and develops decision making processes. The activity involves a high degree of motivation and observation, and develops self discipline, confidence and self-reliance.

Initiative exercises

Through initiative exercises in the outdoors, young people are challenged by having to complete a task together. To accomplish this, the exercise requires the sharing and exchanging of ideas; problems having to be solved and decisions made. To achieve the task, the group has to gel together so that the task may be carried out in the shortest space of time in the most efficient way. This requires each individual to think of themselves not as an isolated unit but as a member of a team where group co-operation, team spirit and cohesion become the highest priority. The activity also develops the skills of sharing, compromise, negotiation, tolerance, adaptability and flexibility. Initiative tests, while primarily useful to develop group interaction, are a most useful vehicle for the reinforcement of particular skills especially verbal reasoning and creativity.

Outdoor studies

Outdoor studies embrace a wide range of projects such as woodland, seashore, pond, moorland, stream, forest, village and urban environments. Studies in the outdoors help develop childrens' educational skills of literacy, numeracy, creativity, communication and observation. Through first hand experiences, young people are able to reinforce specific skills acquired in the conventional subjects of biology, geography, history and maths. Several adventurous activities can also be used to develop children's environmental awareness and study skills. Outdoor studies provide opportunities for the development of sensory awareness, for recording, problem solving exercises, developing communication skills and for the enhancement of group cohesion, team spirit and co-operation.

Night exercises

Traditionally, these activities have been used as a vehicle for the development of personal and social characteristics. Through the excitement and challenge of nocturnal problem solving exercises, young people develop initiative, self reliance, self confidence and self discipline. Through this activity, group relationships are strengthened, team spirit is developed and group co-operation and cohesion is reinforced. Night exercises heighten a sensitivity to the natural environment, and verbal and general communication skills are enhanced.

Canoeing

Both flat water and white water canoeing create unique opportunities for personal, social and environmental awareness to be developed. Through canoeing activities young people become aware of their own strengths and weaknesses and those of others. They develop a responsibility both for themselves and others, group co-operation, team spirit, and group cohesion is reinforced. Through this activity, groups can undertake a wide range of outdoor study projects to include recording and measurement of depth and flow; opportunities are available for elementary surveying, for the study of hydrology, flora and fauna and other environmental issues. Canoeing not only strengthens interpersonal relationships but develops self confidence, self reliance, initiative and trust. It provides opportunities for the reinforcement of specific learning skills, particularly those of numeracy, communication, problem solving, decision making and creativity.

Climbing and abseiling

These activities are very challenging. Both provide unique opportunities for the development of personal characteristics, particularly self discipline, self confidence and self awareness. Through climbing, a wide range of integrated learning vehicles are possible. For example, the activity develops environmental sensory awareness and the locations used provide natural opportunities for glacial studies, geographical, geological and mathematical concepts to be developed and biological studies to include topics in flora and fauna. Climbing provides a vehicle for the development of creative writing, aesthetic awareness and art. It can be used to reinforce the specific learning skills of communication, numeracy, literacy, problem solving and decision making processes.

Gill scrambling

Gills are fascinating habitats offering unparalleled situations for intensive adventure. They are also unique environments illustrating ecosystems of times past, and flora dating as far back as the last glacial interphase. This activity which involves journeying up and through a water worn gorge, generates spontaneous excitement and challenge, providing opportunities for personal, social and environmental awareness to take place.

In terms of personal development, young people develop self reliance, discipline, confidence and awareness, initiative, trust, dependence and co-operation Decision making and problem solving processes are learned. This activity reinforces group cohesion, team spirit and group responsibility in addition to enhancing an awareness of the natural environment. Gill environments provide opportunities for a range of outdoor study projects to be undertaken. These include stream studies, surveying, hydrology, plant biology, the study of small mammals, and enhance the learning skills of creative writing, science, numeracy and communication.

Assault courses

Aerial ropes, nets, barricades and zip wires are the kinds of apparatus which are used to challenge resourcefulness, develop initiative and enhance self confidence. Tasks and activities set in this context reinforce the personal characteristics of young people. While the exercises are of tremendous challenge, the activity develops self reliance, self discipline, self awareness and trust. Opportunities are provided for decisions to be taken and problems to be solved. Inherent in this activity are the skills of personal physical competence.

Raft building

Raft building has very similar objectives to those of initiative exercises. Both are vehicles which are used to develop young people's personal and social characteristics. Decision making and problem solving objectives lie at the very heart of this activity. However, there is also a wide range of opportunity for particular skills to be developed. These include the skills of communication and creativity. Several outdoor study projects may be combined with this activity to include fresh water studies, pond studies, and mathematical studies to develop concepts of measurement, recording and surveying. Normally the objectives associated with this activity are to do with the development of young people's personal and social characteristics. Socially, this activity helps to develop group cohesion, co-operation, team spirit and group interaction. Personally, young people develop self confidence, self reliance, trust, initiative, observation skills, flexibility, adaptability and decision making processes are reinforced.

Caving/mine exploration

One of the most potent vehicles for personal and social development and for integrated learning in outdoor education can be found in the activity of caving or mine exploration. Young people generally find this activity the most challenging and most rewarding of all the adventurous pursuits. Potential exists for a host of skills to be developed. These include creative writing, numeracy, science, communication, decision making and problem solving. In addition the subterranean environment provides unique opportunities for a wide range of outdoor study projects. These range from surveying studies, involving mathematical concepts to studies in geology, biology, hydrology, geomorphology, and archaeology. Studies of flora and fauna may be compared and contrasted in the entrance, twilight and total darkness zones, by the use of simple line or belt transects.

As with gill scrambling, this activity is a potent vehicle for personal and social development. Young people learn to be responsible for themselves and others, and team spirit, group cohesion and co-operation are reinforced by experiences. The personal characteristics of initiative, self confidence, discipline and awareness are developed together with ability in decision making and problem solving processes.

Dinghy sailing

Dinghy sailing provides the opportunity for young people to develop aspects of their personal and social characteristics and promotes an awareness of the natural environment. It can be used to reinforce the specific skills of scientific discovery, verbal communication and those connected with numeracy and competence. Unlike many of the other adventurous pursuits, sailing requires an intellectual understanding of wind direction, change, and interpretation. This activity may be used as a vehicle for a range of outdoor study projects to include surveying, measuring, navigation, lake studies, biological studies, geographical studies and to develop mathematical concepts. Dinghy sailing increases group cohesion, responsibility, co-operation and awareness. The activity helps to develop initiative, leadership, self confidence, trust and self reliance.

Board sailing

In contrast to dinghy sailing, board sailing is a very individual activity which develops aspects of personal rather than social characteristics. The activity requires a high degree of motivation for success and in the early stages is dependent upon commitment, resolution and an understanding of the complexities of wind direction and change. Board sailing develops self reliance, discipline, awareness and confidence. It requires decisions to be made and problems to be solved, the development of observation skills together with sensory awareness. Through this activity the skills of creativity and competence are reinforced.

Skiing

Skiing is a dynamic and very popular activity with young people. It has similar objectives to board sailing. Primarily, the activity strengthens aspects of young people's personal development and reinforces the characteristics of self reliance, discipline, awareness and confidence. As this activity is often undertaken in small groups, skiing also reinforces aspects of social development. It fosters group cohesion and generates group responsibility. The activity may be used in a variety of ways to develop environmental awareness. aesthetic appreciation, and develop the skills of observation, decision making and problem solving processes.

Opportunities for developing an integrated learning approach to teaching

Outlined on the following pages are a range of specific projects and explorations which can be undertaken in the context of a number of the more traditional outdoor and adventurous activities. Projects are categorised under several broad headings to include:

1.   Cave and mine projects.

2.   Water-based projects.

3.   Gill projects.

4.   Hill and fell projects.

1. Caving and mine exploration projects

Introduction

The underground world of caves offers a unique environment for much integrated learning to take place. It is completely different from anything on the earth's surface. Undertaking a journey below ground provides opportunities for recreation, study and adventure. It enables young people to experience the mystery of the unknown and the ever present possibility of making new discoveries.

Ideas for integrated learning

Youngsters are often highly excitable the first time they enter a cave. Fear of the unknown stimulates the senses, providing opportunities for much useful work to be developed. Initial experiences could be reinforced by re-creating the environment graphically through art, drama or creative writing.

Exploration of a cave system also provides many opportunities for groups to record and observe. Groups may either wish to carry out a survey of the system, or to record and observe the different species of flora and fauna of various parts of the cave.

(a)   Surveying or mapping

The surveying of a cave system can be carried out at various grades depending on the type of tools and the effort involved. To carry out a survey does not require expensive equipment or the use of highly sophisticated instruments.

According to the Cave Research Group there are seven grades of survey. Accuracy is the yardstick. They are as follows:

- Grade 1: a plan from memory.

- Grade 2: a plan roughly to scale with estimated distances and heights.

- Grade 3: a plan made with a simple compass and measuring cord.

- Grade 4: a plan using a prismatic compass and measuring tape.

- Grade 5: a plan made with a prismatic compass, clinometer and steel tape measure.

- Grade 6: (same as 5) but using tripod.

- Grade 7: (same as 5) but using a theodolite.

Method

Simple equipment is appropriate to achieve an acceptable standard survey at Grade 3 level and should include the following:

- a tape measure;

- a 'silva' compass;

- a note book;

- pen or pencil.

A survey requires recording lines, bearings and angles. Each part of the cave system should be measured and relate to a number of survey points.

e.g. Survey Point A - B	Compass bearing	70 degrees
	Angle of slope	+ 5 degrees
	Width of passage	1 metre
	Length of passage	10 metres 20 cm
	Height of passage	2 metres

(b) Observing living things

Studying the living things which exist in a cave system provides children with numerous possibilities for making exciting discoveries. Animal forms are much easier to find than fungi or lichens, which are often microscopic. Before embarking upon a study of the underground environment, it is important that students appreciate that two different worlds exist in the cave system. That part of the system at the entrance is known as the threshold or the entrance zone. Its limit is as far as light may penetrate. That part beyond, completely devoid of light, is known as the total darkness zone. A greater abundance of life will be found in the entrance zone than in the total darkness zone.

To undertake this project students will need to carry a small outfit of apparatus for identification purposes, which should include the following:

- a magnifying glass;

- two very small water-colour paintbrushes;

- one small tea-strainer;

- a small notebook and pencil;

- a glass jar;

- a tape measure.

To record all forms of flora and fauna within the cave requires the use of a metric tape measure. This is placed along the floor of the cave so that all insect life and vegetation can be recorded at specific points. In this way students will soon appreciate those factors that determine the existence of living things underground.

(c) Studies in hydrology

Caves provide unique opportunities for the study of hydrology. Groups wishing to undertake such a study could for example trace the flow of water through passages and convert information discovered either onto their own survey or onto a cave survey which has already been prepared.

(d) Studies in geomorphology

Cave exploration lends itself to the study of limestone formations and their distribution.

Geomorphological studies may involve groups studying the extent of specific formations within the system. These could range from a study of the stalactites and stalagmites, limestone rocks, cave pearls, moonmilk, heleclites and many other types of pool and deposits. Opportunities also exist for the study of the physical development of passages, to determine whether or not these were formed in the vadose or phreatic zones.

(e)   Historical studies

Both caves and mines lend themselves to historical studies. It may be possible to undertake some research to ascertain if the system was the home of Bronze Age people. The cave, for example, may have provided a refuge for people escaping foreign occupation, or been the site of a show cave in the Victorian era.

All mines have a unique and interesting history from which students could undertake a wide variety of studies. They could be encouraged to trace the evidence of the working patterns of mines by examining levels and adits and observe both building remains and spoil heaps to deduce how, when and for what purpose the mine was used. Further research will lead to young people identifying the living conditions of those who worked at the site and enable them to answer many questions. For example, where did the miners and their families live? What was the level of their pay? What were their conditions of service? Who owned the mine? During what periods was the mine prosperous and economic? When did it close?

The suggestions listed above are but a few of the possibilities which this activity may provide for integrated learning.

2.   Water based projects

Introduction

Journeys involving canoe, sailing dinghy or raft provide unique vehicles for young people to embark upon a challenging adventure, associated with some aspect of integrated learning.

In using water based activities to stimulate learning it is important that leaders are not only familiar with the craft to be used, but also are qualified to teach the specific activity and are fully conversant with the safety procedures. In developing projects of integrated learning, teachers will also need to point out the limitations of different craft in certain water conditions to pupils, alert them to the logistical problems, and ensure that safety codes are adhered to at all times. Weather and water conditions will undoubtedly determine whether or not projects can be undertaken. While large peaceful lakes will more readily lend themselves to more quiet reflective projects, slow running rivers will provide scope for other investigations.

Any recording of information whilst on flat or moving water will often have to be carried out in fairly damp/wet conditions. It is therefore important that leaders ensure students have the appropriate equipment to write with and on - for example, pencils work far better in cold/wet conditions than biros. People also lose efficiency in wet/cold conditions so leaders should ensure that the students check details or measurements while still in the field.

Ideas for integrated learning

Flat water activities using either open Canadian canoes, kayaks, rafts or planing dinghies lend themselves quite naturally to a wide range of integrated learning projects. Open lakes provide a unique resource for combining adventurous activity with the opportunities for carrying out first hand investigative work and for developing young people's awareness of the environment. Projects range from either depth sounding of a lake, surveying, sketching, mapping of a bay or island, studying fresh water animals and plants, land use surveys, pollution counts or simply as a vehicle for creative writing.

(a) Mapping of a bay or island

Many people assume that to undertake a survey of a bay requires complicated equipment and a knowledge of complex maths. This is not so. Simple survey work may be introduced by encouraging students firstly to draw a straightforward map of the perimeter of the lake and the adjacent features. This may include sketching a cliff back-wall, the marshy areas, and the inlet and outflow streams. Experience indicates that those involved in such a mapping exercise become involved in spin-off activities such as the study of plant communities around the lake, photography and/or sketching of the landscape and possibly even the compilation of a bathymetric map.

Reconnoitring

Before undertaking any survey it will be necessary for groups to reconnoitre the area and locate obstacles and blind spots. This is best done by either simply sailing or canoeing round the bay to be surveyed, or by sitting at a convenient, and if possible, elevated vantage point and drawing a rough plan of the lake.

Once this has been done, it should be possible to decide where to locate 'stations', or points around the lake shore which the group will survey.

Method 1: Tape and compass traverse

Equipment

Several sticks and poles
1 x 50 metre tape
1 compass (preferably of the sighting type)
A note book

Having established a series of stations or points around the bay it should be possible to take bearings from one station to the next, to measure the straight line distance between the stations and to take 'off-sets' (measured distances at a right angle to the straight line) to the lake shore or other prominent features. This can also be coupled with bearings from stations, or at noted distances between stations, to prominent features such as nearby mountain tops.

All of the information required should be recorded in a notebook and a map can be drawn up later in the day. The use of photographs from stations may well aid the memory in drawing up a map if the former option is taken.

This method has the obvious advantage of requiring little equipment to be carried, and that a more detailed map can be constructed at a later date. The main disadvantage is that it is possible to make incorrect notes and such errors do not become obvious until it is too late to rectify them without a return visit.

Method 2: Plane Table Survey

Equipment

1 x 50 metre tape
1 compass
A note book, pencils and sharpener
A rubber
Some bamboo canes with flags (10)
1 plane table
1 tripod
A spirit level

Scale rulers
An alidade (sight rule)

Basically a plane table is a drawing board covered with plain paper, mounted on a tripod, levelled in the horizontal with a spirit level and on which sighting lines, or rays, are drawn from a number of stations to other stations by using the alidade, or sighting rule. In theory the method appears complicated, but practically it is one which when grasped by young people has great appeal. The map, by means of a series of intersections of the rays from different stations, grows before the eyes of the surveyors. Additional detail between stations can be sketched in or fixed by tape traverse as outlined previously. Neat traces of the map can be completed at a later date and the information obtained supplemented with sketches and/or photographs.

(b) Soundings of a bay

Many lakes and bays are as yet unsounded and the challenge to undertake an original venture still remains, with its special opportunities for enterprise, teamwork and careful measurement.

Equipment

3 large buoys (with weights and rope attached)
3 x 50 metric ropes
3 x 20 metric tapes
Several sticks, poles or paddles
A map of the lake shore
A note book
A sounding line
30 bits of bright tape

Method

Establish a network of three shore stations marked with paddles/sticks or poles. Out in the bay lay three buoys approximately 50 metres from the shore and opposite the shore stations. Then using a kayak or Canadian canoe extend lines from each buoy to the shore. At intervals of five metres, attach pieces of coloured tape to the ropes running from shore to each buoy. This will provide 30 sites for depth soundings. Encourage teamwork and set each group the task of measuring and recording the depth at each coloured marker. From the readings taken it should be possible for a cross section to be drawn up at a later date using details taken on site.

(c) Temperature change

In a similar way to the method previously described for lake soundings and using similar equipment, students could compare and contrast the range of water temperature. Using thermometers, comparisons can be made at specific points to ascertain the water temperature - at the bottom of the lake, at a depth of three metres and on the surface.

The results may be converted on to a large map in a similar way to the previous project. The temperatures for one area could then be contrasted with another, to raise questions as to why differences occur.

(d) A study of animals and plant life

Using either Canadian canoes or kayaks students could be encouraged to carry out some original investigative work on animal and plant life. For this project to be successful specific areas will have to be clearly defined. Leaders will have to examine the sites well beforehand selecting suitable areas where contrasts can easily be made. For example a marshy shore could be compared and contrasted with a rocky shore and used to raise questions as to why different animals and plants live in differing habitats.

To achieve an effective study of animals and plants the best method to use is the line transect. This requires that a buoy with rope and weight is placed in the water some ten metres from the shore. A ten metre tape is extended from the shore to the buoy. Students should be encouraged to record what they see using pond nets at metre intervals and compare and contrast results with other areas.

(e) Land use survey

One way to ensure that students undertake a journey with their eyes open is to introduce a land use survey. Using a 1:25,000 OS Basemap, encourage children to identify for what purpose the land is currently used at points along the perimeter of the shore. By using a simple 'key', writing can be kept to a minimum. Such a survey will raise questions about the reasons for the existence of different land use patterns and provide opportunities for discussion.

(f) Shoreline discovery

Shoreline discovery projects work exceptionally well with upper primary and lower secondary pupils. Below is a list of prompts which may be used as a framework to encourage children to really focus upon the shoreline environment and stimulate observation and awareness.

1.   Draw a rough map of the lakeside.

2.   List all the objects that you see.

3.   Are all the stones of similar size?

4.   Turn them over - what do you see?

5.   Are there tide marks? Why are there differences?

6.   Does the land slope gently or steeply?

7.   Note anything you see growing on the shore.

8.   How far from the water is the nearest tree/grass?

9.   Is there any evidence of living things?

10.   What is the soil like? sandy/clayey/or stony.

11.   Place a metric tape from the water's edge to the grassland - note everything you see at one metre intervals.

12.   Are there any differences/similarities?

13.   Try to give reasons for differences/similarities.

Orienteering

Orienteering is a fast growing dynamic activity involving the challenge of journeying to and from various specific points identified on a map, in the shortest space of time. Lakes provide unique opportunities for this activity to be undertaken. Orienteering competitions set up at different locations on the shores of lakes accessible only by boats or canoes, provide children with an absorbing and exciting challenge. The activity may be used to reinforce a range of learning, enhance mathematical concepts and promote group and individual development.

3   Gill projects

Introduction

Gill scrambling is a fast-growing adventurous activity in which participants journey up and through a gill or gorge. It involves the techniques of scrambling, bouldering and rock climbing. Most gills have unique vegetation and in contrast to elsewhere in the fells they have remained relatively undisturbed by man for a very long time. Because of the combination of a cool wet climate and variable soils, they are unique ecological environments which must be treated with a great deal of respect. Leaders should ensure that students keep to the bottom of the gill for all integrated projects, in order to avoid environmental damage.

Ideas for integrated learning

The environment of a gill provides opportunities for a wide range of integrated learning experiences to take place. The scope for projects that may be undertaken is wide. Projects range from survey work, mapping and cross sections to measurement of current speed and pattern. The potential also exists for studies of flora and fauna, stones, pebbles and even aspects of geomorphology. The challenging atmosphere of a gill develops sensory awareness and provides pupils with the motivation to undertake a wide range of integrated projects.

A   Making a plan of part of a stream

Streams running through gills provide many excellent opportunities for surveying. To survey part of a stream and produce a simple plan can be a challenging experience in which pupils measure and record heights, depths and distances. It is also a useful exercise to reinforce group work, and mathematical concepts.

Equipment

Two measuring tapes
Graph paper
Note book - pencil

Points to note

1. Choose a part of the stream which is fairly shallow and illustrates contrast.

2. Set a base line along one side of the stream, a little distant from the water's edge.

3. To determine the width and make a plan of the stream, measure offsets at right angles from the base line at metre intervals to the first bank and then the far bank, either directly onto graph paper or by simply recording data into a note book.

4. To bring the plan alive, encourage pupils to sketch in details, i.e. cliffs, sandbanks, stones and trees on the base map.

Teachers should introduce this project primarily to encourage children to ask questions. For example - why are steep cliffs found at a particular place but not in others? Why is sand evident in some parts? What is the current doing? Does this have an effect upon the development of the stream?

B   Measuring the flow of a stream

Equipment

Oranges
Stop watch
Note book
Metre tape

Points to note

So often when journeying up and through a gill, young people take very little notice of the speed of flow. To measure flow is very straightforward. It is a fascinating project much loved by students because of the opportunity it affords not least of all to splash about in the stream!

(a) Students should be encouraged to work as a team, each member having a specific job. Basically four people are required to measure flow; one as a timer, one as a recorder, one as a thrower and one as a fielder.

(b) Teachers should select a part of the stream which is fairly free of rapids, large boulders and strong eddies which will have an adverse effect upon flow.

85

(c)   A tape measure is placed along the bank of the stream for a distance of 20 metres. Student A places the orange in the water opposite the end of the tape and starts the stop watch. Student B records the time when the orange passes the 20 metre mark signalled by student C. Student D collects the orange from the stream.

(d)   To determine the rate of flow this exercise should be repeated ten times, and the speed estimated by means of averaging out the results.

(e)   Students should be encouraged to compare and contrast results with other parts of the gill, and think about the factors which affect flow.

C   Measurement of depth

Equipment

Tape measure
Measuring rod
Note book and pencil

Points to note

1.   Extend a tape measure across the stream.

2.   Using the measuring rod, record the depth at every half metre across the stream.

3.   Results can be converted into a cross-sectional diagram.

4.   Sites can be compared and contrasted with other sections of the stream to raise questions as to why differences exist.

D   Pebbles in a stream

At the edge of the stream there will be a lot of different pebbles and stones. Encourage the pupils to look closely at them, grouping them into size, pattern, shape, colour and texture. Get them to look for the hard and soft pebbles - warm and cold colours, smooth and jagged shapes, plain and patterned stones. Using a quadrat (a half metre square marked off in 25 subsquares), ask the pupils to consider the percentage of different sorts, sizes, shapes and colours of pebbles.

Some suggested areas of study/questions:

Weight

Are some stones heavier than others size for size? Can they be arranged in order of weight? What shapes are there?

Smoothness

Is there a test for smoothness? Where were the stones found? What makes them smooth? Collect some pebbles.

Hardness

Which pebbles are the hardest? Can you think of hardness tests - scratching with a variety of things?

Pond dipping/ stone turning

1. Turn over some stones in the stream and check for living things. Many will be small. Record what you find. Always replace stones exactly as you found them.

2. Put any living things into a jar for closer study. When you have finished put them back into the water.

E   Living things in a stream

Within all streams there exists a preponderance of living things that provide an immediate fascination for most young people. During certain times of the year at different points in the stream there will be much evidence of Caddis, May and Stonefly larvae. Pupils will require little encouragement to look for evidence of these living things. They should nevertheless try to answer questions relating to why living things exist in a particular part of the stream and not in others. It is more important for pupils to suggest reasons why living things are located in certain parts of the stream than for them to identify organisms accurately.

It may help if quadrats are used, to compare and contrast different locations in order to work out the percentage of differing species which exist at a given site.

F   Plant Colonies

The sides of mountain gills have unique ecosystems, which are invariably rich in plant species. The greatest concentration of plants are often found some little distance from the water's edge.

In order to determine the range of different plants and any succession one of the most effective methods to use is the line transect. A metre tape is placed on the bed of the gill running up the bank. Students may identify different species of plants at 10 cm intervals and compare and contrast their results with other areas of the gill. By using a line transect in conjunction with a quadrat at several sites, students are able to determine the percentage of cover of specific plants and contrast differences. It is essential that students approach this project in an enquiring manner. They should ask questions as to why various plants exist in one area and not in others. What factors determine plant colonisation? To what extent does temperature, light, moisture, canopy and soil affect colonisation?

It should always be borne in mind that these habitats are often the last refuge of many plant species and as such should be treated with the utmost care.

G   Soil Sampling

Pupils can take soil samples from different places in the stream. They should allow the particles to settle. Get them to state what they see and compare and contrast results with other parts of the stream. Questions should be asked relating to why different types of sediments are evident at different points of the stream. Ask pupils to take soil samples some distance from the stream. Do samples contain any small creatures? If so what? Are there differences in texture, colour and rock? Through such a project youngsters will be able to make first hand observations which will lead them to understanding much more of the complexities of the gill environment.

4   Hill and Fell Projects

Introduction

Undertaking an expedition into the hills and fells will provide unique and unparalleled opportunities for young people to explore a wide range of possibilities for integrated learning. All too often groups tramp over moorland and fell without ever stopping to consider the rich natural surroundings through which they journey.. Countless opportunities are wasted, as groups often set themselves a specific distance or target, and time often prevents the possibility for investigative or observational work to be undertaken.

Ideas for integrated learning

The mountain environment is perfect for integrated learning. Outlined below and on the following page are a limited sample of the varied projects which can be attempted with young people. The section includes a study of walls, the habitats of living things, mines and quarries, a study of archaeology, human effect on the landscape, and building design, structure and materials. So often, when one is walking on the fells, a little time spent in looking at something, which often warrants no more than a glance, can produce a multitude of ideas. All that is required for these ideas to flow is a little sense of wonderment and a curiosity about the world in which we live.

A   Walls

Running across many moorland fells is a network of dry stone walls, of different composition, construction and age. Listed below are a number of questions which young people could think about. The ideas are not exhaustive and include: walls as features of the landscape; walls as used by humans; walls that provide shelter for plants and animals.

Walls as features of the landscape

1.   Where are the walls sited? Compare the actual distribution of the walls with those shown on old and current OS maps.

2.   What state of repair are the walls in? Categorise the walls into those which have fallen down, those falling down, those in use with repairs, those that are new. Are the walls in these various states due to farms merging, sheep on the mountainside or the greater use of fencing?

3.   How old are the walls? This may be determined to some extent by their shape and method of construction, or by using old maps. How weathered or overgrown are they?

4.   What are the walls made of and where did the material come from? If the walls are found on the high fells there may be evidence of nearby quarries. If the walls are in the low fells, stone may have been gathered from streams or rivers, or perhaps cleared from the fields as shown by the presence of clearance cairns. Geology maps may provide clues as to the source of the building material.

5.   What variation is there in wall type? Look for the presence of 'hogg holes', 'rabbit smoots' and 'wall heads'. Measure the width, height, batter and length of walls and comment on the style of

construction. Is there a relationship between wall type and steepness of slope?

Uses/functions of walls

1. What are the functions of walls? Sort the walls into those that provide shelter for livestock or act as barriers to prevent straying; act as channels to move livestock down the mountainside; act as Parish or pasture boundaries, or have a combination of several functions. How are these walls distributed across the area?

2. What improvements could be made to the location of walls and their type of construction to help (a) the farmer and (b) the visitor?

Walls that provide shelter for plants and animals

1. What lives on walls? Note the types, abundance and distribution of plants and animals on the walls. Are they found living in cracks or water courses near the top or bottom of the wall?

2. Why do the plants and animals live where they do? Examine the type of stone, the orientation of the wall, its exposure and inclination, age and roughness of the stone surfaces. If it is raining, watch where the water is running since plants may be associated with the water courses.

3. Do the walls in the area support the same plants and animals?

B   Habitats of Living Things

Background

By and large there are three vegetation communities which dominate the fells of upland areas. They are:

(a)   bracken

(b)   mat grass

(c)   bog.

Above the 400 metre level bracken often gives way to patchy grassland with associated mosses and lichens. These plants can tolerate the thin soil and exposure found at these altitudes. The well-drained valley floors provide good grazing land which is often 'improved' with the use of artificial fertilisers which enrich the soil with nitrogen, phosphorus and potassium. The fells themselves are grazed by sheep which may seriously inhibit the growth of germinating seedlings of some species. Bracken is not palatable to sheep and therefore grows to cover large areas. Boggy, poorly drained areas are hostile environments to most plants and are dominated by 'bog moss' (Sphagnum) species.

Some questions for consideration

1. Why do certain plants grow in this locality?

2. Is there some change in geology/aspect/slope which affects plant distribution?

3. Why does this plant grow in association with this other plant?

4. Has some outside agency, e.g. people affected the area in which particular plants grow?

5. Do sheep have any effect on plant communities? Are the plants on this hillside the same as those on another?

Generally the aims of this type of study are comparative. Young people should compare and contrast habitats of living things in different areas and try to discover why plants exist at some sites and not at others.

C   Mines and Quarries

Abandoned mines and quarries are common in many upland parts of England and Wales. Underground workings are usually dangerous but there are often remains at the surface and exploring these may provide the basis for many interesting integrated projects. Examples include railway tracks, mine buildings and water-powered machinery and its associated water courses.

Safety

Open shafts and quarry faces are clearly visible hazards. Mine areas often contain hidden dangers as well. The mouth of a 'level' or tunnel running into a hillside may appear enticing to the young explorer, but its innocuous looking dirt floor may well rest on rotting timbers a century or more old which conceal a chasm below.

How to locate suitable areas

Ordnance Survey maps at scales of 1:25,000 or larger show most abandoned workings. In the field the first sign of a working is often its spoil heap. Mines and quarries produce far more spoil than usable material, and because planning regulations were less strict hitherto, mine entrances are frequently marked by large unlandscaped heaps of rubble. To reduce transport costs, the ore was often processed at the site, as a result of which the waste from the processing plant may augment other spoil.

Examples of projects

a) Watercourses

Upland areas usually have high rainfall. Before the industrial revolution mine machinery was often water-powered. Unless miners could site the equipment beside a suitable stream they had to construct watercourses or 'leats' across country. Typically these consisted of ditches a metre or so deep with a wall on the downslope side to contain the water. Generally they have gentle gradients and so snake round hillsides following contours. Where the leat left the stream or reservoir there was a sluice and at the opposite end a storage pond to provide an even flow of water to the waterwheel.

Possible projects could include:

- Plotting routes of watercourses on existing large-scale maps (e.g. 1:10,000).

- Preparing a map of the watercourses using simply survey techniques.

- Measuring the widths, depths and gradients.

- Locating sluices and storage ponds.

- Locating reservoirs.

- Noting construction methods.

b) Railways and tramways

In post-industrial revolution mines and quarries, ore was generally carried by trucks running on rails. These were moved by manpower, ponies, locomotives or cables from fixed machinery. The track beds were usually of solid construction so that their remains, often grassed over, may frequently be seen today.

Possible projects could include:

- Plotting tracks on an existing large-scale map.

- Preparing a map of the tracks using simple surveying techniques.

- ◆ Measuring widths and gradients, types of track.

- ◆ Locating bridges and fixed machinery.

- ◆ Discovering the motive power used.

c) Mine and quarry buildings

Many workings have associated buildings such as explosive and equipment stores, machinery houses, offices and workers' cottages. The condition of these is very often ruinous but their location may provide clues as to their past use. For example, a power house at the bottom of a steep pipeline supplied with water by a leat leading from a stream; or a terrace of miners' cottages on a south-facing slope some distance from, but within easy access to, the mine workings

Possible projects could include:

- ◆ Plotting location of buildings on existing large-scale maps.

- ◆ Preparing large-scale plans (at scale 1:1000 or larger) of selected buildings.

- ◆ Describing architecture and construction; present day adaptation or use.

d) Spoil heaps

Spoil heaps come in two types. The first type is normally the residue left after the processing of ore and the useless rock produced in tunnelling to reach the ore. The second usually lacks unusual minerals and resembles the local rocks. The rocks in the first, often contain minerals (in Britain most often quartz) and, depending on the processing techniques used, have frequently been crushed to smaller size than the second. When the processing has produced a slurry of fine waste mixed with water the heaps have flat tops and terraced sides. This is due to the accumulation of the waste layer by layer in ponds enclosed by low dams.

Spoil heaps are useful because they provide clues to the size of the workings (the larger it is the greater the volume of spoil) - and to the processing techniques. For example at Greenside Lead Mine near Glenridding, processing techniques have changed over the years. The older spoil heaps contain comparatively large fragments that have been picked through by hand. The younger heaps are of much finer material processed by machine and pumped onto the tip as slurry.

Possible projects might include:

◆ Plotting locations of spoil heaps on existing large-scale maps.

◆ Estimating the volume of spoil heaps by simple survey techniques.

◆ Finding the average size of particles in a heap by measuring a sample.

◆ Searching material for signs of the mineral mined.

◆ Suggesting ways of reducing or removing 'eyesore' spoil heaps.

D   Archaeological Remains

The fells of northern England are rich in archaeological remains. They include remains of coppice woodlands, kilns, Roman roads, shielings, bronze age dwellings, ancient pack-horse routes, and farmsteadings.

1.   Coppice woodlands

When walking up a long valley it is a useful exercise to plot the areas of woodland that have been coppiced. Pupils can record the remains of industries that have been associated with the woodlands; for example: charcoal burning 'pitstead' tracks leading through and to the woods etc.

Research into coppice industries will initiate questions about how people lived in the past - how woodland industries evolved, how charcoal was made - trade links with other areas and woodland related industries. Recording need not be complicated, and involves the use of 1:25,000 map, a 20m or 30m tape measure and a 'Silva' compass.

2.   Kilns

Studying kilns is very similar to investigating coppice woodlands, only the raw materials are different! Potash kilns are often found in bracken infested areas, and required bracken and birch twigs (potash was used in the textile industry). Lime kilns are usually situated near out-cropping limestone - but not always !

3. Pack-horse routes

Young people can be encouraged to observe and record the bridges, lengths of made up track and revetment, track state, small buildings and enclosures seen on the routes.

4. Roman roads

A fine example is High Street in Cumbria. This runs between Troutbeck and Tirril (near Penrith), 29 kilometres (18 miles) of high fell track. Projects could include detailing any prominent surfaces or sections, (e.g. where there has been erosion or landslip) and looking for other evidence such as forts or milestones. Information could be recorded on standard 1:25,000 maps.

5. Shielings

Shielings are summer settlements used mainly in 'wild country' areas in the past for the pasturing of stock to allow lowlands to regenerate.

Integrated study projects could involve the study of maps, and possibly aerial photographs, to locate likely sites prior to visiting the area and recording them accurately on 1:25,000 maps.

D A Woodland Project

Britain is rich in its many types of coniferous and broad leafed woodlands. Many opportunities exist whilst groups are journeying into and through upland areas to observe the different varieties of woodland. This suggested project is designed to raise the consciousness of young people towards woodlands and highlight the importance and need for management in order to ensure the survival of woodlands in the future.

1. Split the group into pairs and encourage each pupil to explore and develop their reactions to the woodlands. Ask them to consider the following:

♦ Listen - what do you hear?

♦ Look - how much colour and light is there?

♦ Feel - take off your shoes - how does the ground feel?

♦ Taste - what might be a general taste - sweet or bitter? Use your imagination.

♦ Smell - how many smells can you smell? Are they good or bad?

Ask each pupil to consider all these aspects and write down their findings. Encourage them to share their perceptions with other members of the group.

2. Encourage the group to consciously determine those areas where work is needed to improve the woodland and get them to survey the area and develop a working management strategy.

- Are there few or too many trees - what can we do about it?

- Are the trees all the same age - and how does this affect the structure of the wood?

- Is there any animal life - how can we improve it as a habitat for them?

- Ground flora - can we improve it so that more will grow?

- What possible uses could this woodland have?

- Why is it here and what benefit is it to man?

- Draw up a list of things to do to improve the woodland immediately.

Conclusion

This chapter has attempted to illustrate the many ways in which outdoor and adventurous projects can be more than just a focus for purely physical development. It has highlighted a myriad of projects and ideas which can be developed with young people while engaged in adventurous activities. The fact that adventurous activities offer unique opportunities not only for social and personal development and physical learning, but also for cognitive development, underlines the fact that all outdoor experiences can be viewed as an integral part of the National Curriculum.

Chapter 7

The value and potential of 'adventurous journeys' at Key Stages 3 and 4.

> "If any man shall demand of me the cause of this my voyage, certainly I can show no better reason than is the ardent desire of knowledge, which hath moved many other to see the world and the miracles of God therein."
>
> *Varthema Ludovico, quoted 1576*

INTRODUCTION

Given the opportunity to reflect upon some of life's rich moments, most practitioners committed to the outdoors would agree that often the most profoundly memorable experiences - those having the greatest impact - are likely to be those which have taken place during the course of an expedition or an adventurous journey. To embark upon a journey of adventure, is one of life's most valuable and enriching experiences.

There are many sceptics who would say - what is it about journeying which makes it so special? Why is it such a powerful medium? Why do adventurers achieve so much satisfaction from their exploits? In what ways are 'journeys' relevant in education? Can they be justified?

To undertake an adventurous journey can offer pupils of all ages and ability scope to widen their horizons of life, at every level. Whatever the experience, the journey will give rise to an increased awareness of self, others and the environment. It will bring opportunities to face up to new challenges, come to terms with the unknown; it will involve a degree of risk and uncertainty, and require self-reliance in pitting one's skill, knowledge, experience and fortitude against the natural elements.

Adventurous journeys also offer opportunities, possibly unrivalled in any other sphere of life, for people to work as a member of a team, where each person becomes, to some degree, dependent upon other colleagues in playing their part in working towards the successful outcome of the venture. Such interdependence can develop a camaraderie within the group and equally a loyalty, often leading to life-long friendships; outcomes which are in many ways unparalleled in other forms of experience. To undertake an adventurous journey also gives rise to opportunities to travel in terms of time and space; away from all the known supports of western society, of family ties, of friends, of home, of job; away from the routine of bells, meetings, commitments, where even time takes on a different and often inconsequential perspective.

Journeying in the National Curriculum

The educational benefits of establishing 'journeying' as a feature within the framework of the school curriculum is axiomatic. Some would argue that in the context of the National Curriculum, such a notion is unrealistic.

While the National Curriculum is very prescriptive in terms of programmes of study and attainment targets for pupils of the ages of 7, 11, 14 and 16, there still is considerable scope for individual teaching styles and for teacher enterprise. Although the attainment targets do appear almost immutable, they are not specific in terms of teaching approaches. The routes and vehicles to achieving many of the programmes of study are still open to some personal interpretation by teachers. Teachers should not lose sight of this fact, but strive towards maintaining what in recent years, has become a very exciting and increasingly acceptable practice of using 'journeys' as a viable and valued component of the curriculum, in a growing number of schools particularly at Key Stages 3 and 4.

Writ large in the physical education programme of study for outdoor and adventurous activities at Key Stage 4 is the notion that pupils who choose this option will be required to undertake a 'journey' safely to encompass one or more activities (*Figure 7.1*). There is an expectation that journeying gives rise to meeting and overcoming challenges, and provides opportunities for being involved in complex techniques. An understanding of nutrition and the effect of climate on the body should ensue.

One has only to read through the National Curriculum science and geography documents to see how relevant are many of the programmes of study in the context of adventurous journeys. For example, guidance notes for geography state that *"pupils should develop knowledge and understanding of the ways in which human activities affect the earth"*. The programme of study for science states that *"pupils should develop skills of planning and carrying out explorations, investigations and tasks and interpreting and evaluating*

98

outcomes... develop the ability to work effectively as part of a group in the planning, carrying out, reporting and evaluation of an investigation or task". These references support many of the very principles that adventurous journeys do stand up to scrutiny, and can be justified at Key Stages 3 and 4.

Outdoor and adventurous activity

Key Stage 4

Programme of study

A   To prepare for and undertake a journey safely encompassing one or more activities, e.g. canoeing, fell walking, rock climbing, in an unfamiliar environment.

B   To develop their own ideas by creating challenges for others.

C   To apply increasingly complex techniques and safety procedures appropriate to the activity or activities undertaken.

D   To understand more of the effects of nutrition and climatic conditions on the body through the activity or activities undertaken and be aware of and respond to changing environmental conditions.

Figure 7.1

Putting ideas into practice

To undertake any adventurous journey, at whatever level, demands a high degree of planning and a clearly devised strategy. In terms of the National Curriculum, the only way that the concept of 'journeying' as a vehicle for learning might even be considered by the senior management team within a school, is likely to be dependent upon the way in which the whole experience attends to, and can be justified on sound educational grounds. The strategy which is outlined has been drawn from current practice, as it exists in several schools. It should be noted that although the suggested model was originally designed specifically for inclusion as part of a 'Personal and Social Education Module', in the TVEI Extension for Year 9 and 10 students in the secondary phase of education, the principles can be easily adapted for use in the primary sector.

Teaching and learning styles

Underpinning the whole process of preparation, execution and evaluation of the adventurous journey should be the notion that the whole experience is utilised as a powerful medium for personal and social development. Through a "supported self study" approach to learning, the young people involved in the project should have an expectation to:

♦ work closely alongside a tutor;

♦ work alongside other colleagues;

♦ enter into a binding contractual agreement in terms of participation, expectations and methods of evaluation;

♦ determine their own mode of, and level of journey through consultation and negotiation.

Aims

Any course should enable students to work progressively towards the development of the necessary skills, attitudes, leadership and teamwork qualities required for the safe completion of an extended journey, either over land, on water or in another context. Through the process of "supported self study", students should be encouraged to devise their own schedules of training and preparation.

Duration

The whole course should ideally cover a period of between two and three school terms, to include planning, preparation, training, execution and evaluation of the journey.

Components

The course should ideally consist of five components, to include:

♦ 10 half day sessions: for members of the group and the tutor to meet together.

♦ 10 half day sessions: for students to develop specific components, by means of a 'supported self study' programme.

♦ 2 × 2 days residential experience: for students to develop the necessary physical skills required for the journey and to create group cohesion.

♦ The journey: this should aim to last between 2 - 3 days.

♦ Evaluation of journey: the production of an assignment.

Specific course components

These should include:

1.   Introduction to the project

Strategy of working, operation, the contract, tutorial system.

Developing group identity.

2.   Residential 1

Variety of team building exercises.

Introduction to a wide range of activities.

3.   Identification of the journey

Choice guided by consultation/negotiation.

4.   Planning

Feasibility of journey.

Practical considerations.

Dietary considerations.

5.   Fitness

Related to specific journey.

Personal fitness programmes.

Individual/group strengths/weaknesses.

6.   Skills

Progressive development of all skills required.

General skills: navigation, weather, campcraft, rescue.

7.   Safety

Theory and practice.

Objective and subjective dangers - risk assessment.

Students identify monitoring strategies.

8.   First aid

Practical work in related activity.

Theoretical work.

9.   Residential 2

Development of necessary technical skills for successful completion of journey.

Team building.

10.   Conservation

Impact of venture on environment.

Devise a practical project.

11.   The journey

To last at least three days and two nights.

12.   Evaluation

To what extent were objectives achieved?

Personal/group developments.

13.   Production of log/record of journey

Written, photographic.

Collage, art.

Audio-visual presentation.

14.   Final review of project

Learning which took place.

Outcomes of venture.

Where do we go from here?

Review of the process

The scheme outlined has been successfully operated in a number of schools for at least five years. It has been integrated into at least three secondary schools and one special school with outstanding results. During those periods when the young people were undergoing their own training programme and devising their own specific 'journeys' of various lengths, using a range of different modes of travel, anxieties ran high. While some apprehension was highlighted both by staff and parents alike in the initial period of the project, most would agree that the experiences had an enormous impact upon students and helped them to develop in a variety of ways.

The success of the ventures have been largely dependent on the quality of the teaching, the commitment of parents and staff, and the thorough preparation by the young people themselves. Projects of this nature are highly valued by all those involved. Ventures have enabled a number of youngsters to aspire to even more challenging, intensive and demanding self reliant journeys, in this country, on the continent and further afield.

The diversity of the "journeys" has been varied. They have ranged from:

♦ a mountain bike traverse of the Cheviots;

♦ a linear traverse from coast to coast on foot;

♦ a circumnavigation of Lake Windermere by canoe;

♦ a coastal journey from Stranraer to Maryport using Wayfarer dinghies;

♦ a journey from John o' Groats to Land's End using public transport;

♦ a Pyrenean expedition on foot;

♦ a journey from Barrow to Carlisle on horseback;

♦ a passage from Grange in Borrowdale to Workington, using open Canadian canoes;

...to mention a few.

"The scope and opportunity for embarking upon any adventurous journey should only be limited by the imagination of the individual."

Experience suggests that, whilst some students have required much guidance on what is practical - given in some cases a limited background, knowledge, motivation and imagination - the majority of youngsters participating have entered into schemes of this nature with maturity, enterprise, sensitivity and responsibility - all qualities regarded as intrinsic to this approach to teaching and learning.

Further considerations

Outlined in the final part of this chapter are a number of important issues which leaders may wish to consider in setting up a journeying option as part of the PE curriculum for Key Stages 3 and 4. Details relate to organisation and management, safety and 'in loco parentis' responsibilities which are relevant to all journeying options and projects in the context of:

1. water-based activities;

2. land-based/rock outcrop activities;

3. subterranean-based activities.

1. Journeys in the context of water-based activities and projects

(Guidelines for groups wishing to undertake canoeing, kayaking or sailing)

Open Canadian canoeing, kayaking and sailing all provide a wide range of adventurous journeys that can be undertaken. With all water activities there will always be inherent dangers, and it is essential that participants are trained to a high standard of personal competence before ventures of this nature are undertaken. It is vital that an integral part of training includes a comprehensive programme of safety principles and procedures. Self reliance and independence lie at the very heart of any adventurous approach to journeying and exploration, and safety considerations must always be given the highest priority.

Safety

Participants should be able to demonstrate practical competence in handling the selected craft. They should have a thorough knowledge and proven experience of deep water rescues, first aid, artificial respiration, and be competent swimmers. All groups should carry emergency food, spare clothing, first aid, spare paddles, repair kit, throwing lines and towing lines, wear approved life jackets or buoyancy aids, and crash hats, as appropriate. They should be familiar with the equipment they carry, fully conversant with rescue procedures and made aware of the inherent dangers of the activity by doing risk assessment.

Responsibilities

(a) Participants: should ensure that the expedition they intend to pursue has the full support and approval of an experienced sailor or canoeist (as appropriate), preferably one who holds senior instructor status, who has intimate knowledge of the area to be journeyed. They should discuss the route with the expert in the planning stages so as to benefit from their experience and local knowledge. Each participant should not only inform parents of the details of the journey but also have gained their approval. In the case of canoe or kayak groups, they should also ensure that access agreements have been obtained, both from local land owners and the BCU local coaching organiser, before embarking upon the journey.

(b) The adult/supervisor: the person having responsibility for the sailing or canoeing journey should themselves be competent at the activity or in the craft selected by the group. The adult should ensure that approval has been given by parents/ guardians and that access permits have been made between landowners and officials. The person responsible should be entirely satisfied that the group is competent to cope with the prevailing conditions, and that each member has the training and experience to undertake the journey.

Ideas for exploration

Throughout the many parts of the United Kingdom, there exists an extensive network of rivers and canals on which groups might wish to undertake a journey of exploration. The British Isles, surrounded by a fascinating coastline, also provides limitless opportunities for groups to undertake a journey using either Canadian canoes, kayaks or sailing craft.

Throughout the adventurous journey participants should seek to achieve clear objectives. They may like to consider using the journey to conduct one or a number of projects based upon first hand enquiry. Projects might range from surveying and measurement involving a detailed study of an area, to compiling a waterways or coastal guide. Options might well include mapping a bay or island, taking soundings of a bay, recording temperature change or comparing and contrasting the range of animals and plants along the route.

2. Journeys in the context of land-based/rock outcrop activities and projects

(Guidelines for groups wishing to undertake rock climbing)

Rock climbing is a highly specialised form of adventurous activity involving a high degree of skill and competence. The activity carries with it a strong element of potential risk, and requires those supervising or leading to have an understanding of their abilities, a great depth of experience and a comprehensive knowledge of safety procedures.

Safety

Unaccompanied journeys which involve young people undertaking some element of rock climbing should only be attempted if those taking part are extremely competent - having a wide experience of the activity - and also have a comprehensive working knowledge of belaying techniques, methods of life lining, abseiling and rescue techniques. They should be familiar with modern equipment and techniques and be fully aware of the inherent dangers.

Conservation

Young people using rock climbing as a journeying option should take great care not to damage, deface or tamper with the natural habitats of flora and fauna which exist on rock faces. Explorers should try as far as possible to leave the crag/cliff as they found it and have a deep respect and concern for the environment in which they are exploring.

Responsibilities

(a) Participants: they should ensure that the project which they intend to pursue has the full approval of an experienced mountaineer who is familiar with the specific area in which the venture is to be undertaken. Details of the crags/cliffs to be climbed should be discussed with this adult, and plans of the exploration should have his/her approval. It is important that participants not only inform parents of the details of the exploration, but also have gained their approval and that of the landowners before proceeding upon the venture.

(b) The adult/supervisor: the person responsible for the expedition should themselves be a rock climber. They should ensure that the venture has been approved by an expert, by parents and by the landowner. They should be entirely satisfied that the group is properly equipped, and that each member has had sufficient training and experience to undertake the project. The supervisor should also ensure that a leader has been appointed within the group.

Ideas for exploration

Although most cliffs, outcrops and crags lend themselves to a wide variety of possible ventures, the activity of rock-climbing can realistically only provide opportunities for either surveying and measurement projects, or for a detailed study to be undertaken and a guide book compiled of the area under research. Exploration projects which might compare and contrast vegetation, geology, lichens and even fauna, while extremely valuable and interesting, are very difficult in practice, due to the precarious nature of the activity.

3. Journeys in the context of subterranean-based activities and projects

(Guidelines for groups wishing to undertake caving and mine exploration)

To explore the beauty of the underground environment gives rise to a sense of wonder, achievement and comradeship which is very different from any other form of outdoor activity. However it should be recognised that all caves, and mines especially, are potentially dangerous, hostile environments; they are always dark, frequently wet, cold and muddy, arduous to explore and require a particular level of experience by those who undertake ventures of this nature. Caves may be structurally and geologically treacherous.

Safety

It must be stressed that unaccompanied journeys underground should never be attempted by young people unless they have a thorough knowledge of the potential hazards and are suitably experienced cavers.

Conservation

It is imperative that those undertaking this journeying option take very good care not to disturb the delicate environment through which they travel. Samples of rocks, animals and plants should never be taken. Make sure that all evidence of the visit is removed.

Responsibilities

(a) Participants: those undertaking journeys of this type should ensure that, prior to the expedition, the cave or mine in question has been visited, is well-known and that the whole venture has been discussed with and approved by an experienced person, who themselves are familiar with the "system" to be explored. Detailed plans of the journey should be left with the adult responsible, who should take all the precautions of informing parents and landowners of the group's intentions, and of the times when they will be underground.

(b) The adult responsible: should be entirely satisfied that the group is properly equipped, has the relevant level of experience, and that each member has sufficient skill and strength to carry out the expedition.

Ideas for exploration

Expeditions into a cave system provide many unique opportunities for groups to record, collect data, and observe. Groups may either wish to carry out a survey of the system, or to record and observe the different species of flora and fauna of various parts of the cave.

Conclusion

Outdoor and adventurous 'journeys' fit very comfortably with the revised orders of the PE National Curriculum and with aspects of the science and geography programmes of study. Through a supported self-study approach and framework, adventurous journeys mirror much of the underlying philosophy of the TVEI Extension and post-16 education, "to encourage young people to take responsibility for their own learning through the spirit of self-discovery and enterprise". For these reasons teachers should take every opportunity to introduce and develop programmes of this nature, not only to create greater breadth and balance in an otherwise narrow curriculum, but to provide young people with relevant experiences, through the process of self discovery, to learn something about the environment and about themselves and others. More importantly it is hoped that through the process of journeying, young people may appreciate that through first hand experiences, some of life's issues can be addressed in a very real, practical and enjoyable way.   .

Section 3

Outdoor environmental studies in the National Curriculum

Chapter 8

A theoretical framework for outdoor environmental studies in the National Curriculum

INTRODUCTION

Outdoor environmental studies is considered by many, to be a dynamic approach to learning. By means of a range of field study projects and activities, which are primarily based upon a child's physical, spiritual, social and environmental interaction with the outdoors, can lead to the progressive development of attitudes and skills. Such is the view of the Schools Council Project (S.C.P 1980).

Outdoor environmental studies in the context of the National Curriculum should aim to involve pupils in decision making and the formation of a code of behaviour about issues concerning environmental quality. Teachers should recognise that:

♦ First hand exploration is essential to all outdoor environmental studies.

♦ The environments studied should be both local and less local and should range from wilderness to inner city, both at home and abroad.

♦ The development of pupils' knowledge, understanding, attitudes and skills must run parallel to one another.

♦ The development of pupils' understanding of natural processes and human features can greatly enhance a sense of wonder and awe about the environment.

♦ In developing environmental understanding, the aim should be to produce a desire in young people to respect and care for the environment in a practical way. This implies conservation in the broadest sense.

Outdoor environmental studies has relevance across the curriculum. Many of the programmes of study and level descriptions in all core and foundation subjects can be achieved through studies out of doors. *Figures 8.1, 8.2 and 8.3* illustrate a range of particular topics to include woodlands, litter and lakes and ponds, all of which can be best achieved through outdoor environmental studies.

113

Studies in woodlands

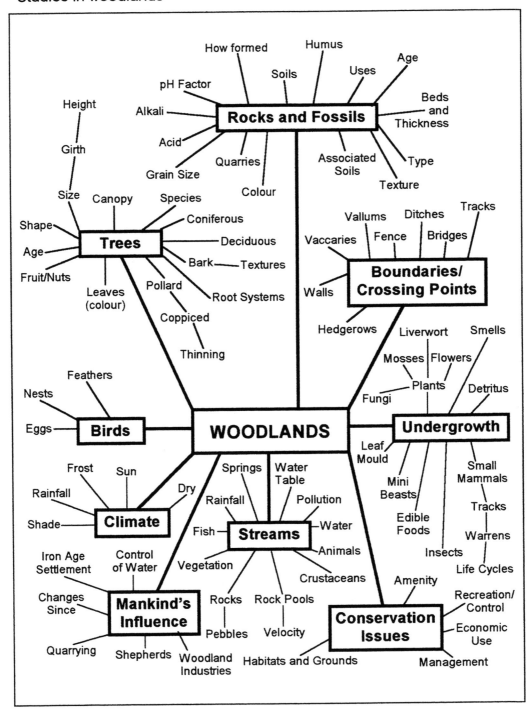

Figure 8.1

114

Litter studies

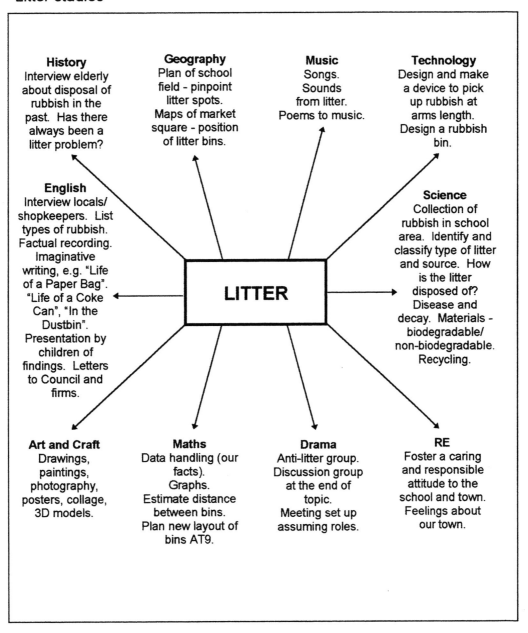

History
Interview elderly about disposal of rubbish in the past. Has there always been a litter problem?

Geography
Plan of school field - pinpoint litter spots. Maps of market square - position of litter bins.

Music
Songs. Sounds from litter. Poems to music.

Technology
Design and make a device to pick up rubbish at arms length. Design a rubbish bin.

English
Interview locals/ shopkeepers. List types of rubbish. Factual recording. Imaginative writing, e.g. "Life of a Paper Bag". "Life of a Coke Can", "In the Dustbin". Presentation by children of findings. Letters to Council and firms.

LITTER

Science
Collection of rubbish in school area. Identify and classify type of litter and source. How is the litter disposed of? Disease and decay. Materials - biodegradable/ non-biodegradable. Recycling.

Art and Craft
Drawings, paintings, photography, posters, collage, 3D models.

Maths
Data handling (our facts). Graphs. Estimate distance between bins. Plan new layout of bins AT9.

Drama
Anti-litter group. Discussion group at the end of topic. Meeting set up assuming roles.

RE
Foster a caring and responsible attitude to the school and town. Feelings about our town.

Figure 8.2

Studies of lakes and ponds

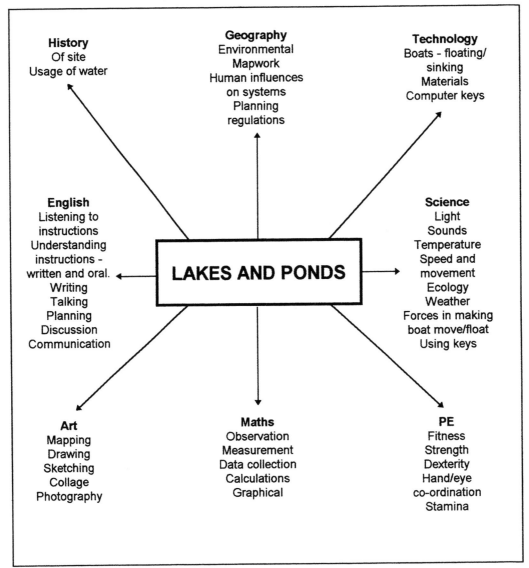

Figure 8.3

Approaches to teaching and learning

Teachers will need to give some consideration to the most appropriate styles of teaching and learning. One of the most effective models for developing outdoor environmental studies is based on the notion of raising awareness, developing knowledge and understanding, and developing skills (G. Cooper, 1991). This process can lead to attitude changes and the actions necessary to conserve the environment *(Figure 8.4)*. An explanation follows.

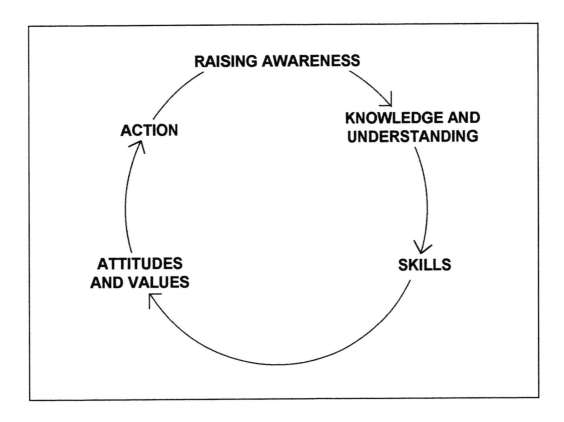

Figure 8.4

Step 1   *Raising Awareness*

There are many opportunities in the outdoors to encourage environmental awareness. Challenging activities where motivation is high can help to introduce young people to environmental issues. Strong personal feelings towards the environment can be developed through adventure, artistic or sensory activities. A self-reliant journey into a natural environment can trigger personal, social and environmental awareness.

Step 2   *Knowledge and Understanding*

Outdoor environmental studies provide first-hand experiences of environments. It engages real situations and issues and gives relevance to topics such as agriculture, energy, industry, building design and planning. The environment is experienced through direct sensory contact. Information is gained from primary sources through

117

observation and discussion. Learning is by doing and leads to greater appreciation and understanding. Students can be introduced to the natural processes which take place in the environment. They should appreciate that social, economic and political systems affect the nature and quality of our environment.

Step 3   *Skills*

Outdoor environmental studies allow students to develop skills of investigation. They are encouraged to define questions, develop hypotheses, collect, present, analyse and interpret information and draw conclusions. Studies often involve data collection and the use of information technology.

There are opportunities to explore and discuss environmental issues. These issues may be approached through adventure, problem solving, field investigation, art or drama. Students can develop personal responses and values and these can be communicated through such means as writing, drawing, discussion and role play.

Step 4   *Attitudes and Values*

Outdoor environmental studies aim to develop personal, social and environmental awareness. Through real problem solving situations in the outdoors, students develop personal and social skills. They learn to respect evidence and the beliefs and opinions of others. Activities based on adventure and creativity often lead to a greater awareness of the environment and a concern for other living things. On occasions, experiences can be inspirational. They can lead to a change in attitudes to the environment and a commitment to conservation.

Step 5   *Action*

There is also scope to encourage practical improvements to the environment. Through outdoor environmental studies, students may experience environmental problems such as water pollution, footpath erosion and urban decay. This can sometimes lead to their involvement in finding solutions. It could mean taking steps to influence decision-makers, working with conservation organisations and undertaking practical tasks to improve the environment.

Outdoor environmental studies involves:

♦ *UNDERSTANDING* - of how the human world depends on, and closely relates to, the natural world and how both interact.

♦ *AWARENESS* - of how human beings affect the environment, built, local, and world - and how it affects us.

♦ *RESPONSIBILITY* - in showing concern and care for the environment in a practical way.

Using outdoor environmental studies to address National Curriculum subjects

Environmental Studies can be thought of as comprising three interlinked components *(see Figure 8.5)*:

♦ education *about* the environment (knowledge)

♦ education *for* the environment (values, attitudes, positive action)

♦ education *in* or through the environment (a resource)

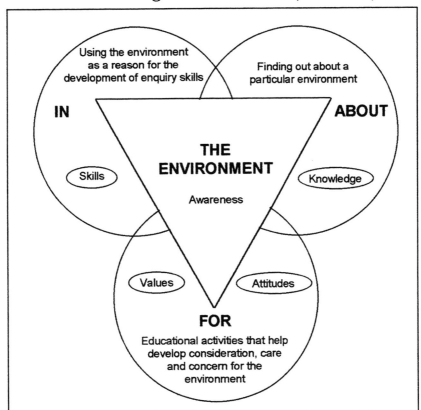

Figure 8.5

1. Education about the environment

A basic knowledge and understanding of the environment can be developed through any one of the following topics:

♦ climate/weather/weathering;

♦ soils, rocks and minerals;

♦ water;

♦ materials and resources, including energy;

♦ plants and animals;

♦ people and their communities;

♦ buildings, industrialisation and waste;

♦ woodlands.

For the most part, these topics will be taught through subjects of the National Curriculum, and in particular through the programmes of study for science, technology, geography and history, though not exclusively.

Geography

Environmental studies permeates the whole of the Geography National Curriculum. In particular Environmental Geography has three important strands:

♦ the use and misuse of natural resources;

♦ the quality of and vulnerability of different environments;

♦ the possibilities of protecting and managing environments.

NCC Curriculum Guidance also highlights that:

> "geography's distinctive concern for area studies at a range of scales, from the local to the global, is particularly significant for Environmental Studies."

Where environmental issues are concerned, national boundaries are of little importance. The problems of global warming and acid rain cannot be solved by any one country. This is also true for the problems caused by mass tourism. The Alps, for example, form part of our European heritage and their protection requires co-operation on an international scale. Pupils should therefore be helped to understand the relationships between countries in terms of space, resources and the effects of their activities on the environment.

Science

The Programmes of Study for science also present opportunities for learning about the environment. For example, energy sources, the processes of life and the effects of human activity on the environment.

The programmes of study for science frequently describe the use of environmental contexts as starting points. For example, the programme of study for Key Stage 2 states:

> *Pupils should explore and investigate at least two different habitats and the animals and plants that live there. They should find out how animals and plants are suited to these habitats and how they are influenced by environmental conditions including seasonal and daily changes and measure these changes using a variety of instruments. They should develop an awareness and understanding of the necessity for sensitive collection and care of living things used as the subject of any study of the environment. They should be made aware of the competition between living things and their need for food, shelter and a place to reproduce. They should study the effects of pollution on the survival of living things.*

Technology

Within Technology, 'Design Technology' can be usefully applied to Outdoor Environmental Studies as it is concerned with using informed judgement to seek practical solutions to certain problems. In relation to education about the environment, AT1 (Designing) and AT2 (Making) are particularly relevant.

The programmes of study for design technology illustrate possible ways of setting work in an environmental context. For example, one activity in the programme of study for Key Stage 2 is "investigate the effects of design and technological activity on the environment". Other examples are the design and construction of wild gardens, bird boxes and bird feeders.

The potential also of information technology, to help pupils develop their understanding of the environment is limitless. The scope for data handling and for generating ideas using IT, is immense.

History

The study of history assists pupils to appreciate how the environment has been shaped by human activity as well as natural change. Pupils can apply historical skills to interpret written sources and physical remains which give clues to long term changes in the environment.

History develops a respect for evidence. Visual evidence is all around the pupils in clues that are waiting to be discovered; alterations to buildings, road patterns, street names, signs, gravestones, field names and patterns, churches, castles and railway stations. The past is very much part of our present.

Children can learn much from the past that will enable them to be responsible decision makers of the future. People create history and it is people who play an important part in defining the way in which our involvement in the environment determines our modes of living.

Art

Sight is a function, seeing is an art, and it is our duty to help children to develop the art of seeing. The aim of teaching awareness of the environment through art is both to help children better understand the world around them, and through that experience, the world within them. Drawing a closely observed tree or plant, an aspect of some industrial complex, or the sweep of a hillside can provide profound knowledge of the shape, form, structure and details of the various elements which make up the source of information. Likewise the experience of moulding and manipulating materials, building and restructuring materials to represent some aspects of the observed environment provides an excellent opportunity for the maker to consider how forms, fibres and fabrics may affect the functions which take place within them. Art provides a vehicle for pupils to exercise an aesthetic appreciation of the environment in a very practical way.

English

The outdoor environment has often been used as the basis for language work, be it a discussion of a controversial issue, a factual report on a visit or a descriptive, possibly emotional response to an element of nature. Environmental Studies, while not explicitly identified within the National Curriculum syllabus for English, is inseparable from it. Moral attitudes and aesthetic values are often more effectively inculcated than when taught, and this is the special property of fable, myth, poetry and story.

Mathematics

Mathematics has many applications and uses as reflected fully in the National Curriculum programmes of study.

The environment in which we live is a ready provider of problems. It is a resource for the delivery of content. As we use mathematics to help clarify our understanding of the world we inhabit, so too do we gain insight into the structure of the subject. There should be opportunity for pupils to decide what quantitative attributes are important, what to measure, how to measure, how to display, interpret, code, analyse, generalise, predict and evaluate.

Music

Many of the skills involved in music education are general to other areas of development; some, such as working with rhythms and making melody are frequently powerful catalysts in developing aspects of creativity that are not triggered off by other areas of educational provision.

Within music, pupils can explore and enjoy both the urban and natural environment. There is much scope for developing skills associated with analysing and creating music which are based upon exploring sounds of the town or country; the sounds of the sea, the wind in the trees, other natural sounds and those manufactured in the environment.

Physical Education

Good health, like the natural environment, is something we may not appreciate the value of, until it is lost. There are close links between physical well being and the well being of the environment. It is in the field of outdoor education particularly that the environment and physical skills come together as factors of equal importance. It is in the interests of all to ensure a wise and sustainable use of the environment through developing a positive attitude of stewardship in pupils. The environment should not become yet another burden for young people to carry, rather a thing of joy and a source of pleasure and absorbing interest. By linking physical education and environmental awareness, pupils are provided with the opportunity to develop sensitivity to and appropriate concern for the environment, while at the same time learning to use it to best advantage through first hand experiences.

Religious Education

All religions have within them implicit and explicit teachings about the environment. Where a religion has been the main faith of a society these ideals help shape perceptions at a precognitive level, even of those who do not subscribe to a faith. To many in the west, the natural environment regrettably has been seen to be mastered and to be exploited for the benefit of mankind. Within the Christian faith there is a tradition that God's love extends beyond mankind to the whole of creation. Religion very much affects the way we see the world, understand our place within it and therefore behave towards it.

Modern Languages

Language usually aims to offer insights into the culture and civilisation of another country as well as dealing with the mechanics of the language. Recent examples of issues affecting more than one country are the problems of air pollution, acid rain, poverty, malnutrition, the use of aerosols and their damage to the ozone layer, nuclear explosions, pollution and global warming. International solutions to environmental problems are recorded in the media. They all help to raise these issues with young people and reinforce the relevance of acquiring language skills as a means of understanding more fully the way in which problems can be overcome.

2. Education For The Environment

Education for the environment is concerned with:

♦ finding ways of ensuring a caring use of the environment now and in the future

♦ finding solutions to environmental problems, taking into account the fact that there are conflicting interests and different cultural perspectives

♦ being informed about the choices which have to be made.

All pupils are, to a greater or lesser extent, involved in every day activities which affect their environment. For example, they are already inhabitants, consumers and followers of leisure pursuits. As children these activities are likely to take place within a relatively narrow range of social contexts - home and family, school, neighbourhood and peer group. As adults their activities will become more extensive; they will become producers and decision makers in the workplace, local, national and international communities.

Each curriculum subject can be used to help pupils develop insight into human behaviour and its effects on the environment. A programme for outdoor environmental studies which draws on the whole curriculum will give pupils the opportunity to consider environmental issues from the perspectives mentioned earlier - physical, geographical, biological, sociological, economic, political, technological, aesthetic, ethical and spiritual. This approach will provide breadth and balance and encourage pupils to explore their own ideas and values as well as developing open-mindedness and respect for the views and beliefs of others. For example, English, art, music and drama can play an important part in developing aesthetic appreciation of the natural environment. They offer the opportunity to understand the design aspects of the environment and the conflicts which can arise between aesthetic, utilitarian and economic considerations.

Study of history, geography and religious education has a particularly important part to play in helping pupils to clarify their values towards the outdoor environment.

3. Education in and through the environment

The emphasis on outdoor environmental studies should primarily be upon enquiry and investigation by the pupils themselves. First hand experience is essential. Fieldwork has an important part to play in all phases of education. It provides opportunities for drawing on the environment as a stimulus for learning, at the same time as developing an awareness and curiosity about the environment itself.

The Geography National Curriculum states that:

> *"Fieldwork allows pupils to carry out investigations in depth in response to key questions and to develop a range of skills, some of which are transferable to other areas of the curriculum and to life outside school. Pupils learn to clarify their objectives; to collect relevant data in a systematic way; to make decisions; to solve problems; to appreciate the values and aspirations of others and to work individually and co-operatively within a group."*

First hand experience is an essential part of helping all pupils to develop a personal response to the environment and to gain an awareness of environmental issues. This can start in the school itself, in its grounds and immediate locality, progressing to visits more distant, contrasting localities in the United Kingdom and in other countries.

Chapter 9

Approaches to outdoor environmental studies in primary and secondary schools

INTRODUCTION

Many schools make extensive use of environments to engage pupils in first hand learning experiences out of doors. The following models highlight the good practice which exists in many schools in their use and range of outdoor sites to promote environmental awareness and good learning. Sites include a countryside woodland centre, a coastal location, a castle, a stream in an upland valley and a farm. The examples illustrate how outdoor environmental studies and projects can be fully integrated into the National Curriculum, and extend children's learning. All the exemplars highlight a number of activities, all of which are referenced to National Curriculum programmes of study.

Model 1 "A Coastal Visit": Key Stages 1 and 2

Staff from a rural primary school decided to visit a coastal 'country park' during the summer term. The teachers wanted to use the visit to increase pupils' understanding of the principles of *adaptation and pollution* and embarked upon a range of projects to illustrate these concepts. All teachers in the project found the visits enormously valuable in extending children's knowledge of maths, geography and science concepts.

Fieldwork Site	Environmental activities carried out
Rock pools	♦ Rock pool dipping ♦ Observing living things ♦ Recording observations ♦ Using 'keys' to identify animals and plants ♦ Comparing specimens in high and low water pools ♦ 'Prey' and 'predator' observations ♦ Sketching rock pools ♦ Mapping rock pools using graph paper ♦ Comparing and contrasting habitats (rocky shore/sand areas) ♦ Observing tidal changes

Fieldwork Site	Environmental activities carried out
Dunes	♦ Observing plants and their differences ♦ Plant succession and colonisation ♦ Using keys to identify plants ♦ Line transects (recording cover every metre) ♦ Belt transects (recording % cover every 5 metres) ♦ Soil analysis
Rocky Shore	♦ Observing pebble sizes/shapes/colour ♦ Enviroscope 'litter survey' ♦ Sorting and classifying objects ♦ Collecting, recording and interpreting data

Seashore Ecology

Many of the activities and projects associated with the seashore can be linked directly to the programmes of study in the revised National Curriculum subjects of science, maths, English and geography. Outlined on the next page are some examples:

128

Rocky Shore Studies	Programmes of Study covered:

Science: Key Stage 1

Investigations:	♦ Exploring ♦ Making deductions ♦ Recording observations ♦ Making simple comparisons ♦ Using drawings to represent findings
Living things/processes:	♦ That animals use senses ♦ Changes affecting plants/animals ♦ Adaptation of plants and animals to environment

Science: Key Stage 2

Investigations:	♦ Making comparisons ♦ Making predictions ♦ Use tables, bar charts, graphs to present results
Living things/processes:	♦ Life processes in animals and plants ♦ Growth affected by water, temperature, light ♦ Significance of root systems in plants ♦ Animals and plants can be identified using keys ♦ Different plants and animals are found in different environments ♦ That plants and animals are suited to their environment ♦ Food chains

Maths: Key Stage 1

Number:	♦	Counting/collecting objects up to 10
	♦	Sort and classify a set of objects
	♦	Collect, record and interpret data
Shape and space:	♦	Purposeful context for measuring
	♦	Describe and discuss patterns
	♦	Use simple measurement instruments

Maths: Key Stage 2

Using Maths:	♦	Simple probability
	♦	Use diagrams and maps
	♦	Searching for patterns
Number:	♦	Develop effective methods of computation
	♦	Recognise co-ordinates
	♦	Solve problems
Shape and space:	♦	Apply measuring skills
	♦	Use co-ordinates
	♦	Use appropriate units of length/measurement

Geography: Key Stage 1

Thematic study:	♦	Express views on environment
	♦	Appreciate that environments change
	♦	Assess quality of environment
	♦	Suggest improvements to the environment

Geography: Key Stage 2

Thematic study:	♦	Transportation/erosion
	♦	Temperature/wind speed
	♦	Ways of combating pollution
Skills:	♦	4 figure references
Places:	♦	Physical features

Model 2 "Stream Studies in an Upland Valley": Key Stages 1 and 2

Subject co-ordinators of Geography and Science from a large primary school in a market town, decided to carry out a joint fieldwork project with pupils of Year 3 and 4. Two full day visits were organised. Both teachers found the joint planning co-ordination and organisation of the fieldwork activities invaluable in terms of developing team teaching, avoiding duplication of work, but principally, as a vehicle to help pupils make connections across subject boundaries. The field visits were considered to be of great value in developing children's understanding of science and geographical concepts.

Fieldwork Site	Environmental activities carried out
The Stream	◆ Stream dipping ◆ Observation of living things ◆ Classification of living things ◆ Using 'keys' to identify animals ◆ Habitat surveys ◆ Representational drawings of animals using natural substances ◆ Representational models of animals using natural materials ◆ Observation of pebbles in the stream (size/texture/colour)

The Stream Bank	◆ Cross section of a stream ◆ Plan of stream ◆ Measuring speed of flow ◆ Representational drawing of stream

Freshwater Ecology

Many of the activities and projects undertaken in freshwater be it either in a pond or stream can be directly linked to the programmes of study in the revised National Curriculum subjects of science, maths, English, art and geography at Key Stage 1 and 2. Outlined overleaf are some examples.

Freshwater Studies	*Programmes of Study covered:*

Science: Key Stage 1

Investigations:	♦ Exploring
	♦ Making deductions
	♦ Recording observations
	♦ Making simple comparisons
	♦ Use of drawings to represent findings

Living things and processes:	♦ First hand experience of living things
	♦ Changes affecting plants/animals
	♦ Adaptation of plants and animals to their environment
	♦ Different environments affect animals/plants
	♦ Living things can be grouped according to observable features

Science: Key Stage 2

Investigations:	♦ Making comparisons
	♦ Making predictions
	♦ Controlled experiments - fair testing
	♦ Use tables, bar charts, graphs to represent results
	♦ Draw conclusions

Living things and processes:	♦ Life processes in animals and plants
	♦ Growth affected by conditions
	♦ Animals/plants can be identified using keys
	♦ Different animals and plants are found in different environments
	♦ Plants/animals are suited to their environment
	♦ Food chains

Maths: Key Stage 1

Number:
- Counting/collecting objects up to 10
- Sorting and classifying a set of objects/living things
- Collect, record and interpret data

Shape and space:
- Purposeful context for measuring
- Look for and discuss patterns
- Use simple measurement instruments

Maths: Key Stage 2

Using Maths:
- Simple probability
- Use of diagrams and maps
- Search for patterns

Number:
- Develop effective methods of computation
- Recognise co-ordinates
- Solve problems

Shape and space:
- Apply measuring skills
- Use co-ordinates
- Use appropriate units of length/measurement

English: Key Stage 1

Speaking and listening:
- Describing events
- Observations and experiences
- Listening carefully to others
- Showing an understanding
- Developing word games
- Participating in activities

English: Key Stage 2

Speaking and listening:
- Sharing ideas
- Developing insights
- Describing events
- Observing situations
- Participating in activities
- Offering explanations

```
┌─────────────────────────────────────────────────────────────────────┐
│ Art: Key Stage 1                                                      │
│                                                                       │
│ Investigating and          ◆  Recording observations                 │
│ making:                     ◆  Experimenting with different textures: │
│                                ◆   colour                             │
│                                ◆   line                               │
│                                ◆   tone                               │
│                                ◆   shape                              │
│                                                                       │
│ Art: Key Stage 2                                                      │
│                                                                       │
│ Investigating and          ◆  Direct experiences                     │
│ making:                     ◆  Recording observations                │
│                             ◆  Experimentation                        │
│                             ◆  Use of artefacts                       │
└─────────────────────────────────────────────────────────────────────┘
```

```
┌─────────────────────────────────────────────────────────────────────┐
│ Geography: Key Stage 1                                                │
│                                                                       │
│ Geographical skills:       ◆  Undertake field work activities         │
│                            ◆  Develop mapping skills                  │
│                            ◆  Make maps of real and imaginary places  │
│                            ◆  Use a variety of scales                 │
│                                                                       │
│ Thematic study:            ◆  Express view of the environment         │
│                            ◆  Appreciate that environments change     │
│                            ◆  Assess the quality of the environment   │
│                            ◆  Suggest improvements to the             │
│                               environment                             │
│                                                                       │
│ Geography: Key Stage 2                                                │
│                                                                       │
│ Geographical skills:       ◆  Observe geographical features          │
│                            ◆  Collect and record evidence             │
│                            ◆  Analyse evidence, draw conclusions      │
│                            ◆  Make plans and maps                     │
│                            ◆  Use a variety of scales                 │
│                            ◆  Measuring direction/distance            │
│                                                                       │
│ Thematic study:            ◆  Transportation/erosion                  │
│                            ◆  Effect on the landscape                 │
│                            ◆  Ways of controlling pollution           │
│                            ◆  Conservation                            │
│                            ◆  Physical features                       │
│                            ◆  Water pollution                         │
└─────────────────────────────────────────────────────────────────────┘
```

Model 3 "A Woodland Study": Key Stage 2

Teachers from an urban primary school wanted to use the resources of a 'country park' which had a rich diversity of habitats to include a native woodland, a pond, formerly an old quarry and meadow, to increase children's awareness and understanding of living things and processes. Several day visits were organised involving Year 6 pupils and a range of activities were undertaken. It was very clear from the quality of work produced that the experiences had not only been very valuable, but had greatly increased children's understanding of living things and provided a resource from which a great many investigative surveys could be undertaken back in the classroom.

Fieldwork Site	Environmental activities carried out
Woodland	♦ Observation/recognition of trees ♦ Use of keys for identification ♦ Tree surveys in an area ♦ Estimation of heights/girths ♦ Effect of 'canopy' on plant life ♦ Food chains ♦ Bark rubbings/plaster casts ♦ Sun collectors, plant munchers/animal munchers ♦ Animals in the leaf litter ♦ Leaf prints - shapes, sizes, colours ♦ Forest foods ♦ Seeds and seedlings ♦ Seasonal changes ♦ Living things on bark/trunk/branches ♦ Tree dating ♦ Plan of wood
Pond	♦ Pond dipping ♦ Observation of living things ♦ Classification - animals/plants ♦ Use of keys for identification ♦ Pollution surveys ♦ Prey and predator observations ♦ Mapping pond ♦ Food chains

Woodland and Water Ecology

Many of the activities and projects associated with the woodland and pond environment can be linked directly to the programmes of study in the revised National Curriculum subjects of science, maths and geography. Outlined below are some examples.

Science: Key Stage 2

Investigations:	◆ Making comparisons
	◆ Making predictions
	◆ Using tables, bar charts and graphs
	◆ Drawing conclusions
	◆ Controlled experiments - (fair testing)
	◆ Explore a local habitat
Living things and processes:	◆ Life processes in animals and plants
	◆ Growth affected by water, temperature, light
	◆ Root systems in plants
	◆ Structure of plants
	◆ Identification of plants/animals using keys
	◆ Food chains

Geography: Key Stage 2

Skills:	◆ Observe geographical features
	◆ Collect and record evidence
	◆ Analyse evidence
	◆ Make plans and maps
	◆ Measure direction/distance
Thematic study:	◆ How people affect environments
	◆ Conservation
	◆ Water pollution
	◆ Habitats

Maths: Key Stage 2

Using maths:	◆ Extend appreciation of position, movement and direction
	◆ Use a wide variety of tools to develop mathematical skills and concepts
	◆ Discuss, describe, compare, explain aspects of mathematics work

---

Model 4 "Farm Visit": Key Stage 3

Teachers from a large high school were involved in developing a programme for Year 9 pupils based upon a farm in the National Park. With the help of the National Parks Education Officer, teachers were able to access data and information so that the visits could be as beneficial as possible in developing pupils' learning. The topic although part of a geography module was relevant in delivering a number of other curriculum areas to include science, maths and English. Pupils visited the farm on several occasions and developed a range of work in a number of topics. Outlined below are some of the activities in which they were involved.

Fieldwork Site	Environmental activities carried out
Farm	<ul><li>Mapping of the farm</li><li>Plan of the farm buildings</li><li>Analysis of farming practices</li><li>Type of machines used</li><li>Observe building materials</li><li>Make an audit of farm buildings, animals, workers, machinery</li><li>Assess variety of stock</li><li>Observe breeds of sheep and cows</li><li>Work out average milk yields</li><li>Assess milking methods today and how these have changed over the years</li><li>Identify routines of the farmer</li><li>Note calendar of crop growing/stock raising</li><li>What markets are served - and where</li></ul>
Farming	<ul><li>Analysis of fields, shape, size</li><li>Note variety of crops grown</li><li>Crop rotation</li><li>pH tests of soil</li><li>Access and conservation issues</li><li>National Park pressures</li><li>Influence of humans on landscape</li><li>Food chains/food webs</li><li>Interdependence of living things</li><li>Growth of animals and plants</li></ul>

Farm Studies

Many of the activities and projects undertaken in and around farms can be directly linked to programmes of study in the revised National Curriculum subjects of science, maths, geography and English at Key Stage 3. Outlined below are some examples:

Farm studies	*Programmes of Study covered:*
Geography: Key Stage 3	
Skills:	◆ Identify geographical questions and issues and establish an appropriate sequence of investigation
	◆ Identify evidence, collect, record and present it
	◆ Analyse and evaluate evidence, draw conclusions, communicate findings
	◆ Undertake fieldwork survey
	◆ Use of map and maps at a variety of scales
	◆ Use 1:25,000 and 1:50,000 maps to interpret land features/relief
	◆ Use of symbols and keys
Settlement:	◆ Reasons for the location, growth, nature of settlements
	◆ Types and patterns of rural land use
	◆ How conflict can arise over use of land
Environment	◆ In areas of scenic attraction how conflicting demands on areas and use can arise
	◆ How attempts to plan and manage environments are undertaken
	◆ How considerations of sustainable development, stewardship and conservation affect environmental planning and management

Science: Key Stage 3

Life processes:	
	◆ Animals and plants have organs that enable life processes to take place
	◆ That there is variation with species and between species
	◆ How keys can be used to identify animals and plants
	◆ Different habitats support different plants and animals
	◆ Food chains/food webs
	◆ Factors affecting the use of population including predators and competition for resources

Maths: Key Stage 3

Using and applying Mathematics:	
	◆ Use and application of maths
	◆ Work on problems that pose a challenge
	◆ Select, trial and evaluate a variety of possible approaches to solve problems
	◆ Use diagrams, graphs and symbols appropriately to convey meaning

Model 5 "Medieval Castle Visit": Key Stage 3

Humanities staff from a large urban based middle school were anxious to provide pupils in Year 7 with first hand experiences of medieval history, particularly in relation to 'medieval society' HSU ([1] d, e, and f). They made contact with the Living History Co-ordinator at one of the English Heritage sites to arrange a day visit and discuss an appropriate programme of activities.

Although the primary focus was very much upon raising pupils' awareness of the issues facing people living during medieval times, the programme for the day was largely cross curricular and involved a number of the activities overleaf. Both teachers and pupils found the day to be enormously beneficial. Despite the fact that the day required a great deal of preparation and follow up work, the experiences were rated as entirely valid and very worthwhile, both by staff and pupils.

Fieldwork Site	Environmental activities carried out
The Castle	*Before the visit* ♦ Designing and making medieval costumes ♦ Researching medieval society: food, farming, crafts, culture *During the visit* ♦ Cooking their own food ♦ Preparing a banquet ♦ Eating (medieval style) ♦ Candle making ♦ Stone masonry ♦ Badge making ♦ Calligraphy ♦ Embroidery ♦ Singing songs of the period ♦ Making music ♦ Maypole dancing ♦ Playing medieval ball games ♦ Acting out a knighting ceremony ♦ Making banners

Living history experiences

Many of the projects listed above can be directly linked to National Curriculum programmes of study, not only in history, but also for technology, art, maths and English. Outlined below are some examples.

Living History Studies	Programmes of Study covered:
History: Key Stage 3 Medieval society:	♦ The structure of medieval society to include the role of the church, farming, crafts, trade, ceremonies ♦ Medieval health and disease ♦ Arts and architecture, to include castles, buildings, paintings, artefacts

Art: Key Stage 3

Investigating and making:	♦ Designing and making images & artefacts
	♦ Paint making
	♦ Sculpture
	♦ Develop ideas from direct experience and imagination, selecting, recording and analysing from first hand observation
Knowledge and understanding:	♦ Recognise the diverse methods and approaches used by artists, crafts people and designers
	♦ Relate art, craft and design to its social, historical and cultural context

Music: Key Stage 3

Performing and composing:	♦ Sing and play a variety of music
	♦ Plan, rehearse, direct and present performances
Listening and appraising:	♦ Relate music to its social, historical and cultural context
	♦ Identify how musical styles and traditions change over time and from place to place

Technology: Key Stage 3

Designing and making:	♦ Designing skills
	♦ Making skills
	♦ Preparing food
Knowledge and understanding:	♦ Materials and components
	♦ Structures
	♦ Products and applications

Physical Education:	
Key Stage 3	
Dance:	♦ To compose and perform dances that communicate the artistic intention
	♦ To perform and create dances in a range of styles
Games:	♦ To undertake a variety of roles in playing games

Conclusion

All the examples in this chapter demonstrate that the value and purpose of engaging pupils in first hand experiences out of doors is beyond question. The educational visits selected, to a range of sites, have illustrated the enormous benefits and potential of learning about the environment through direct experience. The examples have shown that pupils' understanding of specific concepts has been increased by their exposure to real live situations, in a way that would not have been quite so effective in the classroom. The issue for the teacher is not whether learning through first hand experiences out of doors is relevant to National Curriculum programmes of study, but in deciding the particular focus of the visit. Teachers will have to 'hone' down what it is they want the children to learn, by identifying clear objectives for visits. They will need to design the activities so that specific learning objectives can be met, and evaluate experiences to ensure that the aims have been achieved. In this way learning about the environment through direct experience will remain a most potent medium of teaching.

Chapter 10

Opportunities for developing a wildlife area in the context of the National Curriculum within school grounds

INTRODUCTION

The National Curriculum poses many challenges for teachers in planning and delivering a range of relevant, appropriate and first hand learning opportunities for pupils, throughout all Key Stages. Implicit in the requirements is a strong emphasis, particularly upon the need for the development of investigative and enquiry based approaches to teaching and learning. Explicit in many of the programmes of study for science, for example, is the notion that pupils should "undertake practical investigations and that they should have access to appropriate natural resources to enrich their understanding of concepts and processes." In the geography orders there is strong reference to "fostering an enquiry-based approach" and that "pupils should be encouraged to undertake practical investigations which involve measurement and recording." The same is true for mathematics and for technology. In many of the programmes of study for all subjects, there is strong reference to practical first hand experiences.

The potential of school grounds is almost unlimited in providing pupils with unique learning opportunities throughout the length and breadth of the National Curriculum. At least 50 per cent of the National Curriculum can so easily be taught through the medium of school grounds and at least 25 per cent can best be achieved through direct, first hand experiences out of doors, not just in PE, but in science, mathematics, technology, English, geography and even religious education. Schools throughout the country are beginning to recognise this and in recent times there have been many examples of exciting, innovative schemes which are up and running, which demonstrate that school grounds can be transformed and used effectively as outdoor classrooms.

Learning opportunities

The concept of developing wild areas, provides untold opportunities for children to extend and deepen their understanding of nature, the natural world; its rhythms and flow and begin to develop a relationship with it, in the context of their own learning. The creation of a range of habitats can provide many opportunities to enrich learning throughout the National Curriculum. Outlined below are a number of possible opportunities that can be developed. School grounds can provide:

- opportunities for first hand experiences out of the classroom leading to heightened motivation and an interest in the living world (science);

- opportunities to increase pupils' understanding of ecological processes, concepts, plant succession, food chains, and other aspects of natural habitats (science);

- opportunities for observing living things and to regularly record and monitor changes in growth and decay (science);

- opportunities for undertaking enquiries and investigations (science, geography);

- opportunities for close observational drawing (art);

- opportunities for speaking and listening, and for the development of communication skills and group work skills (English);

- opportunities for generating ideas, in terms of designing an area and for evaluating proposals (technology);

- opportunities for recording, measuring, handling and interpreting data (mathematics);

- opportunities to develop an understanding of climatic conditions and weathering wind patterns (geography);

- opportunities to develop an understanding of conservation and promote environmental sustainability (geography)

- opportunities to communicate in a target language (modern foreign language);

- opportunities to listen and appraise and compose a sequence of music (music);

- opportunities to develop an understanding of the spiritual dimension of the natural world (religious education);

- opportunities for mapping and surveying an area (geography);

- opportunities for designing and constructing bird boxes (technology).

In order to create opportunities for pupils to be engaged in some of the learning objectives outlined in the previous paragraph, schools will have to decide which habitats are the most appropriate to develop, both in the short and long term.(Figure 10.1)

Habitat creation

- ♦ Constructing bird and bat boxes.
- ♦ Developing a pond.
- ♦ Formation of a wetland area.
- ♦ Planning a nature trail.
- ♦ Establishing a tree nursery.
- ♦ Constructing a stone wall.
- ♦ Planting a hedgerow of natural species.
- ♦ Constructing a weather station.
- ♦ Creating a mini beast log pile.
- ♦ Establishing a rockery.
- ♦ Developing a herb garden.
- ♦ Creating a compost and vegetable plot.
- ♦ Creating a traditional cornfield.
- ♦ Making bird feeders.
- ♦ Establishing a heather garden.
- ♦ Developing a sensory trail.
- ♦ Constructing footpaths and stepping stones.
- ♦ Creating windbreaks.
- ♦ Creating seating.
- ♦ Developing mounds and tunnels.
- ♦ Establishing raised flower beds.
- ♦ Planting out bushes.
- ♦ Constructing a 'hide'.
- ♦ Developing a texture trail.
- ♦ Establishing a fallen tree/log area.
- ♦ Developing interconnecting footpaths.

Figure 10.1

Habitat creation can be hugely variable, and will largely depend upon a wide range of factors to include; cost, climate, exposure, soil, security, space, supervision and a whole host of other considerations. Outlined in figure10.1 are a sample of some of the different habitats which schools may like to consider. Some of the benefits which can be gained from the creation of habitats are outlined in figure10.2.

What can wildlife areas do for your school?

♦ It can provide an immediately accessible *outdoor classroom* for much of the National Curriculum.

♦ It can enable pupils to *understand* about wild living things, wild places and how they can influence them - for better or worse.

♦ It can enable pupils to *value* and care for nature rather than abuse and vandalise it.

♦ It can enable pupils to *support* the natural environment in their actions at school and home as well as work on other areas outside the school grounds.

♦ It can give pupils safe, *direct experience* of living things and natural features on their own school doorstep, without relying on television programmes or other secondary source material.

♦ It can help pupils to *work together* and so develop social, organisational and communication skills.

♦ It can strengthen links with the *local community* and new businesses as providers of advice, labour, materials and adult supervision.

♦ It can lead to young people and the local community developing *new interests* and commitments for wildlife and sustainability.

♦ It can make the school grounds a more *attractive* and stimulating environment.

♦ It can be *fun!*

Figure 10.2

Involving others

In starting out schools will need to seek much advice. Any proposals will have an impact on other interests and schools will need to consult widely at an early stage in planning, and get others involved in their proposals, to avoid difficulties later.

Staff and pupils

Continuity and long-term interest is often best served by staff and pupil involvement. Ask for their help throughout the process, from the initial recording of existing features in the school grounds and in collecting ideas and alternative proposals. Their ideas will help in the preparation of a simple management plan (*Figure 10.5*).

Advisory staff

During preliminary enquiries get in touch with the LEA office and speak to the adviser/inspector with responsibility for environmental education, or an appropriate advisory teacher.

Ground staff

The creation of wildlife areas will have some effect on the school grounds maintenance programmes. Schools will need to maintain a good working liaison with ground maintenance contractors or playing field staff. Their co-operation and technical advice can prove invaluable.

Conservation organisations

These will include the local Wildlife Trust, the Urban Wildlife Group, the British Trust for Conservation Volunteers, or the Groundwork Trust. Do contact these specialist groups for specific practical advice on the most suitable seeds, plants, other materials and tools. Also discuss with them the future management and ecology of the proposed areas. Some voluntary organisations are often able to arrange site visits to schools, so make every effort to include them at an early stage of planning.

147

Parents and neighbours

Obtain ideas and practical help from parents and neighbours at all stages of the development. Hidden talents, professional and amateur, are often apparent where least expected. Keep them informed and, if possible, involved in the school grounds development. Some 'features' may seem to be no more than a case of neglect to those who do not understand. A screen of trees and shrubs or a mown grass strip may be desirable in defining new 'wildlife' areas. Remember, good communication will help to create a sense of community concern and responsibility.

Site design and plan

How should you start developing the school ground's wildlife areas?

With pupil help, schools should consider carrying out a simple survey of the grounds taking full account of existing buildings and vegetation.(*Figure 10.3*)

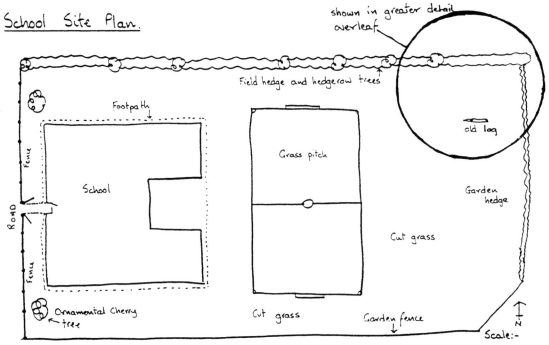

Figure 10.3

The wildlife area

♦ Consider incorporating any natural features such as hedgerows, trees or shrubs into the future plan. Be careful not to damage existing wildlife in planning and developing the areas. Gradual development of the grounds may be wisest at the start, leaving some creative work such as planting and digging for future children in the school.(*figure 10.4*)

♦ Look over the school fence or wall. It may be that there is an area of wilderness on the other side. This may influence the location of specific wildlife areas which may benefit from the movement of creatures and seeds, and the eventual natural colonisation of the school grounds.

Consider:

♦ Access to the areas from the classroom for all age groups, and the advantages of the visibility of the areas from one or more classrooms.

♦ Suitable safe spaces for investigating and working (such as around a pond) in the areas, having some consideration for the wildlife present.

♦ The situation of the areas and the nature of the soil, the shape and aspect of the grounds (mounds, damp hollows, shaded areas, prevailing winds). Do the areas act as a litter trap?

♦ Neighbouring houses and gardens, as the spread of weeds may be a problem.

♦ The presence of drains, power cables/pipes, nearby play areas, buildings, roads and footpaths.

♦ Service points. For example, is there a nearby tap, long hose, or are there plenty of 'water carriers' to water plants in the summer?

♦ Areas which are at least susceptible to vandalism. Is the school ground overlooked by houses so that out of school hours a friendly neighbour can keep an eye on the wildlife areas? Is there an internal quadrangle to provide a secure location for a pond or wetlands habitat, accessible only with the supervision of a teacher?

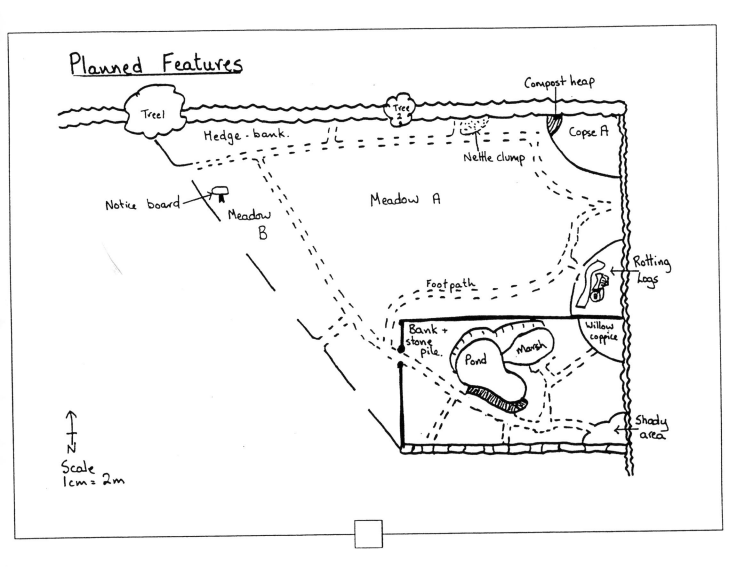

Figure 10.4

- The size of the grounds. Develop wildlife areas which, if need be, could be expanded in time when additional resources permit and interest grows. Much will depend on the intended educational use of the areas, future management and the time and resources available. Relatively small areas can be suitably developed and managed to allow an increase in wildlife which would then be valuable for study. Staff and pupils in small urban schools could consider developing areas a few metres in size. This may involve digging up some of the tarmac and filling the areas with sub-soil, constructing raised beds/ponds, or using sinks/barrels containing soil or water. Always think about regarding the entire school estate as a resource for learning about the environment and in providing opportunities for the establishment of local wildlife.

The design

Having completed the survey and chosen the areas for development with the pupils, schools will be in a position to start designing, using the advice and views of the people already consulted. A good design will allow the grounds to be developed in a way which will benefit both wildlife and the people using it. Teachers may find it helpful at this stage to visit similar wildlife areas in a nearby school *(Figure10.3)*.

Consider:

- obtaining a large scale map of the school and grounds (ask the Property and Estates Department), so that you can add to it or use it to make a simpler version; or get the pupils to draw their own map

- having a master plan onto which you can plot progress in the areas, as well as working plans, which can be duplicated for the pupils' use (*Figure 10.5*).

- Choosing a limited number of features.

When designing the layout of the areas it is tempting to try to include as many features as possible. Diversity is often considered the key when creating wildlife areas but it is wise not to include too many different features in unreasonably small spaces.

151

Ensure:

- The shape of the wildlife area allows the grounds maintenance staff to mow adjacent areas with relative ease. Don't forget they may also mow inside the wildlife area.

- That a path system is included to avoid excessive disturbance to particular features. Consider the width of the path if it is to be mown. Think about access and the movement of pupils.

- That a mown grass strip around the edge of the grounds is considered to separate neighbouring gardens from the wildlife areas. This can prevent the dumping of rubbish and complaints about weeds.

- That there are not too many small habitats adjacent to each other. One habitat will affect another and they will require a lot of time and effort to keep them going. Habitats such as ditches, hedges and meadow strips are very useful. They often fit around the edge of school grounds and do not compete with other uses such as games or car parking. They can be lengthened when required and provide plenty of space for pupils to manage or investigate them.

- That you use local plant species where possible - although some species such as "buddleia" may be introduced for specific educational purposes. Your design of the wildlife areas should take account of the plant species to be introduced and have these listed. Seek advice on the most appropriate species.

5 Year Plan

YEAR 1	YEAR 2	YEAR 3	YEAR 4	YEAR 5	
Winter Approach Education Department Playing Fields. Start Site Survey.	**Winter** Plant Copse A – if not already done. Rebuild stone wall.	**Winter** Replace losses and remainder of Copse A if not done. Fencing of pond areas.	**Winter** Plant replacements in Copse A, if not already done.	**Winter** Plant tree replacement in Copse A and willow coppice.	1st Willow Coppice cut in 2-3 years.
Spring Continue survey. Apply for grants for liners etc.	**Spring** Arrange meadow mowing regime and compost heap. Dig marsh and fill.	**Spring** Dig pond and later colonise with plants. Paint wall.	**Spring** Plant ferns in shady area.	**Spring** Introduce new wild flowers to meadows after growing indoors.	
Summer Survey – continue. Arrange for hedge bank to be left uncut.	**Summer** Add plants to marsh. Apply for grants for pond liner.	**Summer** Establish growth on protective bank around pond. Paint wall.	**Summer** Use pond! Continue mowing regime.	**Summer** Have an open day for parents! Reflect on progress so far.	
Autumn Continue survey. Make notice board for site. Arrange for long grass to be cut on hedge bank. Arrange delivery of rotting logs.	**Autumn** Consider effectiveness of mowing regime. Count tree losses in Copse A. Paint wall.	**Autumn** Continue mowing regime. Count tree losses.	**Autumn** Count tree losses in Copse A. Repeat wall painting if necessary.	**Autumn** Introduce more rotting logs if needed. Count tree losses in Willow coppice.	
	Winter Replace tree losses and plant remainder of Copse A. Paint wall.	**Winter** Plant tree replacements in Copse A.	**Winter** Plant replacements in Copse A. Plant Willow coppice.	**Winter** Replace tree losses in Willow coppice. Consider new wild flowers for bank/meadow.	
Winter Start to plant Copse A – 6 trees.				**WRITE A NEW 5 YEAR PLAN**	Include any additional feature you would like, e.g. tree nursery, benches.

Figure 10.5

153

Conclusion

Where ever possible teachers should try to give pupils every encouragement to become involved in the creation the school wildlife areas at all stages. In this way pupils will begin to take some responsibility not only for the environment, but for their own learning. Give pupils a chance to make contact with nature as well as the freedom to explore their surroundings in a personal way. It will provide opportunities for them to launch into many areas of the curriculum. Most importantly, it will give them a chance to develop caring attitudes towards the living world so that they can play an informed and responsible role in its conservation and development. A sense of ownership may help prevent any potential vandalism. Obviously, wherever young people are involved, safety becomes doubly important, so do ensure that all necessary precautions are taken and that you are aware of health and safety guidelines.

Whatever you decide to do, try to plan ahead. Don't try to accomplish everything in the first year. Developing a wild area takes time. Think ahead and think long term! The plan outlined in Figure 10.5 may give you some ideas about planning for the short, medium and long term developments to ensure that the creation of wildlife habitats can be sustained as a continuously evolving project.

Chapter 11

Exploring nature with children in the National Curriculum (Key Stages 1 and 2)

INTRODUCTION

There are many, many things in nature which are indescribably beautiful both in characteristic, structure and shape. The myriad of animals and plants throughout the natural world, whose colourings, detail and form are almost beyond the scope of our articulation and full appreciation. It could be the beauty of a springtime blossom or the fragility of a tiny lichen clinging onto its life source; the intricate structure of a spider's web shimmering in the sunlit dew or the grace and majesty of an encircling high flying bird of prey in search of its quarry; the unsettling roar of wind through the trees on an autumn night, or the immense power of a waterfall in full spate, unleashed, crashing down upon the rocks below. None of us can dismiss the fact that at one time or another, we have been touched by the various moods, forces and wonder of nature. Its immense mystery opens up to us, its stunning purity reminds us of a spirituality of a life force that is much greater than the affairs of mankind.

Exploring nature with children has become something of a way of life for many engaged in the teaching of young children out of doors. With the advent of National Curriculum many programmes of outdoor learning have not only focused upon the acquisition of fieldwork skills to develop knowledge and understanding of scientific, geographical, historical and even mathematical concepts, but sought to develop other ways of enhancing children's observational skills. Indeed it could be argued that without developing pupils' observational skills at an early age as part of the fundamental foundation of all outdoor learning, young people become impoverished and are never really able to develop their conceptual understanding of the natural world.

Exploring nature with children is not so much about the what or the how of nature, it is much more to do with developing childrens' senses and sensitivities to nature's rhythms. It attempts through a wide variety of activities and projects to stimulate curiosity and encourage the widest use of the 'senses'.

Outlined on the following pages are a number of activities and projects which have been used with children very successfully to raise both their levels of consciousness of the natural world and also increase their observational skills. None of the activities are intensive in resource requirements, conversely most are very simple and require the minimum of preparation. Supporting the ideas and projects is a matrix outlining both a reference to a number of the programmes of study at Key Stages 1 and 2 for science, geography, art, maths and English, and a number of other generic learning outcomes.

Having seen the awe and wonder expressed on many children's faces, and witnessed their curiosity and excitement of living things and of their response to the natural world, largely as a result of this particular approach to the teaching and learning of outdoor studies, I am utterly convinced of its value. Furthermore I believe that all those who are engaged in teaching out of doors have a duty, and a responsibility, of passing on to the next generation, something of the mystery and rhythms of the natural world. Sharing nature with children is not only an excellent teaching vehicle and an appropriate starting point but provides an excellent foundation for all learning, in, about and for the environment.

Teaching and learning strategies

In putting together these ideas I fully acknowledge the wisdom, inspiration and writings of the original author and proponent of "Sharing nature with children" - Joseph Cornell. He put forward five tenets of good outdoor teaching and learning. These were:

♦   Teach less and share more.

♦   Be receptive.

♦   Focus the child's attention on detail.

♦   Look and experience first; talk later.

♦   Infectious enthusiasm should permeate all teaching.

1. Teach less/share more

In addition to encouraging children to learn about the bare facts of nature; the names of animals, plants and birds, it is also important that teachers challenge children to observe various life forms. For example, how an animal or plant adapts to its environment, how it survives winter conditions; by looking at leaf or root structures, and the detail of flowering plants.

It is also important that teachers share their inner thoughts and feelings with children. For it is only by sharing our thoughts and feelings that we begin to communicate and inspire in others a deep love and respect for the natural world.

2. Be receptive

Being receptive means listening and being aware. It is one of the most important teaching skills to develop when working with children out of doors. All exposure to the outdoors brings a spontaneous enthusiasm from children, which when skilfully developed, can often ensure that good learning takes place.

As teachers we always need to be super sensitive to the questions, the comments, the exclamations made by children. We need to respond to their moods and feelings and exploit these to ensure that their curiosity and wonderment is sustained.

Above all as teachers, we need to be alert to what is happening in nature and focus pupils' attention accordingly. Something of interest is always happening. We need to develop time-strategies that provide opportunities for us to stop, to look, to listen, instead of rushing on in a vain attempt to complete our own agenda.

3. Focus the child's attention

Initially, children are often so taken up with the natural world that they easily flit from one point of interest to another, in a haphazard way. At the start of any experience in nature it is important that teachers set the tone of the session and ensure that they focus the childrens' attention without delay; by asking questions and by structuring the session. Many children are not used to watching or listening to nature. They will often need help and guidance to focus in upon detail. This approach will gradually lead them on to developing a keenness for close observation and through support, begin to foster an independence to learning.

4. Look and experience first, talk later

On nearly every occasion nature's wonderful and spontaneous happenings will take over any input from the teacher. Children will often be in awe of the spectacle unfolding before them. It may be a hovering dragonfly, or a lone deer grazing in a clearing; an army of soldier ants on the move, or a caterpillar struggling up a plant. Children have a marvellous capacity for absorbing themselves in whatever is happening on the real life stage of the natural world. As teachers, we must ensure our teaching strategies are sensitive to the moment. We should learn not to be so preoccupied with children being able to specifically name animals and plants by 'class' and 'species', but rather ensure that we exploit the moment of discovery, by encouraging a real and genuine relationship to develop. In time this relationship will naturally lead to a thirst for knowledge and understanding. The important thing, particularly in young children, is to cultivate that discovery spirit and the emotional responses of awe and wonder.

5. Infectious enthusiasm

Children largely learn through example. This is never more apparent than when children are actively engaged in the great outdoors. As teachers of nature, we must always strive in our teaching to pervade a genuine infectious enthusiasm for everything that we love and believe in. If we are not fully absorbed by the natural world, we cannot expect those we teach to develop any enthusiasm for the forces of nature.

Children are naturally drawn to learning in the natural world, particularly when the teaching is dynamic and enthusiastic. Young people will invariably reach heights of awareness and absorption when it is matched by the enthusiasm and infectious zeal of teachers. It is this characteristic which is perhaps the greatest asset any teacher engaged in teaching and learning out of doors can possess and should strive to cultivate whenever possible.

Some Activities

There are hundreds of possible activities which teachers might wish to use. I have chosen only to draw upon a few to demonstrate the potential of using this particular teaching and learning approach, with pupils at Key Stages 1 and 2.

1. The unnatural trail - *Observation exercise*

Equipment: 10-15 unnatural objects, balloons, bulbs, litter, ribbons, badges, stockings. Twenty metres of footpath in a wood.

Split the group into two halves. One half should sit and wait in a clearing, while the other half set out the trail.

Half the group are given 10-15 objects to place alongside the track between two known points, not hidden but in unusual places.

When all the objects have been set out let pupils join the other group but don't let them tell the others what they have done or where they have placed the objects.

Half of the group then set out along the track and record on paper as many of the unnatural objects as they can see. The other group of children monitor how successful they have been. After completion the groups change; one setting out another trail, the other trying to locate and record the unnatural objects they see (*reference J. Cornell, Sharing Nature with Children, page 40*).

2. Earth windows - *Sensory exercise*

Equipment: none

Find an area of woodland covered in leaf litter. Get pupils to lie down and cover themselves and each other in forest debris leaving a window over the face. Use enough leaves and sticks to give a feeling of being down inside the earth. Tell the pupils that you will give a signal when it is time to get up out of the earth. Encourage them to lie quietly and try and get everyone buried quickly. Ask them to get up slowly and quietly so as not to disturb the quiet they should have experienced.

Discourage panic about insects crawling over them, by asking them what it might be doing or where it is going. Ask them to listen, smell, look and feel. When the activity is finished get the pupils to discuss how it felt, what they saw, heard and smelt (*reference: J. Cornell, Sharing Nature with Children, page 21*).

3. *Leading a friend to a tree - Sensory exercise*

Equipment: Blindfolds

Put pupils into pairs. One is sighted, one is blindfolded. The sighted child turns their partner around several times to lose their sense of direction. The blindfolded partner is led about 20-30 metres to a tree. The 'blind' pupil is encouraged to explore the tree and to feel its uniqueness. "Rub your cheek on the bark." "Is this tree alive or dead?" "Can you put your arms right around the tree?" "Are there branches, lichens, signs of animals, mosses?"

When the blindfolded children have finished exploring their tree, their partners lead them back to where they started by a different route. Make it fun by suggesting they be led over imaginary logs and through thickets and bracken. Upon removal of the blindfold pupils must try and find their tree (*reference: J. Cornell, Sharing Nature with Children, page 26*).

4. Sound Map: Sensory exercise

Equipment: Pencils, card (1 for each child).

Teachers need to select a site where there are a variety of sounds, i.e streams, wind in trees, birds etc. Pupils are told to find a special 'listening place', where they can record the sounds they hear. The children should be fairly widely dispersed from one another. Give each child a card and a pencil, tell them to listen carefully and as they hear different sounds to plot the details on the card, relative to their own position, by the use of a simple 'key': Tell the children to close their eyes. Explain that cupping their hands behind their ears provides a reflective surface for catching sounds!

After 5 minutes call the pupils to return to base. As they arrive ask them to share their "maps" with their friends, explaining the sounds they heard. Ask then how many sounds they heard, what were the best sounds; the worst sounds? Which sounds were new to them? (*reference: J. Cornell, Sharing the joy of Nature page 74*).

5. Duplication (Kim's game): Observation and memory exercise

Equipment: 2 handkerchiefs/dusters or towels

Encourage the children to collect ten natural objects such as stones, pebbles, seeds, leaves, pine cones and parts of plants. Lay the objects out on a handkerchief and cover them with a cloth.

Gather the group around and tell them, "Under this cloth are ten natural objects you'll be able to find nearby." Lift the cloth for 25 seconds so that they can take a good look and try to remember everything they see.

After looking at the objects the pupils spread out and try to collect ten identical objects, keeping their findings to themselves.

After five minutes of searching, call the pupils back, and dramatically pull out objects from under the cloth, one at a time, telling interesting stories or giving information about each one. As each object is presented ask the pupils if they found one just like it.

If this game is repeated several times it has a noticeable strengthening effect on the pupils' concentration and memory. (*reference J. Cornell, Sharing Nature with Children, page 44*).

6. "Solo Spot" - Sensory exercise

Equipment - none

Encourage the pupils to explore an area of woodland on their own: to experience the natural world away from others in a calm, personal situation. The exercise of a 'solo spot' is the relaxation of being alone without being lonely, having the freedom to experience the natural world without disturbing it or being disturbed by others, but with the security of having friends nearby.

Suggest to the children that they try to remain still for a short while, listening to the sounds, smelling the air, touching the ground, either observing things about them, or simply keeping their eyes closed.

Call the children back after a period of five minutes and ask them to share their experiences and observations with each other. (*reference J. Cornell, Sharing Nature with Children, page 112*).

7. *Blind Line - Sensory exercise*

Equipment: Blindfold for every pupil, 75 yards baling twine/rope, which needs to be laid out beforehand

Sit the pupils down behind a wall. One teacher (or parent if no teacher) stays with the group, the other goes to the end of the line. All pupils are blindfolded. Ask pupils to feel the ground around them, what do they feel? How does it feel?

Guide the pupils one at a time to the start of the trail. Instruct them to keep at least one hand on the rope and follow it until they reach the parent or teacher at the other end. Encourage the children to try to remember what they can feel, smell and hear on the way. Leave a gap between each pupil. Discourage them from talking out loud.

When all is finished, wind up the line after the last pupil. Ask them what things they noticed as they came along the line. How did they feel about being blindfolded? What they felt underfoot and around them, what they smelt and what they heard. Encourage the pupils to share with each other their reactions. (*reference J. Cornell, Sharing Nature with Children, page 29*).

Sources of Activities

The activities outlined on the previous pages have been drawn from a range of sources. Acknowledgement is given to Steve Van Matre and Joseph Cornell, both pioneers in this field. Details of several further activities; how to carry them out, what props need to be gathered or created, are further described in other publications. Two of these, "Earth Magic" and "Snow Walks" are published by IEE and can be obtained from P.O Box14, Mortimer, Reading, RG7 3YA. Two others "Sharing nature with children" and "Sharing the joy of Nature" are published by Exley, 12Ye Corner, Watford, Hertfordshire, WD1 4BS.

National Curriculum

Many of the activities and projects which are associated with exploring nature with children can be referenced to the programmes of study in the revised National Curriculum subjects for science, geography, art and English. Outlined below are some examples where elements of the programmes of study can be achieved through direct experience with the natural environment using some of the activities outlined.

Programmes of Study covered:

Science Key Stage 1

Investigations: AT1

♦   Exploring using appropriate senses

♦   Making deductions

♦   Recording observations

Living things/processes: AT2

♦   Parts of a flower

♦   Seeds

♦   Local environment - changes affecting plants/animals

♦   Adaptation of plants and animals to the environment

Science Key Stage 2

Investigations: AT1

♦ Making comparisons - seeing patterns

Living things/processes: AT2

♦ Plant growth - affected by water, temperature and light
♦ Seed dispersal
♦ Food chains

Geography Key Stage 1

Thematic Study

♦ Express views on the environment
♦ Appreciate that environments change
♦ Quality of the environment
♦ Improvements to the environment

Geography Key Stage 2

♦ Thematic Study
♦ Investigate how environments change
♦ How people affect environments
♦ Ways of combating pollution

Art Key Stage 1

Investigating and making

♦ Recording observations

♦ Experimenting with different texture, colour, line, tone, shape

Art Key Stage 2

Investigating and making

♦ Direct experience (observation)

♦ Experimentation

♦ Use of artefacts

English Key Stage 1

Speaking and listening

♦ Describing events

♦ Observations and experience

♦ Listening carefully to others

♦ Showing an understanding of what they know

♦ Participating in drama activities

♦ Developing word games

English Key Stage 2

Speaking and listening

♦ Sharing ideas

♦ Developing insights

♦ Describing events

♦ Observing situations

♦ Participating in drama

♦ Role play activities

Conclusion

Exploring nature with children is a dynamic approach to the teaching of environmental concepts. It is not so much about the what or the how of nature. It is much more to do with developing children's awareness of the rhythms of nature. It is a way of enabling pupils to develop a relationship with the natural world. It is about encouraging them to develop an understanding about our rich and diverse natural heritage. Exploring nature with children, is not just appropriate in meeting the programmes of study of the National Curriculum, it should be a "must" for every teacher struggling to find ways of relating difficult concepts and ideas to children. For those not already committed to this approach to teaching and learning, I urge them to "have a go" and experience for themselves the dynamic of this effective pathway to first hand learning.

Chapter 12

Inspirations: Examples of good practice to illustrate ways in which outdoor environmental studies can enrich many areas of the National Curriculum

INTRODUCTION

Inspirations is a collection of examples of good practice which aim to provide teachers with a range of ideas for involving children in first hand experiences out of doors. It has been written to graphically illustrate how environmental studies can enrich many areas of the National Curriculum, and be used as a vehicle for investigative learning.

Inspirations is a practical resource pack of ideas which demonstrate how environmental studies as a cross curricular theme may meet many of the requirements of the programmes of study and attainment targets of the National Curriculum. The intention is that this chapter should provide teachers not only with a bank of ideas for developing cross curricular topics but also act as a key resource for those wishing to implement topics which have a central discernible core of environmental content.

The suggested activities are particularly designed to stimulate children's investigation, enquiry and communication skills. A wide variety of ideas is provided to provoke children to question, choose sources for investigations, collect and record information and for presenting results, orally, visually and in writing. Special attention is given to the cross curricular skills of problem solving, investigation and communication; all essential and important elements which run throughout the whole of the National Curriculum.

The ideas, while not specifically age related, are designed to fit in with, and span, the general range of expectations for Key Stages 1-3. No attempt has been made to grade the activities formally or to identify specific levels of attainment in relation to Core or Foundation subjects. The major purpose of this chapter is to provide teachers with a range of useful ideas to develop children's learning in the context of the natural or built environment.

Contents   **Page**

HISTORICAL SITES – Using a site to investigate aspects of the past.

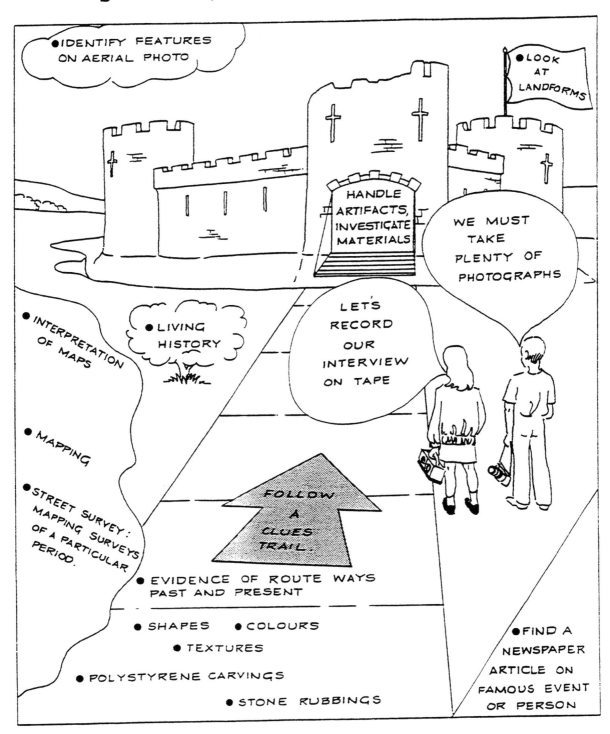

KEY STAGES 1 AND 2

RIVER STUDY – Fieldwork on local river.

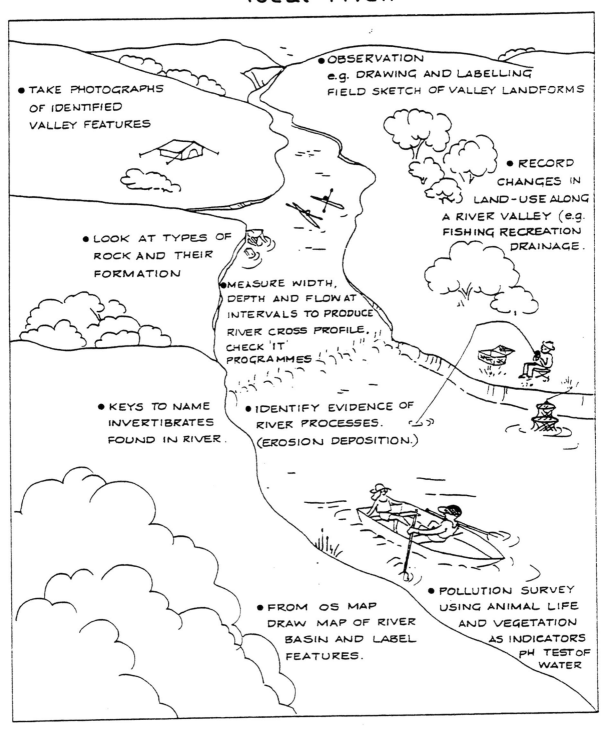

- TAKE PHOTOGRAPHS OF IDENTIFIED VALLEY FEATURES

- OBSERVATION e.g. DRAWING AND LABELLING FIELD SKETCH OF VALLEY LANDFORMS

- RECORD CHANGES IN LAND-USE ALONG A RIVER VALLEY (e.g. FISHING RECREATION DRAINAGE.

- LOOK AT TYPES OF ROCK AND THEIR FORMATION

- MEASURE WIDTH, DEPTH AND FLOW AT INTERVALS TO PRODUCE RIVER CROSS PROFILE. CHECK 'IT' PROGRAMMES

- KEYS TO NAME INVERTIBRATES FOUND IN RIVER.

- IDENTIFY EVIDENCE OF RIVER PROCESSES. (EROSION DEPOSITION.)

- FROM OS MAP DRAW MAP OF RIVER BASIN AND LABEL FEATURES.

- POLLUTION SURVEY USING ANIMAL LIFE AND VEGETATION AS INDICATORS PH TEST OF WATER

KEY STAGE 3

INVESTIGATE CHURCHES AND GRAVEYARDS

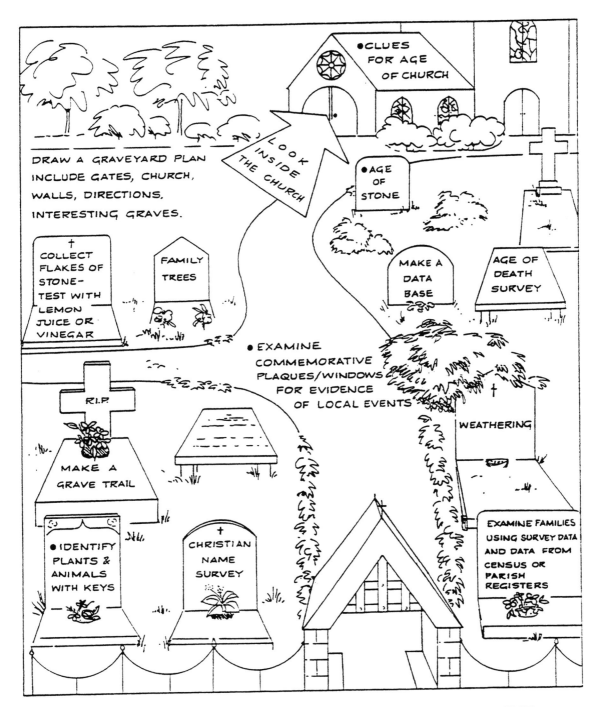

USING EVIDENCE TO FIND OUT ABOUT THE PAST IN THE LOCAL AREA. (KEY STAGES 1 AND 2)

STREAM STUDIES
STRUCTURE AND PROFILE

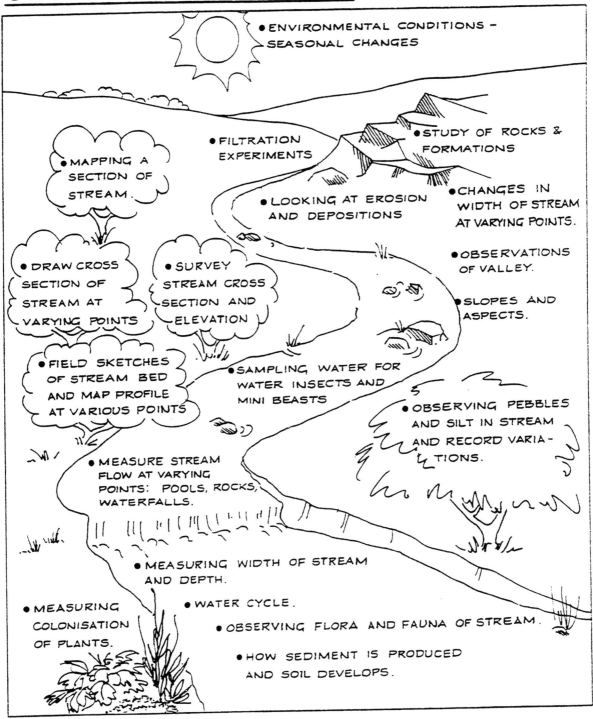

- ENVIRONMENTAL CONDITIONS - SEASONAL CHANGES
- FILTRATION EXPERIMENTS
- STUDY OF ROCKS & FORMATIONS
- MAPPING A SECTION OF STREAM.
- LOOKING AT EROSION AND DEPOSITIONS
- CHANGES IN WIDTH OF STREAM AT VARYING POINTS.
- DRAW CROSS SECTION OF STREAM AT VARYING POINTS
- SURVEY STREAM CROSS SECTION AND ELEVATION
- OBSERVATIONS OF VALLEY.
- SLOPES AND ASPECTS.
- FIELD SKETCHES OF STREAM BED AND MAP PROFILE AT VARIOUS POINTS
- SAMPLING WATER FOR WATER INSECTS AND MINI BEASTS
- OBSERVING PEBBLES AND SILT IN STREAM AND RECORD VARIATIONS.
- MEASURE STREAM FLOW AT VARYING POINTS: POOLS, ROCKS, WATERFALLS.
- MEASURING WIDTH OF STREAM AND DEPTH.
- MEASURING COLONISATION OF PLANTS.
- WATER CYCLE.
- OBSERVING FLORA AND FAUNA OF STREAM.
- HOW SEDIMENT IS PRODUCED AND SOIL DEVELOPS.

KEY STAGE 2

FARM STUDIES

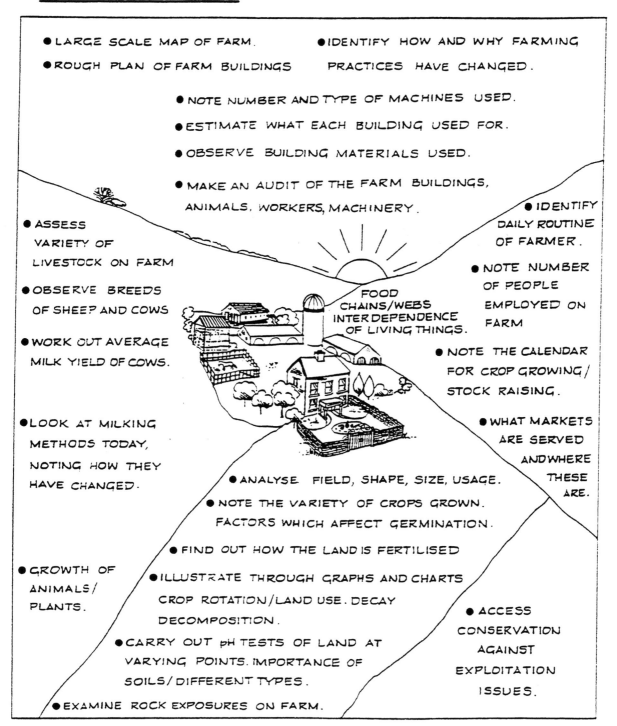

- LARGE SCALE MAP OF FARM.
- ROUGH PLAN OF FARM BUILDINGS
- IDENTIFY HOW AND WHY FARMING PRACTICES HAVE CHANGED.

- NOTE NUMBER AND TYPE OF MACHINES USED.
- ESTIMATE WHAT EACH BUILDING USED FOR.
- OBSERVE BUILDING MATERIALS USED.
- MAKE AN AUDIT OF THE FARM BUILDINGS, ANIMALS, WORKERS, MACHINERY.

- ASSESS VARIETY OF LIVESTOCK ON FARM
- OBSERVE BREEDS OF SHEEP AND COWS
- WORK OUT AVERAGE MILK YIELD OF COWS.
- LOOK AT MILKING METHODS TODAY, NOTING HOW THEY HAVE CHANGED.

FOOD CHAINS/WEBS INTERDEPENDENCE OF LIVING THINGS.

- IDENTIFY DAILY ROUTINE OF FARMER.
- NOTE NUMBER OF PEOPLE EMPLOYED ON FARM
- NOTE THE CALENDAR FOR CROP GROWING / STOCK RAISING.
- WHAT MARKETS ARE SERVED AND WHERE THESE ARE.

- ANALYSE FIELD, SHAPE, SIZE, USAGE.
- NOTE THE VARIETY OF CROPS GROWN. FACTORS WHICH AFFECT GERMINATION.
- FIND OUT HOW THE LAND IS FERTILISED
- ILLUSTRATE THROUGH GRAPHS AND CHARTS CROP ROTATION/LAND USE. DECAY DECOMPOSITION.
- GROWTH OF ANIMALS/ PLANTS.
- CARRY OUT pH TESTS OF LAND AT VARYING POINTS. IMPORTANCE OF SOILS/DIFFERENT TYPES.
- ACCESS CONSERVATION AGAINST EXPLOITATION ISSUES.
- EXAMINE ROCK EXPOSURES ON FARM.

A WORKING FARM - INPUTS AND OUTPUTS

KEY STAGE 3

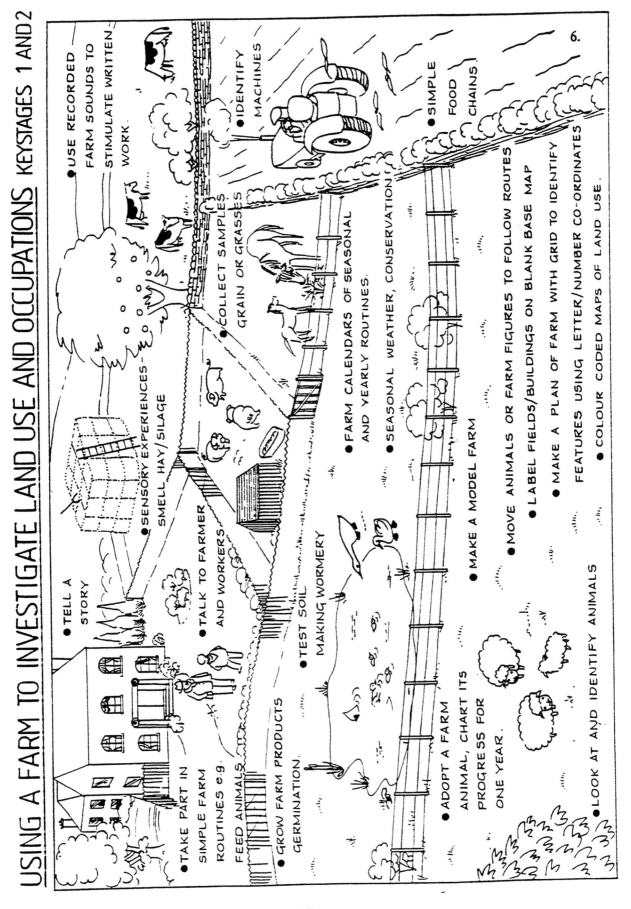

6.

- USE RECORDED FARM SOUNDS TO STIMULATE WRITTEN WORK.
- IDENTIFY MACHINES
- SIMPLE FOOD CHAINS.
- SENSORY EXPERIENCES - SMELL HAY/SILAGE
- COLLECT SAMPLES - GRAIN OR GRASSES
- FARM CALENDARS OF SEASONAL AND YEARLY ROUTINES.
- SEASONAL WEATHER, CONSERVATION
- MOVE ANIMALS OR FARM FIGURES TO FOLLOW ROUTES
- LABEL FIELDS/BUILDINGS ON BLANK BASE MAP
- MAKE A PLAN OF FARM WITH GRID TO IDENTIFY FEATURES USING LETTER/NUMBER CO-ORDINATES
- COLOUR CODED MAPS OF LAND USE.
- TELL A STORY
- TALK TO FARMER AND WORKERS
- TEST SOIL
- MAKING WORMERY
- MAKE A MODEL FARM
- TAKE PART IN SIMPLE FARM ROUTINES e.g. FEED ANIMALS
- GROW FARM PRODUCTS GERMINATION.
- ADOPT A FARM ANIMAL, CHART ITS PROGRESS FOR ONE YEAR.
- LOOK AT AND IDENTIFY ANIMALS

SCHOOL GROUNDS   KEY STAGES 1 & 2

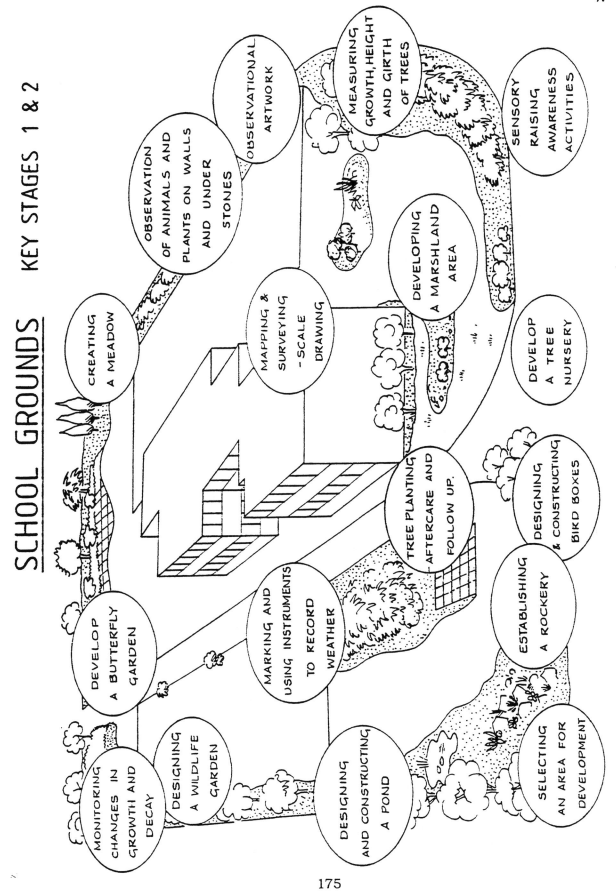

WOODLANDS - A Living Ecosystem

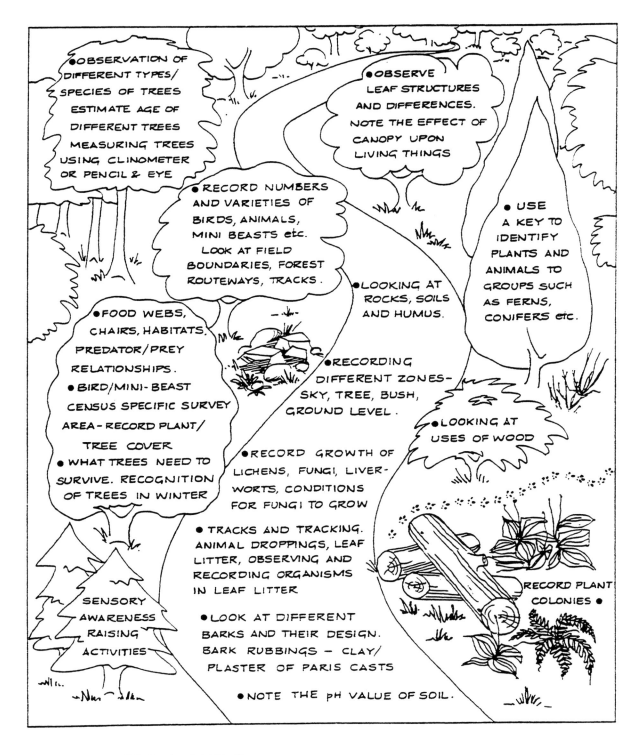

KEY STAGES 1 AND 2

INDUSTRY – Factors Affecting Industrial Development (KEYSTAGE 3)

- SITE VISIT e.g. FACTORY, INDUSTRIAL ESTATE OR TOURIST AMENITY.

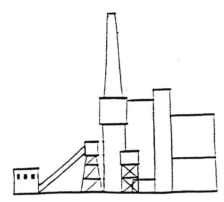

- NEWS REPORT ON AUDIO OR VIDEO CASSETTE

- PREPARE AN INFORMATION PACK OR PORTFOLIO FOR A BUSINESS OR TOURIST BROCHURE

- ON SITE QUESTIONAIRE

- O.S. MAP WORK EXERCISE TO SUM UP LOCATION FACTORS AND PLOT ROUTE TO SITE VISIT.

- RANKING EXERCISE IN PAIRS OR GROUPS e.g. CHILDREN HAVE RETURNED WITH REASONS FOR SITING OF AN INDUSTRY OR TOURIST AMENITY AND THESE CAN BE RANKED. (PUT BAD POINTS ON RANKING SHEET AS WELL AS GOOD POINTS).

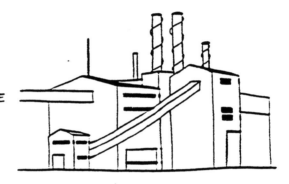

- SPEAKER FROM LOCAL BUSINESS / INDUSTRY

- COMPARISON OF PAST INDUSTRIAL SITES AND PRESENT USING OLD MAPS, PHOTOGRAPHS AND DOCUMENTS.

- CLASS SURVEY OF TOURIST SITES IN NORTHUMBRIA.

ENVIRONMENTAL QUALITY – Using the local area to examine likes and dislikes about the environment.

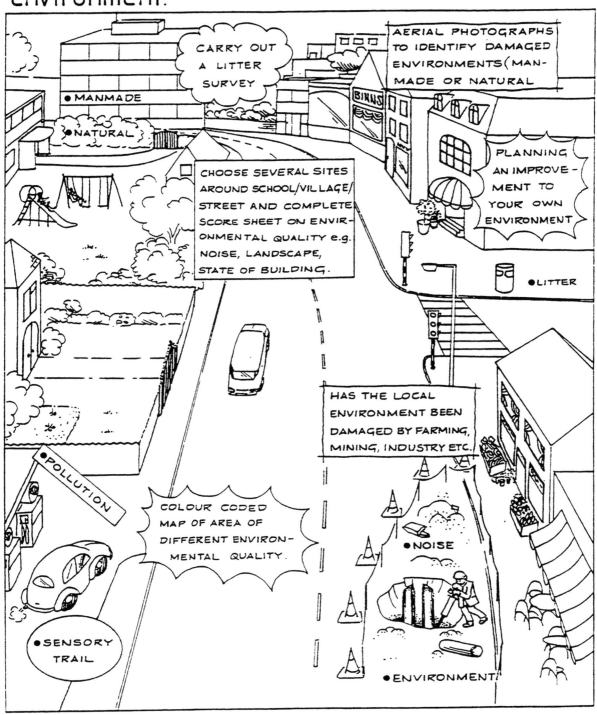

KEY STAGE 2

HOLES AND UNDERGROUND – Studies of various types of holes.

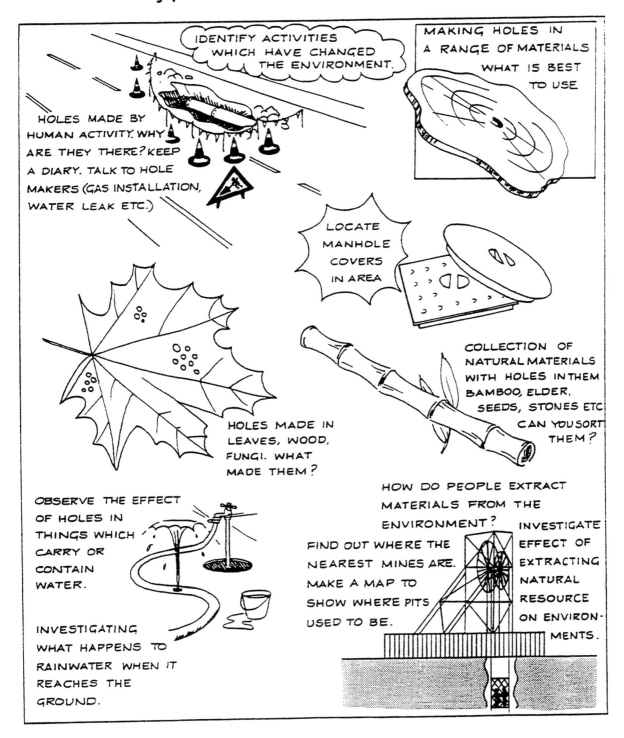

KEY STAGE 2

THE SEASHORE – A Changing Environment.

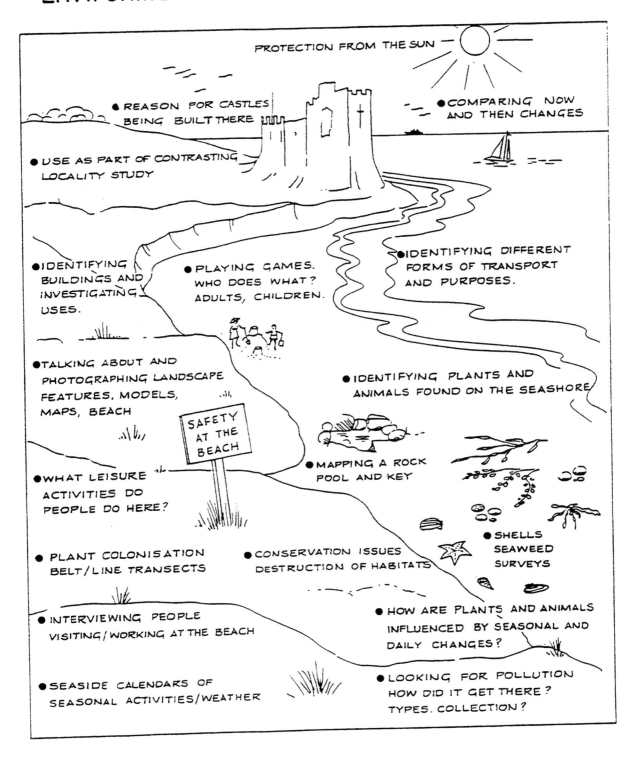

PROTECTION FROM THE SUN

● REASON FOR CASTLES BEING BUILT THERE

● COMPARING NOW AND THEN CHANGES

● USE AS PART OF CONTRASTING LOCALITY STUDY

● IDENTIFYING BUILDINGS AND INVESTIGATING USES.

● PLAYING GAMES. WHO DOES WHAT? ADULTS, CHILDREN.

● IDENTIFYING DIFFERENT FORMS OF TRANSPORT AND PURPOSES.

● TALKING ABOUT AND PHOTOGRAPHING LANDSCAPE FEATURES, MODELS, MAPS, BEACH

SAFETY AT THE BEACH

● IDENTIFYING PLANTS AND ANIMALS FOUND ON THE SEASHORE

● WHAT LEISURE ACTIVITIES DO PEOPLE DO HERE?

● MAPPING A ROCK POOL AND KEY

● SHELLS SEAWEED SURVEYS

● PLANT COLONISATION BELT/LINE TRANSECTS

● CONSERVATION ISSUES DESTRUCTION OF HABITATS

● INTERVIEWING PEOPLE VISITING/WORKING AT THE BEACH

● HOW ARE PLANTS AND ANIMALS INFLUENCED BY SEASONAL AND DAILY CHANGES?

● SEASIDE CALENDARS OF SEASONAL ACTIVITIES/WEATHER

● LOOKING FOR POLLUTION HOW DID IT GET THERE? TYPES. COLLECTION?

KEY STAGES 1 AND 2

BUILDINGS – Uses of buildings and functions and origins of settlements. KEY STAGES 1 AND 2

- USING FICTION TO IDENTIFY DIFFERENT BUILDINGS, TYPES OF HOMES, VILLAGES AND CITIES.

- SHOES
- CLOTHES
- FOOD
- FURNITURE

- STREET SURVEY – USES BUILDING MATERIALS

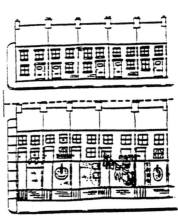

- COMPARISON OF BUILDINGS BETWEEN OWN LOCALITY AND CONTRASTING LOCALITY. (TWINNED SCHOOL LOCALITY OR E.D.C. LOCALITY.)

- PHOTOGRAPH LABELLING DIFFERENT TYPES OF BUILDING.

- IDENTIFY BUILDING FUNCTIONS USING AERIAL PHOTOGRAPHS.

- MAP BUILDINGS WITH COLOUR CODING FOR DIFFERENT AGES TO SHOW GROWTH OF SETTLEMENT.

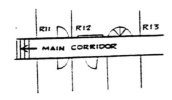

- MAKE A PLAN OF SCHOOL ROUTES ROUND SCHOOL

- WHAT ARE THE BEST BUILDING MATERIALS?

- DIFFERENT TEXTURES

- DIFFERENT SHAPES

- NOTE ANY HISTORICAL SITES

- CARDBOARD MODELS OF BUILDING TYPES – STREETS, HOUSES.

DETERMINE PURPOSE

THE RECLAIMED ENVIRONMENT

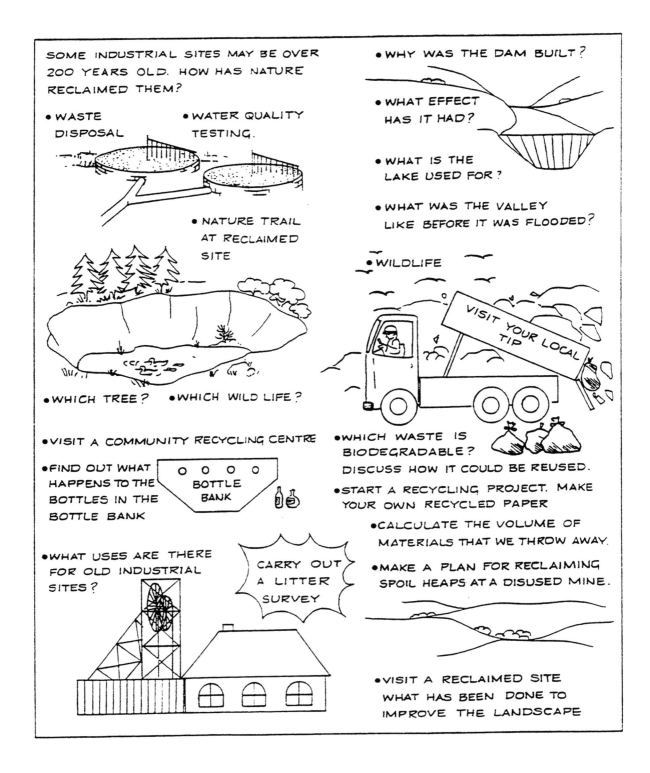

SOME INDUSTRIAL SITES MAY BE OVER 200 YEARS OLD. HOW HAS NATURE RECLAIMED THEM?

• WASTE DISPOSAL

• WATER QUALITY TESTING.

• NATURE TRAIL AT RECLAIMED SITE

• WHICH TREE?   • WHICH WILD LIFE?

• VISIT A COMMUNITY RECYCLING CENTRE

• FIND OUT WHAT HAPPENS TO THE BOTTLES IN THE BOTTLE BANK

BOTTLE BANK

• WHAT USES ARE THERE FOR OLD INDUSTRIAL SITES?

CARRY OUT A LITTER SURVEY

• WHY WAS THE DAM BUILT?

• WHAT EFFECT HAS IT HAD?

• WHAT IS THE LAKE USED FOR?

• WHAT WAS THE VALLEY LIKE BEFORE IT WAS FLOODED?

• WILDLIFE

VISIT YOUR LOCAL TIP

• WHICH WASTE IS BIODEGRADABLE? DISCUSS HOW IT COULD BE REUSED.

• START A RECYCLING PROJECT. MAKE YOUR OWN RECYCLED PAPER

• CALCULATE THE VOLUME OF MATERIALS THAT WE THROW AWAY.

• MAKE A PLAN FOR RECLAIMING SPOIL HEAPS AT A DISUSED MINE.

• VISIT A RECLAIMED SITE WHAT HAS BEEN DONE TO IMPROVE THE LANDSCAPE

KEYSTAGES 1 AND 2

Section 4

Residential Education in the National Curriculum

Chapter 13

The residential experience: A conceptual framework

INTRODUCTION

The importance and relevance of the residential experience as an aid to learning is not a new idea as evidenced by various Government reports and recommendations dating back over 50 years.

> In 1963 the Newsom Report confirmed the conviction of many teachers that a wide range of activities developed in a residential context can provide *"an abundance of opportunities to enhance and extend learning. It is an almost unique environment to promote the social and personal development of young people and to bring teachers and students into closer contact."*

For the purpose of clarification, 'residential' is defined as "Any experience involving an overnight stay away from home". However, the concept behind the word is more clearly conveyed by the Schools Council that:

> *"living and working together, pupils develop a higher degree of social awareness so that by the end of the residential course many pupils know themselves and their fellows more thoroughly than they would have otherwise done."*

The aims of residential education

The aim of the residential experience should be: To provide young people with the opportunity to participate in a series of residential experiences to develop aspects of their personal, social and environmental awareness:

- *Personal development* comes from having to adapt to new conditions and different methods of working. Whether particular facets of personal development are deliberately planned for will depend upon which approach the staff and school adopt.

- *Social development* arises out of living away from home and family, as a member of a small community in a different environment with opportunities for developing contacts with others, in an atmosphere different from that of school.

- *Environmental awareness* will vary widely according to the subject and the nature of the work carried out. Experiences offer something that cannot be done equally well in school.

Learning outcomes

Personal Development

Within the residential experience social and personal development are almost inseparable. But, in many examples of living in a community, a deliberate attempt is made to provide the kind of atmosphere in which personal development may occur. Young people can:

- develop initiative, independence, confidence and self-reliance;
- develop leadership qualities;
- develop a sense of responsibility;
- learn to adapt to unfamiliar situations, environments and people;
- develop openness, consideration, co-operation and tolerance.

Social Development

The social element is intrinsic throughout the whole of the education process and is so fundamental that many might not mention it in stating the aims for a particular unit of work.

In living with a group, large or small, for a period of time away from home, it is hoped young people will:

- develop an increasing understanding and tolerance of themselves and others;
- understand and accept the need for guidelines for living in a small, compact community;
- develop a willingness to contribute to the welfare of the group in activities, leisure, study and domestic chores;
- develop better relationships with their leaders and each other;
- adjust to living in a different community than that to which they have been accustomed;
- learn to accept new challenges; physically, socially and mentally;
- develop a sense of independence and responsibility;
- accept the strengths and weaknesses of themselves and others;

♦ develop a sense of compassion and sensitivity towards other human beings.

Environmental Awareness And Academic Development

The residential experience provides almost unique and limitless opportunities for young people to work in and experience the natural environment. Through contacts made with and in the environment it is hoped young people will:

♦ develop a respect and concern for nature;

♦ gain first-hand practical experiences;

♦ understand more about the environment;

♦ develop an enjoyment of living things;

♦ develop a conservation awareness;

♦ develop an aesthetic awareness;

♦ develop academically and cognitively.

The Value of the Residential Experience

A residential experience provides unique opportunities, often difficult to create in the school environment. Experiences offer students opportunities to embark upon a wide range of investigative learning, cross curricular and specialist projects in the context of the National Curriculum. In such situations, particularly where organisation is kept flexible and informal, students and staff become primarily *people*. Relationships can be established based on personal qualities rather than imposed structures.

The residential gives opportunity for students to re-establish themselves amongst their peers. Prejudices which may have arisen by accident early in a student's school career are frequently overcome in new situations where different resources are available.

Residential experiences lead to 'group' commitment which in turn can lead to an enhanced group identity and to improved personal identities within the group. It also facilitates an increasingly important method of teaching where the understanding of learning processes and the development of learning ability are the main aims rather than the activity. In this context students and staff greatly benefit from a Plan-Do-Review model of teaching and learning.

The residential itself is frequently based on new first hand experiences and invariably involves an impact of intensity and immediacy which cannot be avoided. Situations have to be faced up to and resolved. While similar impact experiences can often be achieved in school, (particularly through outdoor and adventure activities), there the effect is literally more short-lived and hence more 'avoidable'.

Although the words 'immediacy' and 'impact' are used, these do not imply 'brief' or 'instant'. The 'residential' therefore offers students of all ages, time in which to accomplish a wide variety of learning. As such the potential of the residential experience is immense. With the development of recording student achievement, it becomes an increasingly important educational medium. The residential not only helps develop the 'whole person', it also gives insight into individuals' real personalities and hidden potentials.

The residential experience also provides sustained periods of time for staff to concentrate on the individual needs of students and issues relating to specific curricular areas.

Planning, preparation, and follow up through active reviews, are crucial to the successful outcome of all experiences. Figure 13.1 *(Hitchin P / Hunt J 86)*, illustrates a structure for planning and evaluating a residential course.

Curriculum Opportunities Through The Residential Experience

The residential experience offers scope for a wide range of learning to be undertaken and for personal and social development to take place. Apart from the opportunities it provides for personal fulfilment and the development of interests, residential education stimulates the development of self-reliance, self-discipline, responsibility, self confidence and the capacity for sustained practical endeavour. Experiences in a residential setting increase an awareness of self, an awareness of others, enabling the development of tolerance and an understanding of other people's points of view.

The residential experience provides opportunities for many interlinked areas of experiential learning to take place which may feature as part of the National and whole curriculum of a school.

188

(A) Forming the Course Group

(B) Integration Objectives

How does the residential fit in with the rest of the learning programme?

(C) Identifying Learning Needs

What do we need to get out of this course?

(D) Establishing a Framework

"Setting the tone" for the residential course

(E) Setting

for the residential course (standard and type of provision)

(F) Planning

Course budget, programme, accommodation, catering, transport, facilities, equipment, insurance, etc.

(G) Preparation

Group development training, preparatory visits, collecting information, preparing kit lists, equipment, maintenance

(H) Course Programme

Experience
Putting plans into practice, trying things out

Planning
the next part of the programme

Reviewing
the experience

Final Review

(I) Evaluation, reflection

on the course to see how effective it was and how efficiently it was organised in relation to the aims.

(J) Learning Transfer

Applying the experience of the course to new situations

Figure 13.1

Potential areas of learning include:-

- *Outdoor adventure* encourages young people to develop a skill in one or more activities; they develop personal and social qualities and inspire leisure time interests.

- *Outdoor environmental studies* which enables young people to acquire academic skills, knowledge and concepts, they develop an understanding of the natural world and develop an aesthetic awareness, respect, sensitivity and concern for the total environment.

- *Personal and social development* which arises out of the reality of living far away from home and family as a member of a community in a different environment. Experiences demand groups and individuals to come to terms with new conditions and methods of working.

- *Cross curricular and a multi-disciplinary approach* to topic work can often be more effective when prolonged periods of study and investigation are able to take place at a residential centre. Projects which focus upon first-hand experiences out of doors, and which relate to several areas of the curriculum can equally be better achieved when young people are away from the normal every day pressures of home and school.

Through residential experiences many aspects of the whole curriculum can be achieved. Indeed residential education could be considered as the 'key' to unlocking much of the National Curriculum. *(Figure 13.2)*.

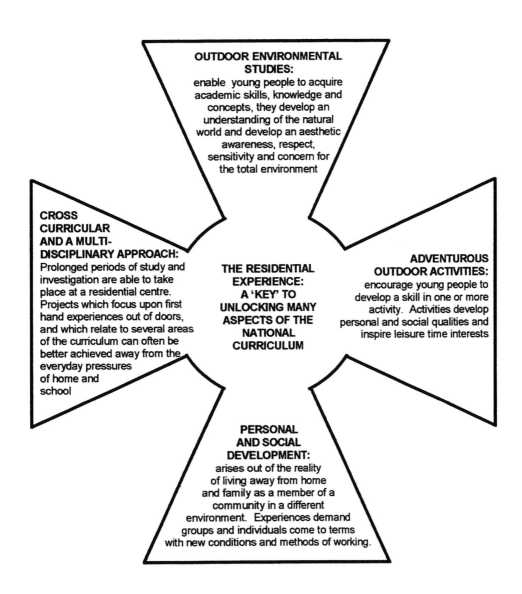

Figure 13.2

Chapter 14

Developing experienced based learning - Establishing course objectives for a residential experience

INTRODUCTION

The nature of the residential experience is characterised by a variety of settings and a wide range of content. Many teachers make use of LEA centres, Youth Hostels, camping barns, self-catering accommodation and private and commercial centres to provide residential and outdoor experiences for pupils. Others make use of the more traditional forms of provision using camping, narrow boats and bothies.

The content and format of a residential experience may be very wide ranging. Many schools use it as a focus for the following projects:

♦ an outdoor and adventurous course comprising elements such as climbing, walking, sailing, canoeing and caving;

♦ to undertake some environmental fieldwork study;

♦ for the purposes of developing an art/drama/music theme;

♦ to embark upon a community project for the purpose of, for example, developing a conservation area or an adventure playground.

The residential situation provides pupils with a very much 'here and now' experience. For all concerned, experiences are very real and involve the everyday tasks of living together, and include:

♦ living skills (coping with everyday life);

♦ personal and social development (people interacting with one another);

♦ leadership and group work skills.

It is for this reason that the residential experience is often regarded as a unique and potent vehicle for personal and social development. It creates opportunities over and above the normal activities undertaken in school, for teachers and pupils to work very closely together and be engaged in first hand experiences which are not only highly stimulating and enjoyable, but more often than not are very memorable. The mere fact of providing a short-stay residential experience for pupils, however, doesn't necessarily ensure that effective learning automatically takes place.

Creating learning opportunities

To create an effective learning climate requires the leader to clearly identify a series of learning aims and objectives for the course. Ideally these should be shared with participants and communicated in a straightforward manner. For each particular activity to have impact, there needs to be a series of intended learning outcomes against which individual development and performance can be measured.

To ensure that learning is ongoing and effective throughout the whole of the residential experience, the leader needs to encourage participants to be as fully involved as possible, not only in the day to day activities themselves, but in all other aspects of the residential. The leader also needs to ensure that time is set aside for the group to undertake debriefing sessions, where participants can be involved in reviewing and reflecting upon their experiences.

When participants are given time and space to reflect upon experiences and are encouraged to articulate how they have coped with the activities or projects they have been involved in, learning invariably takes place. Very often it is by making sense of their own experiences, by talking about and sharing them with others, for example - how they have overcome a problem, or found another way of doing something - do they learn and develop, not only in skills, knowledge and understanding, but as people.

The value and impact of the residential experience depends on a succinct definition of realistic objectives which will vary according to the target group concerned. Most learning objectives, however, should stress not only the acquisition of specific skills, but also the less tangible development of the individual as a person and as a group member.

In specifying objectives, it is important to differentiate between the obvious and prescribed outcomes of a predominantly skill-based or knowledge-based course, and the more pervasive, but less readily defined outcomes of socialisation. For example in fieldwork or outdoor adventurous activities, the learning programmes are normally clearly determined and any degree of socialisation is left largely to the discretion of the individuals participating. Residential experience implies the provision of opportunities for participants in living and working together, to engage in a more intense process of social interaction. It could be argued that in any successful residential programme the boundaries between cognitive learning and social and personal development will be blurred, but to enable this to happen requires skilful and thoughtful planning. Where the primary aims of the residential experience are for social and personal development, the arguments for involving young people at all stages of the planning and running of the residential are compelling. No residential experience is likely to achieve its full potential for learning and understanding, unless both teachers and pupils are fully involved at the same level. All the activities provided as part of the residential experience, should create a medium to extend the learning process rather than be regarded as ends in themselves.

Some suggested aims and objectives of the residential experience

Outlined below are a selection of possible aims for a residential experience. They are exceedingly wide and varied to give the reader some indication of the range of possible aims.

- To enhance the learning process by promoting a greater awareness of the environment.

- To develop problem solving skills and to encourage resourcefulness, responsibility and decision-making.

- To provide a new or unfamiliar environment which will extend the range of experience for young people and provide a background which is sympathetic to their social and personal development.

- To generate circumstances whereby young people are able to gain personal insights which contribute to their self-awareness, maturity and self-confidence.

- To develop the capacity for individuals to work purposefully within groups, adapting their own talents and self-interests to promote group identity and its effective operation.

- To enable young people to review their values, attitudes and social inter-relationships and to enhance their personal contacts with teachers and other adults.

The list of possible aims is far from exhaustive, but can serve as a basis on which more immediate and tangible objectives can be defined. The range of objectives may be extended or limited, depending on the nature and age of target group, the length of residential stay, identification of the appropriate learning outcomes, the experience and calibre of staff, the resources available, and the nature of the residential experience itself.

Possible areas of activity/projects

Outlined below are a range of activities and projects which may be used to further the aims and objectives of a residential experience. They fall into six general categories.

(a)   Environmental fieldwork experiences

These lend themselves naturally to academic fieldwork where processes of analysis, interpretation and conclusion may be utilised to survey environmental problems and construct working hypotheses. However, it is also perfectly feasible to organise different types of projects which invoke similar problem solving skills and group activities. For example, organising and developing a nature trail or designing and constructing environmental habitats will involve cognitive and problem solving skills.

(b)   Physical activities

These can be designed to improve self-confidence and provide a sense of achievement and be presented at levels aimed to stretch youngsters rather than simply to bring them (sometimes traumatically) to a knowledge of their own limitations and fears. Normally such activities include rock-climbing, sailing, orienteering, abseiling, canoeing, camping and expedition work. Each activity may have specific learning objectives which are skill related and personally and socially beneficial.

(c)   Group exercises

These can develop a responsibility for others and help to foster team spirit and camaraderie. Competitive activities in the form of simulations, for example rescues: treasure hunts, expeditions and team games, are normally employed for this purpose. Practical coping/survival skills may best be engendered through the medium of group work and co-operation.

(d) Leadership exercises

These can provide a range of opportunities where responsibility can be delegated. It is always possible to devise a variety of activities which emphasise the skills and problems of leadership and management.

(e) Creative activities

These provide a variety of skills to be developed within the context of an appropriate environment. For example photography, drama, video work, sketching and printing involving some aspect of presentation, can all be developed as part of the residential.

(f) Activities promoting communication skills

These can be developed by providing opportunities for individuals to discuss, argue, justify, present material and by involving young people in activities which require a certain degree of organisation and planning. For example dramatic and musical presentations often require good group work and communication skills to be effective.

Vehicles for effective learning

The residential experience provides first hand and relevant opportunities for pupils to be engaged in 'real' situations. Within the context of a week's stay at a centre, pupils may be involved not only in a wide range of outdoor adventurous activities and environmental studies, but equally they may be engaged in some creative activities. It is important for the leader to appreciate that underpinning all the learning out of doors, pupils will also be involved in a range of domestic practical living skills and in personal and social development.

It is very important that the leader recognises that learning is often on a continuum. It is not necessarily compartmentalised. The team work and group work skills developed in traversing a river, are no less important than when applied to washing up or sweeping the dormitories.

In order to effect good learning it is as important that the leader draws upon the learning potential, not only of all the activities and projects out of doors, but also upon the more mundane activities undertaken by the pupils in their living, sharing and domestic duties together.

Outlined on the following pages are several categories of activity related learning objectives which leaders may wish to consider when planning a residential. They include:

- Living skills.

- Personal and social opportunities.

- Outdoor and adventurous activities.

- Outdoor environmental education opportunities.

- Creative activities.

(a) Living skills

Living skills are those which are associated with a wide range of domestic activities including those undertaken by pupils and teachers before and during the course of a residential experience. They include:

- menu planning;

- shopping;

- cooking and food preparation;

- eating arrangements;

- washing up;

- cleaning up;

- decisions about sleeping arrangements and bedtimes;

- ground rules about behaviour;

- timekeeping;

- personal and group hygiene.

The way these activities are organised, and how duties are shared out, is a matter for the leader organising the learning activities. Group work will always have a significant part to play in the learning process. The matrix below in Figure 14.1 illustrates further points for consideration.

Learning objectives for living skills

POSSIBLE OBJECTIVES	POSSIBLE ACTIVITIES						
	Menu Plann-ing	Shop-ping	Food Prep.	Cook-ing	Wash-ing Up	Eating Arrange-ments	Time Keep-ing
Responsibility for self and others							
Ability to survive independently and in day to day life							
Problem solving							
Awareness and use of time							
Exploration of basic skills that might be used at school/work							

Figure 14.1

(b) Personal and social development

Personal and social development is a natural extension to any social and life skills programme. The residential context provides staff and pupils with extra time to do things for which there is not usually enough time. It involves participants being useful members of a group over a long period and of getting on with other people and taking decisions.   Figure 14.2 highlights several possible objectives for specific activities.

Learning objectives for social and personal development

POSSIBLE OBJECTIVES	POSSIBLE ACTIVITIES			
	Trust exercises, games and role play	Expeditions and challenge activities	Group discussion	Group tasks
Getting to know each other				
Group cohesion				
Self-confidence				
Decision making				

Figure 14.2

(c) Outdoor and adventurous activities

Attitudes of care and concern, mutual respect and confidence can be generated through close and intensive involvement in a range of physical activities. Adventurous outdoor activities can provide a significant and unifying theme, give a sense of direction and purpose to the residential experience and above all provide an immediate impact.

Not all outdoor adventurous activities require teachers to have a high degree of knowledge and skill before they can tutor groups, some activities do. Whatever activities are provided will require thoughtful planning and a careful consideration of the equipment necessary, as well as the safety management by the leader. Outlined in Figure 14.3 are a range of possible objectives associated with outdoor and adventurous activities.

Learning objectives for outdoor adventurous activities

POSSIBLE OBJECTIVES	POSSIBLE ACTIVITIES						
	Camping	Simple map and compass work	Canoeing	Climbing and abseiling	Archery	Rock Climbing	Raft Building
Group performance							
Self reliance							
Initiative							
Self confidence							
Trust							
Skills							

Figure 14.3

(d) Outdoor environmental studies

The principal learning objectives of outdoor environmental studies are to develop pupils' awareness of, and sensitivity to the natural world. One of the purposes of environmental studies, projects and activities should be to develop in pupils some knowledge and understanding of the natural world, and also some level of skill. It may be to do with developing their observational skills or their ability to measure the speed of stream velocity or the use of a quadrat in determining percentage plant cover. It is equally important that the learning objectives should relate to developing pupils' attitudes and values and to enhancing their appreciation, care and concern for all living things as part of their studies. Outlined in Figure 14.4 are a range of possible objectives associated with outdoor environmental projects.

Learning objectives for outdoor environmental studies

POSSIBLE OBJECTIVES	POSSIBLE ACTIVITIES						
	Pond dipping	Woodland studies	Shoreline studies	Fresh water ecology	Moorland studies	Cave environment	Farm studies
Observation							
Awareness							
Knowledge/ Understanding							
Skills (cognitive)							
Attitudes and values							
Group work skills							

Figure 14.4

(e) *Creative activities*

Creative activities provide opportunities for experiential learning about self and others, encourage other skills such as co-operation and communication and explore the latent qualities of creativity in everyone. The starting premise is that within us all, there are skills, talents, ideas, imaginative thoughts, expressions, feelings that are valid and, by exploring different creative activities, we can often learn more about them and develop. The residential experience allows this to be built upon and not fade before it becomes effective. Outlined in Figure 14.5 are a range of learning objectives associated with creative activities and projects.

Learning objectives for creative activities

POSSIBLE OBJECTIVES	POSSIBLE ACTIVITIES				
	Handcrafts	Sketching	Photography	Music	Drama
Experience of handling tools and using materials					
Confidence in ideas					
Listening and communication skills					
Use of imagination					

Figure 14.5

Planning

When planning any programme of outdoor or residential education, teachers and leaders should know exactly what it is they intend to achieve as a result of the experiences. Although learning outcomes cannot always be predetermined or guaranteed, nevertheless this should not prevent leaders from having some idea as to what it is they intend to achieve. Many questions will need to be resolved and will necessitate deciding on the specific objectives of the course; for example: Will the pupils be involved in......................

- The acquisition of a physical/academic skill?
- Personal and social development?
- Raising environmental awareness?
- Developing and reinforcing core curriculum skills?
- What learning will take place?
- To what extent will the group be involved in planning?
- Will the activities designated assist in achieving the objectives?
- Will the experience reinforce learning already introduced?
- How will the students be prepared?
- Will the leader direct or facilitate?

By answering these and other questions, the teacher then enables the activity or project to become a 'vehicle' to allow several objectives, be they personal, social or educational, to be accomplished. In this way, the activity or project reinforces the specific learning skills rather than it being undertaken totally in isolation. Learning objectives can best be achieved when experiences are carefully planned. Wherever possible, students should be encouraged to be involved in the decision making processes and invited to be involved in the mechanics of how, when and where. By so doing motivation will be greatly increased and serve to reinforce the learning which ultimately transpires (*Figure 14.6*).

Planning a residential/outdoor education experience

Group tutors will need to:	
1. Identify the needs of:	♦ the individual ♦ the group
2. Establish learning outcomes:	♦ acquisition of a physical skill ♦ personal and social development ♦ raising environmental awareness ♦ development of core skills
3. Plan an appropriate programme:	♦ as an integrated part of the curriculum ♦ ensuring the activities assist in achieving their objectives ♦ involve students in all aspects of planning ♦ structure to be consistent with planned learning experiences and activities: a) indoor/outdoor b) work based/leisure based c) individual/group
4. Consolidate learning by reviewing achievements:	♦ of the individual ♦ of the group ♦ of the programme
5. Evaluation and appraisal: (post-course/programme)	♦ individual appraisal (profile) ♦ group appraisal ♦ needs - were they met? ♦ objectives - were they achieved? And to what extent? ♦ programme - was it appropriate in meeting the needs and objectives?
6. Follow up and progression:	♦ integration of learning experiences within the curriculum ♦ sequential progression of project/activity

Figure 14.6

Conclusion

In order to get the very best out of the residential experience, teachers will need to be ultra sensitive to the individual needs of young people in their care. They will need to maximise the learning opportunities that arise both in the planned outdoor experiences as well as in the domestic arrangements which occur throughout the week. They will need to be clear about the aims and objectives of the residential experience and seek to utilise the activities as a vehicle to promote good learning. Equally they will need to think carefully about the ways in which experiences are reflected upon, and reviewed throughout the week, in order to ensure that the learning objectives have been achieved. They will need to be skilled in appreciating success and in supporting failure to ensure that disappointment can in some way be translated into a positive outcome.

The learning derived from a residential and outdoor experience is essentially 'experiential'. The opportunities provided throughout the experience offer unique exposure to a range of 'real life' situations. To ensure effective learning takes place there must be opportunities for young people to be involved in the planning and evaluating of all their experiences. As a consequence pupils will develop, learn and grow.

Chapter 15

Analysis of empirical research to demonstrate how residential experiences can contribute significantly to pupils' personal and social development through a structure of plan - do - review

INTRODUCTION

The place of residential education has over the last two decades developed a worthy reputation for confronting young people with a variety of profound psychological, physical, social and academic experiences. But at the same time, the amount of rigorous research carried out within this important area of the curriculum to substantiate the beneficial impact such experiences may have upon the individual is very scant. Until fairly recently few studies had been carried out within the Education System in an attempt to quantify the influences of residential education upon young people. The first part of this chapter sets out to illustrate through the available documented research, evidence to support how a structured approach to residential experiences can contribute significantly to pupils' personal and social development. The latter part of the chapter illustrates how social and personal development is re-enforced particularly when students are involved in their learning, through a plan - do- review approach.

Research Evidence

(a)   Personal development

One of the earliest attempts to quantify the influence of the residential education experience upon personal growth and development in this country was undertaken by Strutt (1966), Tosswill (1964) and more recently Fletcher (1972). They all looked at the British Outward Bound Schools and attempted, in their own way, to illustrate the value of training and its impact upon personal development.

Tosswill conducted the first investigation into the impact of the outward bound experience in 1964. As far as any aspects in the development of personality were concerned, students were seen as having developed in self confidence, tolerance and maturity. While this research project has been severely criticised on the grounds of subjectivity in testing, it did mark the first attempt to quantify the influence of residential experiences upon individual development.

Strutt followed Tosswill a year later, by conducting an investigation to present statistical evidence in support of the influence of an outward bound course on the personality of girls. This was accomplished by comparing the differences between initial and final assessment personality tests administered to a group of girls. The findings indicated that as a result of the experience, both girls' groups appeared to be more stable, more dependable, more critical, more lively, more independent, less sensitive and less conventional.

Fletcher conducted another piece of research into the influence of outward bound training upon the personal development of trainees in 1970. Results from his research indicated that students had grown in self confidence, increased in maturity, developed a greater awareness of the needs of others and increased the ability to mix well.

Two further research projects were undertaken to determine the influence of outward bound training upon personal growth and development, which are worthy of comment. The first of these was conducted by Clifford and Clifford in 1967. Their aim was to examine the 'self concept' of a group of adolescent boys aged between sixteen and twenty-one at the beginning and end of a summer outward bound course at Colorado Outward Bound School USA.

The tests revealed that, as a result of the course, overall changes took place in the self concept of all students in the direction of increased self worth and self confidence.

The second survey of the influence of the outward bound experience upon personal development was conducted by Jickling in 1977. He attempted to determine the specific effect of an outward bound course at Keremas Outward Bound School, British Columbia, upon its participants.

Results show that course members became more warm-hearted, more easy going, and showed greater participation in new situations. They were generally more assertive and also more forthright at the end of the course than they had been at the beginning.

The conclusion to Jickling's research supports the view that the outward bound experience not only provides a worthwhile challenge, but that courses of a similar nature have a profound effect upon personal and social growth and development.

The Outward Bound Trust is not the only organisation to conduct research into the powerful influences which residential education may have upon the development of young people. Payne et al (1970) sought to ascertain the extent to which an expedition to the Arctic influenced the personalities of its members, while Heaps and Thorstenson (1973) set out to study the permanent nature of changes in personality which result from a survival course undertaken in the remote north-eastern corner of the United States. The results of both these surveys are worthy of mention.

Payne and his co-authors looked specifically at changes in the self concept of thirty-six English school leavers who participated in an expedition of one month's duration to Spitsbergen in the Arctic. Research revealed that the members of the expedition were significantly more extrovert than the control group, that participants had developed in self confidence, self discipline, self worth, became more independent and more assertive as a result of the experience.

Heaps and Thorstenson by contrast set out to study the permanence of changes which result from the experience of outdoor education - wilderness, survival training.

Using the Tennessee 'Self Concept Scale', tests were administered immediately before the expedition, during, immediately after and again after a period of one year. The results illustrated a positive score for all the students. Overall levels of self esteem and self concept scores one year following the expedition were significantly higher than before the experience in all cases. This data indicates that not only did students perceptions of their identity, self satisfaction, behaviour, physical self, moral self, ethical self, personal self and value as a family member all become more positive during the expedition, but these aspects of personality were in fact maintained after one year following the experience.

(b)   Personal and social development

Social effectiveness can be regarded from two perspectives. At the person to person level, an individual develops personal awareness, an identity and other qualities. At the person to group level, awareness and acceptance of a person's relationship to the group is involved. To achieve this the individual needs to acquire the sensitivity and relevant skills to operate effectively and creatively within these groups. The Department of Education conference report on outdoor education commented on this aspect of organisation at the person to person level and at the group level by stating that:

"The most important aims of outdoor education are to heighten awareness of, and foster respect for others through group experiences and in the sharing of decisions." (DES (A) 1975)

"This involves an individual, with other members of his group, planning activities, evaluating progress, sharing leadership, domestic duties, and responsibility for the group; co-ordinating activities, representing the group, communicating effectively and helping others." (DES (B) 1975)

Several attempts, particularly during the last decade, have been made to quantify the influence of residential education upon the personal and social development of young people. In order to accomplish this, a variety of tests have been administered by research workers in the field. Evaluation tests have included the use of self concept and self esteem assessment, 'interaction analysis' tests, 'social distance' scale tests and 'Likert-type attitude' scale tests. Such evaluation tests have been utilised to illustrate the degree of influence experiences in residential education may have upon an individual's social awareness, at the person to person and at the person to group level.

One of the earliest pieces of research to be conducted into the social effects of a residential education course was conducted by Becker at Colombia University USA in 1960. Research was undertaken to test whether the social and emotional growth of school children attending a residential course of outdoor activities could be shown to exceed the growth of an equivalent group of school children, who had not experienced a residential outdoor activity course.

From the research evidence, it was apparent that as a group, the children who had attended the residential course experienced increased feelings of self confidence as people, to an extent which was not matched by children from the control groups. The effect was not a transient one, but was evident in even greater magnitude after a lapse of ten weeks and one year later (Becker 1960).

The conclusions to Becker's research suggest that residential education experiences not only can have a marked positive impact upon children's self concept but upon the development of social relationships.

In 1973 Kaplan carried out research into the influences of an outdoor challenge programme upon individual's self concept and self esteem awareness and social interaction, in McCormick Experimental Forest, Michigan, USA.

The results of this research demonstrate that for the young people who took part in the outdoor challenge programme, many appeared to have benefited far more from their experience both in terms of self concept and self esteem than their counterparts in the control group, not only in the short but also in the long term.

In 1978 Wood and Cheffers attempted to follow up much of Becker's research by carrying out an investigation into the interaction patterns of participants in another residential course.

The results of the 'Cheffers' Adaptation of Flanders Interaction Analysis' illustrate that significantly more social interaction could be measured within the experimental group residing at the outdoor education centre, as compared with the results of tests administered to the control group, who had not experienced a period of residential education.

Two other exponents of outdoor education, who set out to demonstrate the powerful influence of the residential experience upon the development of personality and social interaction, are Jones and Carswell. They designed a study to examine whether the residential experiences in outdoor education produce any positively significant social attitude changes in children, as compared with non-residential experiences (Jones and Carswell 1975).

The results of this survey illustrated that all the young people demonstrated positive changes in attitudes not only towards their peer group and to other individuals back at school, but in actual situations, towards their teachers, instructors and even parents. Marked differences were measured as compared to the control group.

Towards a strategy for structuring the residential experience

The combined research data produced by Messrs Kaplan (1974), Becker (1960), Wood and Cheffers (1978) and Jones and Carswell (1975) is very convincing. It provides strong evidence as to the value and powerful influence which outdoor education programmes can have upon aspects of personal development, of social competence, social interaction and social awareness when young people are fully involved in their learning.

What is of particular significance is that in the case of all four of these research projects, evaluations were administered before and after the residential experience, but also on several occasions during the experience. On each research project the young people were to a greater or lesser extent involved in their experiences by planning, doing and reviewing all aspects of their course. Both Wood and Cheffers and Jones and Carswell indicated the profound importance of involving participants in their experiences if these are to have any lasting effect upon personal and social development.

Many educationalists assume that as a result of learning through experience in either a residential or outdoor environment, personal and social development automatically occurs in the lives of young people. That having subjected them to a range of exciting and challenging activities they are in some way changed; that their attitudes are automatically moulded and reshaped! Such an assumption is erroneous and without foundation.

The 1980's witnessed a major revolution in education and training as *experience-based approaches to learning* became an increasingly important feature of school, college and training scheme programmes. This shift of emphasis was mostly in evidence in pre-vocational and social education courses, but with GCSE developments and the advent of GNVQ courses, problem solving and learning by doing seem set to become more and more a significant part of students' school and college lives.

Inevitably *experience-based learning* has been presented in some quarters as the latest educational innovation akin to the introduction of language labs or computers, but in moving towards a more experiential approach, the education and training system is not so much innovating as recognising a basic fact of life; that people are innately 'programmed' to learn from their own experience and that the most effective learning programmes harness this potential, rather than trying to by-pass or short-cut it. Teachers, training scheme staff and group tutors who recognise this, find themselves on the threshold of a challenging but immensely rewarding change of perspective... their roles shifting from teaching students to 'helping people learn and grow'.

This is much more than a trendy change of vocabulary. Helping people to learn means seeing beyond the learners' academic and physical needs (in acquiring particular facts and skills), to enable them to develop as people. It means paying more attention to the *learning processes*, and less towards the *content* of education and training.

While one accepts that it is much more difficult to identify the learning processes compared to the acquisition of factual knowledge and specific skills, experienced based learning involves abilities which cannot be taught in the conventional sense. For example, observation, listening skills and working co-operatively together are all complex learning processes.

Teaching and learning strategies

Experiential learning is *learning by doing*. This approach to teaching relies upon the participants being completely involved in their own learning. It involves young people taking a genuine responsibility for that learning, through being invited to think, share ideas, weigh evidence, consider alternatives, solve problems, make decisions in the light of actions, exercise independence in thought and action, in the planning, execution and reviewing of projects.

Past research into the effects of experiential learning both in outdoor education and within a residential setting, illustrates quite conclusively that in order for activities to affect personal and social development and have greater impact and more relevance, opportunities for *preparation, evaluation* and *reflection* should where possible be carried out (Wood and Cheffers 1978/Jones and Carswell 1975).

This approach represents a different method of teaching and indeed is a fairly new approach for many educationalists. It will inevitably require a change of attitude for many leaders, because the teaching embodies a *facilitative approach* away from the conventional and all too familiar teaching style of *imparting, instructing* and *directing*. For example, such a method of teaching requires the adult to be sensitive enough to draw out from the group personal learning as a result of an activity or experience. It is therefore paramount that in order to enhance the learning process and enable personal and social development to take place, teachers and leaders should seize upon every opportunity to *plan, do* and *review* those experiences in collaboration with young people.

Experiential learning requires teachers to develop a 'holistic' approach to teaching and learning. The task, instead of being the most important aspect of the experience takes no more prominence than the group, the individual or the environment in which the experience takes place. Such an approach relies very largely upon the tutor distilling awareness, both at the person to person level, the group to person level, the effect of the environment upon the group and vice versa. It is in this context that reviewing the experience becomes all important. This is best effected when pupils are fully involved in all aspects of planning.

Planning, doing and reviewing - A Strategy:

In embarking upon any outdoor experience, time should be set aside to *plan*, *do* and *review* individuals' and the group's performance (KOLB 1981). It is vital that teachers and leaders approach this process of learning, in a way whereby each activity or project can be seen in its entirety and not in isolation. The group leader's role is one of a facilitator, enabling individuals to take responsibility for themselves within the framework of the exercise or project. In the early stages the role of the leader should be minimal and objective. When the reviewing session is reached personal learning can be enhanced by tutor support.

In essence there are three stages in the process:

♦ Stage I is the *Planning* stage.

♦ Stage II is the *Doing* stage.

♦ Stage III is the *Reviewing* stage.

Stage I: The Planning Stage

The following points should be noted by leaders when preparing the group for any exercise, project or activity:

♦ Clarify your role as leader.

♦ Indicate your expectations of the group, as facilitator/enabler and observer.

♦ Make sure instructions are clear.

♦ Check on personal and group equipment.

♦ Emphasise the place of the activity in the course.

♦ Clarify individual responsibilities.

♦ Clarify group responsibilities.

♦ Indicate the importance of respecting the natural environment and local community.

♦ Clarify safety procedures and issues.

♦ State importance of timing.

♦ Note importance of personal preparation.

♦ Determine how the key aims and tasks are decided and by whom.

Stage II: The Doing Stage

It is vital that the group take as much responsibility during this stage as possible. The leader should be aware of the following:

♦ Take an objective position.

♦ Avoid interrupting the group.

♦ Allow interaction to develop naturally.

♦ Point out concerns for safety only.

♦ Try not, at this stage, to comment on individual's contribution or lack of it. This should materialise at the reviewing stage.

♦ Allow events to take their own course, even if the group is way out of line (intervene only if practices are unsafe).

♦ Be aware of what is happening to the group:

    (a)   person to person
    (b)   group to group
    (c)   group to person
    (d)   leadership patterns
    (e)   membership patterns
    (f)   isolated individuals.

Stage III: The Reviewing Stage

This stage is a crucial part of the whole process and leaders should sensitively draw out personal and group interaction. Through initial open ended questioning the leader can allow the group to explore exactly what happened and relate it to their own personal development.

The following questions are possible starters. The leader should try to avoid adopting the conventional leader style and only make observations relevant to the reviewing process.

♦ How did the group get started on the job?

♦ How did the group work?

♦ How were decisions made?

♦ Did a leader emerge - how effective was he/she?

♦ Did members listen to one another?

♦ What behaviour prevented or assisted the objective being achieved?

♦ What strengths did each member bring to the project?

- What qualities/skills did each of you lack?

- How did each of you feel during the exercise?

- What have you all learned about yourselves?

- Would you approach the exercise the same way if you did it again?

Teachers should be aware that in some instances, over emphasis on the review stage can be counter-productive.

Conclusion

This chapter has demonstrated by way of research data, strong evidence to support the view that outdoor programmes can have a powerful impact on aspects of the personal development, social competence, social interaction and social awareness of young people in the context of a residential experience. The survey of empirical research evidence widely substantiates this view. The implications for teachers and tutors engaged in working with young people is very apparent. It is clear that the most effective residential programmes are those which are accompanied by clear statements of philosophy and rationale, by thorough preparation, meticulous planning, evaluation and integration of the learning experiences within the curriculum. Good teaching, sensitive leadership and management of the learning process is crucial if young people are to have the opportunity of gaining a deeper understanding of themselves and each other. By encouraging pupils to share and take responsibility for their own learning, residential experiences can offer young people unique opportunities for personal and social development and in so doing make a profound contribution to their education in its widest sense.

Chapter 16

The potential of pupil profiling and records of achievement in residential and outdoor education

INTRODUCTION

Three decades have elapsed since the Newsom Report *Half Our Future* was first published. Within that report, much emphasis was placed upon the notion that "those who stay at school until they are 16 years of age, may reasonably look for some record of achievement when they leave". However many still leave school with no comprehensive record of their overall achievements. Although six out of seven pupils are now reported to obtain G.C.S.E. certificates in at least five subjects, by the time they leave school, one out of nine pupils fail to obtain passes in any subjects. Few possess any record of either their knowledge and skills in subjects or of experiences and achievements which reflect personal qualities and which are not tested by formal examinations. For a large number of children, examination results still have no real meaning or currency in the outside world. Even in the cases of youngsters who do achieve some academic success, what do their certificates tell us about them as people? The answer is very little. Examination certificates illustrate nothing whatsoever about the personal and social characteristics of each individual, or a young person's ability to interact with others, their sensitivity, confidence, patience, imagination, sense of humour, creativity, social competence or even common sense! Outlined overleaf (*Figure 16.1*) is a matrix showing some of the key objectives of residential and outdoor education.

Why profiles and records of achievement?

Most practitioners involved in both outdoor and residential education would argue very strongly that the very essence of learning out of doors is that personal and social development occurs quite naturally as a result of experiences. But many would deny that there is ever the need to evaluate that which has been taught or experienced; that to formalise a young person's attainment by means of undertaking some form of pupil profile or record of achievement is an anathema and subscribes to the notion that the experience itself is in some way invalid. Such a point view, though controversial, has no justification for those who genuinely believe that outdoor and residential education relies upon a different approach to teaching and learning from that which is traditionally prescribed within the formality of the school-based curriculum.

	The objectives of outdoor and residential education	

Through activities and projects - individuals develop an awareness and respect for: themselves / others / the environment

Others - social development	Oneself - personal development	The environment
Co-operation	Motivation	Awareness
Tolerance	Adaptability	Sensitivity
Trust	Self reliance	Concern
Openness	Self discipline	Respect
Honesty	Self awareness	Understanding
Group cohesion	Self confidence	Knowledge
Responsibility	Creativity	Action (conservation)
Team Spirit	Imagination	
Leadership	Loyalty	
Taking Orders	Decision Making	
Sharing	Sensitivity	
Compromising	Taking Responsibility	
Negotiating	Independence	
Interdependence	Patience	
Consideration	Curiosity	
Communication	Humour	
Dependence	Courage	
	Determination	
	Problem solving skills	
	Decision making ability	

Figure 16.1

Sadly, the present education system, with its reliance upon preparing young people to pass examinations, does very little either to prepare them for the real world of work or to face up to the problems of a fast moving and changing society. Do we not sell young people short, if we are able to offer both society and prospective employers no more than a list of formal qualifications? Employers are rarely provided with character references unless they are specifically requested when school leavers apply for jobs. In most cases youngsters who are successful in obtaining a job do so solely upon the success of the interview; the employer having little or no record of his or her profile. This is an appalling dilemma and a terrible indictment upon the record of achievement movement as it now pertains throughout education.

Much of the causes of inertia in education are to do with people's reluctance to change and keep pace both with industrial development and the changing patterns of society generally. Education has failed in its attempt to restructure itself to meet the needs of an ever more complex society. The National Curriculum in schools is largely traditionally *subject based*, *teacher centred* and orientated towards the passing of tests. The curriculum is still obsessed with *content* rather than being concerned with developing the individual and the *processes* by which young people learn and grow.

Structural changes in industry and of the society in which we live, have in recent years led to dramatic changes in the distribution of occupation and different patterns of employment experienced by young people in Britain. The introduction of new technology has required different skills of the workforce, with different levels of ability and knowledge. As further changes occur, young people will need to be even more adaptable and flexible. They will need to be more broadly educated and possess more relevant and transferable skills. Radical changes within the whole structure of the education system as we know it, will be necessary, to provide a curriculum which is more relevant and which focuses upon self reliance, initiative, motivation and the acquisition of problem solving skills. There will be a premium upon people being flexible and adaptable to cope with the processes of change and the consequent demands made upon them.

In a report by the DES on Records of Achievement, the Secretary of State for Education outlined what he believed to be the value of compiling pupil profiles in order to achieve several basic educational aims. Among these he claimed:

(a)　*that profiles would improve pupils' motivation: "There is evidence that some pupils who are at present poorly motivated would aspire to higher standards if they knew that their achievements and efforts would be formally recognised";*

(b) *that profiles would encourage a more relevant curriculum for pupils: "The compilation of a record of a pupil's achievement obliges schools to consider whether the curriculum and organisation offer pupils the opportunity to develop the general, practical and social skills which are to be assessed";*

(c) *that profiles would offer pupils a certificate which is recognised and valued by employers and institutes of further education when the pupils seeks work or admission to a course.*

Creating opportunities for pupil profiling

To ensure that residential education can provide the right climate whereby experiences become a potent vehicle for pupil profiling and recording pupils' achievements, teachers will need to ensure that their *aims* are clearly stated and that *learning strategies* are identified. It is important for leaders, to realise that young people need to be fully involved in their learning throughout the duration of the residential experience; that pupils are provided with opportunities to *reflect* upon activities and be involved in *evaluating* their performance. It will have implications for the *styles of teaching* which are adopted and of the strategies used by teachers to facilitate tutorial sessions.

By defining clearly the specific *learning objectives* for each session, teachers should be able to compile a 'generic' pupil profile for any particular course. The 'profile' should reflect those personal and social skills and qualities that have been demonstrated by individuals in a wide range of activities, throughout the course. Provided *learning outcomes* have been specifically identified, the construction of the 'profile' should be fairly straightforward. Providing the *evaluation* and *review* sessions have been effectively managed, pupils should be able to articulate their progress and have developed the confidence to be involved in the whole process of *self assessment*.

The mechanics of profiling

The group tutor system

Analysis of good practice countrywide suggests that in order to create the right conditions whereby pupils may be involved effectively in their own *self assessment* and *appraisals*, the adoption of the *group tutor system* is crucial. Such a system relies upon a member of staff working alongside, sharing experiences and being fully involved with a specific group of young people, for the duration of the residential experience. Research evidence illustrates conclusively, that the group tutor system provides pupils not only with a valuable reference point, for the duration of the course, but also stimulates group interaction and enhances within the group a sense of co-operation. Some would argue that the 'tutor' is in fact the key to the whole process of personal and social development and of pupil profiling and recording achievement.

The profile/appraisal

One of the most important aspects of using outdoor education and the residential experience in pupil profiling is for tutors to encourage each young person to produce for themselves an appraisal of their own performance as an integral part of any course or programme. The profile should not be written as a log or diary, but relate to a series of statements, in the form of a questionnaire for each of the pupils in the group. The comparison between a pupil's perception of himself or herself and the perceptions of the tutor, or those adults responsible for the group, will not only be of value and provide a focus, but will allow for discussion between pupils and staff. The examples of pupil profile recording sheets found overleaf (*Figures16.2, 16.3, 16.4 and 16.5)* are a sample and range of the graded assessments which have been found useful. In figures 16.2 and16.3 key aspects of personal and social behaviour are highlighted on a five point scale. These range from largely negative responses to positive responses. The object of the profile is that both the tutor and the student complete the questionnaire independently. After completion, tutor and pupil, use the 'proforma' as the basis for discussion. In this way, the pupils are involved in their own profile and retain the right for the tutor to elaborate upon the observations, especially if there are areas of inconsistency and/or disagreement. Figures 16.4 and 16.5 provide further examples for consideration.

The process of pupil profiling provides staff and young people with the opportunity for reviewing experiences and identifying specific learning which has taken place. Tutors and staff should be very sensitive about using negative statements. They should try as far as possible to keep profiles positive and highlight the pupils' attributes rather than focus upon areas of weakness. Figure 16.5 provides teachers with a bank of statements for recording the achievements of pupils during a residential experience. The questionnaire at the end of the chapter has been designed as an "aide memoire" to focus teachers' attention on those aspects which need to be considered before pupil profiling can be established as an integral aspect of residential education.

Pupil profiling

A graded assessment scheme for common areas

1.	Knowledge		
		1.	learned practically nothing
		2.	some understanding
		3.	understood
		4.	understood, can make deductions
		5.	retained and understood all work covered

2.	Group work		
		1.	just never involved/minimal involvement
		2.	follower
	Co-operation	3.	good group member
	Team work	4.	good group member with ideas
		5.	leadership skills - total involvement

3.	Sensitivity		
		1.	insensitive, unaware, immature
		2.	insensitive, intolerant
	Awareness	3.	understands, finds difficulty in assessing
	Tolerance		people
	Relationships	4.	considerate
		5.	thoughtful, understanding, mature

4.	Confidence		
		1.	totally lacking confidence
		2.	nervous/cautious, needs a lot of support
		3.	confident, self assured
		4.	competent, positive
		5.	assertive or aggressive

5.	Communication		
		1.	unable to communicate
		2.	poor but able to communicate
	Forming and	3.	average
	expressing opinions	4.	good
	Speaking	5.	excellent

Figure 16.2

Pupil Profiling Record

NAME _____   GROUP _____

TEACHER _____   DATE _____

COMMENTS

1. _____ 1 2 3 4 5

2. _____ 1 2 3 4 5

3. _____ 1 2 3 4 5

4. _____ 1 2 3 4 5

5. _____ 1 2 3 4 5

PUPIL SELF-ANALYSIS

COMMENTS

1. _____ 1 2 3 4 5

2. _____ 1 2 3 4 5

3. _____ 1 2 3 4 5

4. _____ 1 2 3 4 5

5. _____ 1 2 3 4 5

Figure 16.3

Pupil Profile Form

Profile for: _____

Assessed by: _____

Date assessed: _____

Friendliness	Feels angry against others	Has at least one friend	Friendly to all those he likes	Friendly to new or less able workers	Friendly to all including strangers
Co-operation	Does not mix (is a loner)	Can co-operate when he/she feels like it	Works well with fellow workers	Quick to agree and help others	An excellent team worker - he/she will always help
Caring	Cares only for him/herself	Looks after friends	Cares about team or scheme	Voluntary work for others	Shows deep concern for social issues
Politeness	Rude, inconsiderate	Occasionally says good morning	Considerate to team mates and elders	Polite in all situations	Makes special efforts to put stranger at ease
Adaptability	Hours of patience needed for change	Very slow to learn new basic skill	Moves easily to new role if taught	Quickly picks up new tasks on his own	Uses initiative, can show others new ways

Figure 16.4   (continued over)

224

Speaking ability	Tongue-tied, grunts single words	Can answer direct question with clear statement	Can start a conversation	Can discuss sensibly with equals and superiors	Can speak out competently in large group
Attitude to authority	Truculent - may argue each instruction	Has to be nagged	Will do as told with some grumbles	Accepts all instructions willingly	Helpful, quick to respond, responsible
Staying power	Does not stick at a job more than five minutes	Can work for an hour if interested	Will work for several hours without being driven	Will work well and look around for more	Works happily all day
Tidiness	Throws cigarette ends and waste paper around	Careless but will tidy up if asked	Sometimes untidy but tools in good order	Never throws waste around, clears up as he/she goes	Tidy, good sense of order - will set others straight
Reliability	Frequently late or absent	OK if watched	Regular, safe, sensible	Accepts responsibility, trusted alone	Honest, never late, seldom ill, reliable
Problem solving	Muddled, cannot see the problem	Can see the problem but cannot solve it	Can work out an answer with other people	Can think out a problem on his/her own	Will lead others in problem solving
Decisiveness	Will not decide, wants to be told	Leans on others, follows	Will choose if given help	Given time will make own decisions	Confident and sure, chooses quickly and correctly

Figure 16.4   **(continued over)**

Cleanliness	Seldom washes or combs hair	Some-times washes daily	Always washes before food	Smart, clean, cares about appear-ance	The cleanest and smartest
Self confidence	Does not believe in him/ herself (a loser)	Afraid to express any opinion	Will give his opinion to strangers	Ready to try different tasks	Will tackle any new situation with enth-usiasm
Self respect	Thinks he/she is just rubbish	Aware of some good points	Thinks he/she is worth something	Some pride but has not set high standards	Knows his/her value, has set new higher standards
Courage	Nervous, shy, easily bullied	Tends to be pushed aside	Can hold his/her own with fellow workers	Will stand up for what he/she believes is right	Brave enough to act and speak as believes in any company
Self control	Loses his/her temper quickly	Tries but fails to keep temper	Can get excited but stays reason-able	Talks out problems quietly	Calm, stable, helps others emotion-ally

Figure 16.4

Outdoor and residential pupil profile

Name	Form	School

INITIATIVE

		Date	Agreed statement and contract
(a)	I am quite good at thinking things up		
(b)	If I think something needs doing I can do it		
(c)	I usually do not help unless I am asked to		
(d)	I find it easy getting others to help me		
(e)	I like to think for myself		
(f)	I do enjoy starting things off		
(g)	I would rather think of things and do them myself		
(h)	I do say when I have an idea		
(i)	I very often have ideas but do not like saying		
(j)	I sometimes worry about starting something in case it is wrong		
(k)	I nearly always help without being asked		
(l)	I do not like to interfere		
(m)			
(n)			
(o)			

Figure 16.5

(continued over)

		Date	Agreed statement and contract
Name	Form		School

LEADERSHIP

		Date	Agreed statement and contract
(a)	I like to be in charge		
(b)	I do not mind being told what to do		
(c)	I would rather follow someone than lead a group		
(d)	I am not afraid to suggest new ideas		
(e)	I like talking with people and getting them to do things		
(f)	I do not like people saying things about me		
(g)	I often find my friends follow me		
(h)	I would rather take a back seat than be a 'show off' at the front		
(i)	I can get upset when I do not get my own way		
(j)	People do listen to me because I am reliable		
(k)	I often find people agreeing with what I think is right		
(l)			
(m)			
(n)			
(o)			

Figure 16.5   **(continued over)**

228

Name		Form	School	

PERSEVERANCE

		Date	Agreed statement and contract
(a)	Although not very sure I went through with it		
(b)	An enjoyable activity and easy to play my part		
(c)	I did not see the point of the activity - not worth persevering at		
(d)	I did keep at it though I found it hard going		
(e)	It is a habit of mine to stick at things		
(f)	I tried hard but in the end I gave up		
(g)	I took the rough with the smooth		
(h)	It was boring so I did not try very hard		
(i)	Like me most people were a little scared but I had to go		
(j)	I did try because of my friends		
(k)	I did try because of the teachers		
(l)	I like to be thought of as someone who keeps going		
(m)	I did try at most things		
(n)			

Figure 16.5

(continued   over)

Name		Form	School

CO-OPERATION

		Date	Agreed statement and contract
(a)	I do try to co-operate but often the others don't agree amongst themselves		
(b)	I find it hard to follow someone		
(c)	I enjoyed working in this group		
(d)	I'm not always sure why we should co-operate		
(e)	I always thought there was a better way but the group agreed something else and I got on with it		
(f)	I feel better in a group, you're not 'shown up' the same		
(g)	I am helpful		
(h)	I like working with just a friend and not in a big group		
(i)	I could have done more on my own but as a group everyone had a chance		
(j)	I am good at give and take		
(k)	I am not very good at give and take		
(l)	There was very little to co-operate about		
(m)	I do like sharing things		
(n)	I get on well with adults		
(o)			

Figure 16.5

(continued over)

		Date	Agreed statement and contract
(a)	There are some things I know I can do		
(b)	I do not like people looking at my work when I have finished		
(c)	I do not mind people telling me when I am wrong		
(d)	It is easier for me to work in a group than on my own		
(e)	I like working out problems on my own		
(f)	I am not very good at trying out new ideas		
(g)	I find it easy to tell people when they are wrong		
(h)	Although sometimes I am unsure I try hard to overcome it		
(i)	I enjoy having a go at things I have never tried		
(j)	I do trust myself to get things done		
(k)	I need a lot of support		
(l)			
(m)			
(n)			
(o)			

Name   **Form**   **School**

CONFIDENCE

Figure 16.5

(continued over)

		Date	Agreed statement and contract
Name	**Form**	**School**	

RELIABILITY		Date	Agreed statement and contract
(a)	As a rule I do follow out instructions		
(b)	I like to decide for myself what I will do		
(c)	I do not like letting people down		
(d)	It is important to me that my friends trust me		
(e)	I do what I say I will do		
(f)	It matters to me what people think about me		
(g)	It annoys me sometimes when people cannot sort themselves out and try to blame someone else		
(h)	I do not like other people letting me down		
(i)	I enjoy starting something new but sometimes I drop out		
(j)	When I start a job I like to finish it		
(k)	I sometimes let people down but it's only over small things		
(l)			
(m)			
(n)			
(o)			

Figure 16.5

Staff Checklist

A checklist for records of achievement within residential courses

(a) Staff Development

1. Have all staff involved in the residential (including staff at the residential centre) been involved in a staff development programme, involving use of Records of Achievement? ☐

2. Have all staff involved had an opportunity to consider the danger of subjective value judgements within Records of Achievement? ☐

3. Have all members of staff had an opportunity to recognise their own prejudices and value systems? ☐

4. Do all staff recognise the care that is required in order to avoid unintentionally imposing their own value system and preferred method of recording upon students? ☐

5. Have all members of staff had opportunities to develop their own skills of negotiating and reviewing? ☐

6. Do all staff accept their role to be that of a facilitator rather than organiser? ☐

7. Do staff have the confidence to take the risk of allowing students to have a much greater say in the learning process? ☐

8. Have staff had an opportunity to consider how they would cope with adverse comments and negative feedback by students? ☐

9. Do all staff accept that the Record of Achievement is the property of the student and can only be shown to others with the permission of the student? ☐

(b) Planning the Residential

1. Have staff decided the degree to which students will be involved in the planning (this may be on a continuum from a residential mainly planned by staff to one almost totally determined by students)? Do the students know the parameters? ☐

2. Have staff and students clearly identified the aims of the residential and the best means of achieving these aims? ☐

3. Is there scope for individual needs to be identified and met? ☐

4. Is the programme flexible enough to allow staff to develop opportunities for learning, which were not originally envisaged as part of the programme? ☐

5. Is there scope for every student to draw up an individual learning agenda? ☐

6. Is there scope for staff to create situations which are sufficiently challenging to develop individual potential? ☐

7. Has there been sufficient time to establish mutual trust between staff and students prior to the residential? ☐

8. Have staff from schools had adequate time to work with staff from residential centres so that a joint appreciation of the objectives has been established? ☐

9. Are all the staff involved in the residential in sympathy with the aims and objectives of the residential? ☐

(c) Preparation by Students

1. Has the student been encouraged to set personal learning targets and goals? ☐

2. Is the student aware of the social responsibilities that form part of a residential experience? ☐

3. Has the student been involved in helping to draw up, and appreciating the need for the ground rules for the residential? ☐

4. Is the student aware of what is negotiable and what is not? ☐

5. Has the student worked jointly with staff to determine personal expectations (whether in terms of skill development or personal and social development)? ☐

(d) The Residential Experience

1. Are some of the experiences provided by the residential □ sufficiently open ended to allow unexpected learning to take place?

2. Do staff have sufficient skills to enable students to derive □ maximum benefit from the experience?

3. Does the residential experience have sufficient scope to □ accommodate different levels of ability?

4. Before, during and after the residential, is there adequate □ provision for staff to help students to review the experience?

5. Is reviewing an integral part of the process rather than an □ activity added on later?

(e) Recording the Experience

1. Is the student fully aware of the whole range of methods □ available for recording the residential experience (such as writing, drawings, cartoons, videos, tapes, sketches, collage, 'chuff-charts', photographs, etc.)?

2. Is the student given scope to choose the method of □ recording most suitable for him or her as an individual?

3. Has preparation for this recording taken place before the □ residential?

4. Does the tutor recognise that the progress of recording and □ reviewing is as important as the final record itself?

(f) Reflection

1. Is there the facility for staff to review whether the activities □ provided, achieved the objectives set by staff and students before the residential?

2. Were the experiences provided relevant to the needs of the □ group?

3. Were the members of staff involved in genuine negotiation □ with the students, avoiding the temptation to mould the students' response?

4. Did staff assist the reviewing process by providing a variety □ of vehicles for reflection, e.g. questionnaires, discussion, role play, peer group reviews?

5. Was there adequate time for each student to review his or her experiences with a member of staff? ☐

6. Was the student encouraged to highlight his or her own skills, personal qualities and achievements? ☐

7. Has the student also been encouraged to explore any negative aspects in the context of particular activities? ☐

8. Has the tutor been able to establish good rapport with the student in order to build up a supportive environment in which reviewing may take place? ☐

9. Has the teacher helped the student to draw up a truly individual Record of Achievement by avoiding the temptation to compare and measure students' achievements with each other? ☐

10. Has the student been encouraged to build on experiences and achievements to set goals for future development? ☐

11. Is there any provision to develop these experiences and achievements back at the student's school or college? ☐

12. Has the student been encouraged to develop self assessment and reviewing skills? ☐

13. Has the student been encouraged to take responsibility for his or her own learning? ☐

(g) Commitment by the Participating School

1. Does the school have a cross-curricular residential policy? ☐

2. Does the school management team recognise the place of a residential experience for all within its curriculum? ☐

3. Does the school have a mechanism for incorporating the feedback from residential courses within its pastoral system? ☐

Conclusion

The question of pupil profiling and recording individual achievement as an integral aspect of the residential experience, will always be regarded by some as controversial. Many teachers will always recognise its value and purpose; others will remain cynical of its importance. The residential experience provides a very powerful and an almost unique forum for this type of assessment, in ways not entirely appropriate or best suited within the mainstream of education.

236

Where learning programmes include pupil profiling which take the form of pupil self assessment alongside tutor perception, the impact can be profound. Where pupil profiles are staff directed, and instituted exclusively by teachers, without pupil involvement, the results can be both meaningless and inappropriate. The key, it seems, is to encourage pupil participation from the start and construct profiles by means of negotiation and meaningful dialogue between tutor and the pupil which is ongoing and in a climate of openness and trust.

The fact that so many young people still leave our schools with little or no evidence of a record of personal achievement or profile of personal strengths is regrettable. Within state education we have missed the opportunity of providing students with the wherewithal to audit, through self assessment and evaluation, their own strengths and personal characteristics and record them accordingly. Pupil profiling in the context of the residential experience has been in existence for some time. It has been found a useful tool to effect personal and social analysis. Mainstream education would do well to recognise the contribution which the residential experience can make to pupil profiling and records of achievement in general.

Chapter 17

An example of how a residential experience can be used to engage primary school children in geographical investigations

INTRODUCTION

Many schools make a commitment towards providing pupils with a residential experience at some point in their school career. The focus for a residential experience can be enormously variable and range either from a programme of adventurous activities, to an art and drama week, from a music workshop to environmental studies, or purely as a focus for personal and social development.

The purpose of this specific chapter is to highlight the practice of one rural primary school in particular, which chose to focus much of its residential week upon a town study of a market town. Outlined on the following pages is an example of:

♦ how the school organised the residential visit;

♦ the importance of planning the visit and clarifying the purpose;

♦ the preparation, the visit itself, and follow up work within school;

♦ how specific geography investigations can become part of a visit and how they are developed afterwards within school.

This case study gives an illustration as to how one school planned its residential experience, using a particular topic with a specific focus, which related to "contrasting environments" in the geography National Curriculum.

There are many other ways to organise a residential experience for primary children and schools will wish to determine both topic and focus according to their own needs. Individual schools will need to plan a programme of work which matches their desired aims and learning outcomes for children. The following exemplar highlights the approach adopted by one school in planning and undertaking its residential experience for Year 3 and 4 pupils.

Aims of the residential experience

There are a variety of reasons for taking children on a residential visit, The primary school teachers in this particular case study outlined the following objectives for their residential experience (Figure 17.1)

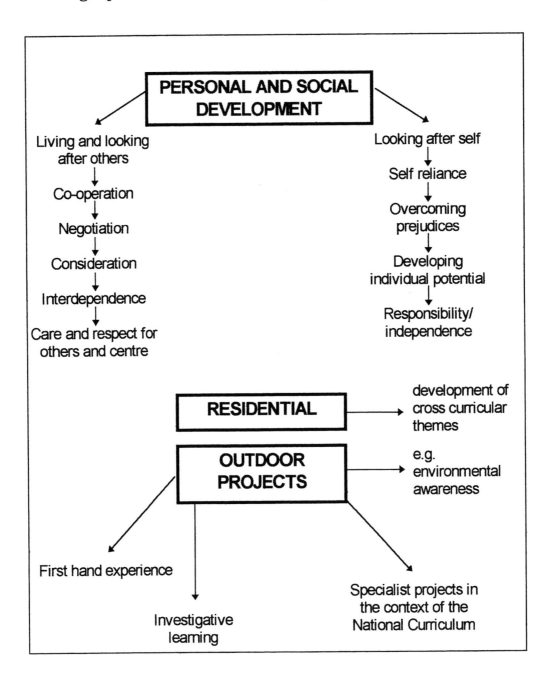

Figure 17.1

The teachers felt that they needed to be clear about the learning objectives and the purposes of the residential in order to ensure the experience would fit in with the rest of the pupils' learning programme.

Once this had been decided the teachers then chose a residential centre which could facilitate their needs and made a booking, accordingly.

General objectives

The residential week was intended to give pupils in Year 3 and 4 the opportunities for:

♦   personal and social development

♦   first hand experiences

♦   investigative learning

♦   geographical enquiries and investigations based on fieldwork activities

Geographical enquiries

It was decided by the teachers that the pupils would study a contrasting locality to their own village by investigating the use of the present 'Mart' in Hexham and consider the implications of its re-location. This was to involve pupils in developing their skills of observation and deduction as well as using:

♦   questionnaires

♦   land surveys

Pupils were also required to carry out an investigation of a river by observing its source and its journey and to consider how it erodes, transports and deposits material. This involved the children in observing and describing landscape features as well as taking measurements of the stream bed at various sites.

Map work skills were to be developed through the above investigations but also through orienteering activities.

The residential visit took place as part of a geography topic about a contrasting locality within the UK and the Deneholm Centre at Allendale was chosen, specifically for the purpose.

Planning

Preparing for the residential visit involved a lot of detailed planning and liaison with various people. Flexibility was needed, particularly in planning, to take account of the needs of the pupils, resources, weather, transport and other mitigating factors. Outlined below are some of the details of planning and liaison which were undertaken.

Planning

Involved organising the:

♦ course budget

♦ centre and accommodation

♦ catering

♦ transport

♦ facilities

♦ insurance

♦ aims/objectives of visit

♦ programme of activities

Liaison with the residential centre

Liaison involved a preparatory visit to the centre to discuss with staff the proposed objectives, together with determining:

♦ A programme to meet the needs of the school and children. Centre staff decided the best areas to do fieldwork and organised transport to and from sites.

♦ Times of meals, opening hours, availability of rooms.

♦ Safety and fire precautions.

♦ Equipment, resources, booklets available to the school at the centre.

♦ Daily duties at the centre during stay.

♦ Room lists so that accommodation could be decided before the visit.

Liaison with parents

A checklist of things to be done was prepared.

- Send a parental notification sheet to inform parents of visit.
- Send letter to parents to obtain written consent and additional information.
- Allow time for parents to save to pay costs.
- Have a parents evening to provide information about centre and its activities.
- Agree standards of individual and group behaviour.
- Seek medical information regarding particular children.
- Provide parents with lists of equipment and clothing needed.

Liaison with children

Teachers would need to meet with pupils and::

- Agree standards of individual and group behaviour.
- Share purposes of visit and programme of activities.
- Explain safety/emergency and fire procedures at centre.
- Give out lists of clothing and equipment needed.
- Discuss domestic arrangements e.g. bedroom lists, group lists and duty lists for maintenance of the centre.
- Explain medical procedures for daily medicines with individual children.

In addition:

- Governors had to approve the visit and permission had to be given by the Headteacher.
- Additional staff had to be recruited from parents or school staff and agreement reached upon the expected behaviour of children and the detailed plans for their role and involvement at different times.
- Both male and female staff were required for mixed groups.
- Preparations had to be checked with the LEA guidelines for residential visits.

Preparation

Preparations for this visit were carried out as already outlined. Staff, parents, children and governors were consulted and additional staff to accompany the children were recruited.

A programme for the week was planned (Figure 17.2).

The children took stamped addressed postcards to the centre so that they could write home upon their arrival. Teachers ensured that pupils were well briefed and that time was spent preparing them for the field study projects in school well before the visit.

Preparation for the river study in school prior to the visit

- The children were introduced to the technical vocabulary (e.g. source, tributary, mouth) relating to the features of rivers by following the journey of a local river on a large scale map and describing it.

- Various pictures of different sections of rivers were used to introduce children to the terms erosion, transportation and deposition.

- Children were shown an example of a cross section and discussed what it showed about the river.

- Safety near a river was discussed.

Preparation for the Hexham Mart study

- The school contracted Jack Lowery, Hexham and Northern Marts to discuss date, time, purpose and structure of the visit.

- The children were given a newspaper article, setting out the issue to be investigated.

Outline programme for the week
An example of a week's programme at a residential centre
Deneholm Centre, Allendale

Monday	leave school 10.00 am	Arrival Allendale 11.15 am Unpack, collect waterproofs and rucksacks	Lunch	4 different walks around Allendale area	Tea	Diary Prepare Hexham work
Tuesday	Hexham - visit to Mart and land use survey Walk through town to Sele Park		Lunch	Visit to Hexham Abbey Questionnaires	Tea	Diary Park Postcard home
Wednesday	2 groups Group A: Walk along river and describe features Measuring and fieldwork activities at sites (Deneholm Centre staff) (swap with B in afternoon)		Lunch	2 groups Group B visit Ashgill Waterfall Why was it formed? (swap with A in afternoon)	Tea	Diary Park/ games
Thursday	2 groups Group A: Killhope Lead Mining Centre (Killhope Centre staff) Group B: Canoeing (2 Deneholm Centre staff)		Lunch	Lunch at Killhope Centre, 2 groups Group A:Canoeing (2 Deneholm Centre staff) River study continued Group B: Killhope lead mining centre (Killhope centre staff)	Tea	Diary Park/ games
Friday	Return waterproofs and rucksacks Orienteering course/ competition within grounds of Deneholm Centre		Lunch	Depart Back to school 2.30 p.m.		

Figure 17.2

Description of fieldwork undertaken

Site visits - Hexham visit - study of a contrasting locality

10.30 am	Arrived in Hexham and walked to Mart from Wentworth car park.
10.45 am	Arrived at Mart. In two groups pupils watched livestock being unloaded, sold in ring and being transported away. Discussed what the Mart is like, how and why people use it.
	Pupils interviewed a person who had bought livestock and a person who works at the mart. Pupils located and identified uses of buildings around the mart on the map.
1.00 p.m.	Walked to Sele Park for lunch. Observed and discussed different buildings and their uses on the way.
2.00 pm	Guided tour of Hexham Abbey.
3.00 pm	Walked to Wentworth car park.
	Carried out questionnaires at different locations on the way.
4.00 pm	Transported back to Deneholm Centre.

The river study

The children were divided into two groups with three adults in each. One of the Centre staff accompanied each group.

The children did one activity in the morning and another in the afternoon. The two activities were:

(i) A visit to Ashgill Waterfall, following a route marked on a map. The children stood behind the waterfall to experience noise, appearance etc. They discussed how it was formed.

(ii) A walk from the source of the East Allen River describing landscape features and looking for evidence of banks being worn away.

At various sites:

♦ pupils explored the bed of the river and measured the flow of the river using floats;

♦ pupils measured the depth of the water and used data to draw a cross section.

Follow up activities

After the residential visit the pupils followed up work in a variety of ways, both at the centre and back at school.

Outlined below are a few examples of the follow up activities used to consolidate and reinforce learning in geography.

Follow up to river study

Activities:

♦ Children wrote about their experience at Ashgill Waterfall (prose or poetry).

♦ Children discussed the large scale effect of material being moved and deposited by the East Allen River and erosion taking place. They described the landscape features and tried to explain how the valley was formed.

♦ They identified the sites visited during fieldwork on an Ordnance Survey map and collated the data into charts to describe what the river was like in different places.

♦ They traced the route of the river and talked about the places it passed on its journey.

♦ Vocabulary used to describe rivers was reinforced.

♦ The children became very interested in pollution of rivers through a newspaper article and discussed what happens when rivers become polluted and why it is important that they are cared for by people.

Follow up to the Hexham Mart visit

Children:

♦ Collated their group's information from questionnaires.

♦ Used Junior Pinpoint to analyse findings.

♦ Drew conclusions from data about reasons why people come to Hexham.

♦ Reported back to class. Suggested possible features/activities wanted by people in Hexham.

♦ Colour coded the map of the Mart site to show the various uses of land at present, e.g. housing, transport, parking, shops, schools, cafe, hospitals.

♦ Discussed the views of people living and using land around the Mart site on the Mart's relocation, and the redevelopment of the site.

♦ Completed a table to show the advantages/disadvantages of the Mart's move for the local residents and local school.

The children continued to develop their Mart investigations using a geographical enquiry process.

They considered:

What might happen on the site.

What effect developments would have.

What other people thought about the proposed developments.

Children:

♦ Used a street plan of Hexham to identify different leisure and work facilities.

♦ Made a tally to show numbers of shops, banks, hotels, swimming pools, leisure centres, supermarkets, car parks etc.

♦ Decided what facilities are not available.

♦ Suggested a variety of facilities/activities which could be developed on the site.

♦ Drew plans of their own ideas on outline maps of the Mart site.

♦ Shared their ideas with the Director of Planning in Hexham.

♦ Discussed the planning process.

Return visit

The school then revisited Hexham to see the outline plans for the building of a Co-op Superstore on the Mart site and met with the Director of Planning at the Council Chambers.

They:

♦ Observed and discussed these plans with the architect who designed the new Co-op building.

♦ Interviewed people about the impact of this proposed development on Hexham.

♦ Interviewed children at Hexham Middle School about their views on the Co-op development.

Finally the children put together a display to show their feelings about the proposed Co-op development. They also displayed other work relating to their residential experience at Deneholme Centre for other pupils and parents to see.

Evaluation

At the end of the experience the staff of the school met together to evaluate to what extent the original objectives had been met: Evaluation took the form of reviewing:-

- Whether personal and social objectives were met.
- Whether first hand experiences met requirements of the National Curriculum.
- Whether the investigative projects were appropriate.
- Whether the geographical enquiries increased pupils knowledge and understanding of geographical concepts.

Conclusion

This chapter has demonstrated the ways in which a particular primary school set about planning preparing and following up their visit to a residential centre. As such it is a model of good practice to illustrate the necessary steps which teachers should take in their overall planning to ensure that first hand experiences can become an integral part of the learning process. Although some might suggest that the pressure of time often prevents this level of planning and preparation, it is clear from the documentation that, largely due to the planning process, some very valuable learning took place which was further reinforced by teachers upon returning to school. Not only were the aims and purposes of the residential experience made unequivocal, but the detailed planning and preparation were exemplary. A large measure of the success of the whole experience was largely due to the commitment and dedication of the school teachers, but also to the very clear relationship that existed between themselves and the Centre staff. Where groups are often very dependent upon the staff and resources of a residential centre, it is essential that a meaningful dialogue is established very early on, in order to ensure that both parties fully understand their involvement in the whole process of curriculum delivery.

Section 5

Related Issues and Topics

Chapter 18

Teaching, learning and assessment strategies in outdoor education

"I hear and I forget
I see and I remember
I do and I understand
...Ask me and I know!"

INTRODUCTION

Outdoor education is an approach to learning which can give greater purpose and reality to much of the curriculum. It encourages first hand experience and can be planned to support and extend the learning opportunities of the classroom, laboratory and workshop. As the structure of the National Curriculum has now bedded down, those responsible for outdoor education will need increasingly to demonstrate how experiences out of doors can contribute specifically and distinctively to the attainments of young people in programmes of study in the core and other foundation subjects, and in relation to *cross curricular themes, dimensions and skills*. Teaching, learning and assessment strategies will need to be clarified by teachers in order to ensure that learning objectives are fully met.

Learning out of doors requires distinctively 'experiential' ways of teaching. These may be summarised as:

♦ using first hand experiences and resources wherever possible;

♦ working outside the classroom;

♦ using one's eyes, ears and other senses in both nearby and contrasting environments;

♦ involving young people in discussion to foster the making of decisions;

♦ encouraging inter-personal relationships and group cohesion opportunities;

♦ providing for physical contact with the natural world;

♦ making sure children behave responsibly in varying environments;

- developing self reliance and children's ability to organise their own work;

- allowing for emotional response, while encouraging an observation and enquiry approach;

- encouraging children to take part in adventurous and enjoyable environmental activities.

These considerations are simple to state but more difficult to organise. They require a distinctive teaching approach and involve 'first hand experience' and 'active learning'. Such phrases have been very much over used and misunderstood. It is nonsense to suppose that children only learn when they are physically doing something. Equally it is nonsense to assume that when children are physically doing something they are learning something. Physical activity does not guarantee mental activity, and it is mental activity which produces learning. It is, however, important to work from children's own experiences, creating a progression from the known to the unknown. This is at the heart of a differentiated curriculum.

Whilst the framework of the National Curriculum with its emphasis on programmes of study and attainment targets is recognised, the taught curriculum will be more effectively delivered if it is based on effective planning which will take into account not only the needs of curriculum delivery, but the needs of individual children.

The teaching and learning strategies outlined within outdoor education cannot be allowed to be ad hoc. Continuity and progression is a crucial principle under the Education Act (1988) and so too the associated assessment arrangements. The nature of much outdoor education is such that the experience and activity often become so important that rigorous planning in terms of curriculum objectives can often be neglected. Sometimes thorough assessment and review is not undertaken. Frequently earlier experiences and activities are not used as the direct foundation for subsequent topics. The models overleaf places teaching, learning and assessment in its proper place as the servant of the Curriculum.

Teaching and Learning Strategies

At the very heart of *all* outdoor education experiences should be the notion of children *"learning by doing"*. Children should be taught to learn by practical experience, the skills necessary for accomplishing any task. They cannot learn simply by being told. Simon Priest in his article *Teaching Outdoor Adventure Skills* graphically illustrates what he considers to be the four most important stages of teaching and learning out of doors (Priest, S. 1989).

The stages involve:

1. speaking (tell)
2. demonstrating (show)
3. simulating (do)
4. confirming (question)

Each of these aspects may be placed on a continuum sequenced as illustrated in Figure 18.1 below. At one end is *speaking*, where the teacher provides information to the learner who listens. Next in line is *demonstrating*, where the teachers shows a particular skill to the learner who watches. Then comes *simulating*, where the learner does the same skill for the teacher to evaluate. At the other end of the continuum is *confirming*, where the learner provides information in answer to the questions posed by the teacher.

For example, witness the outdoor educator teaching knots to a group of novice climbers, cavers, canoeists or sailors. The lesson begins with an input on the basic terminology and topology of knots. The lesson continues with a presentation of several examples of tying common knots and then the group practices tying each of those same knots. The lesson concludes with the confirmation of learning, where the teacher asks a series of questions of the group to ensure that they have understood and can demonstrate the necessary skills.

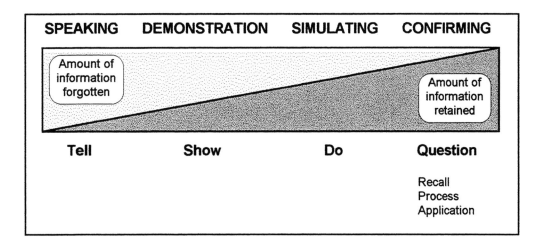

Figure 18.1

The teaching and learning strategies required for the teaching of outdoor education, I suggest, go much further than simply the stages as outlined by Priest (1989). Much learning out of doors requires a distinctively *active learning* way of teaching, which involves young people in planning, doing and reviewing their work. Educators need to recognise that teaching, learning and assessment strategies need to go much further than merely to identify the acquisition of a physical skill, but facilitate the wherewithal for young people to recognise what they have learned about themselves in the area of the "affective" domain. Experienced based learning is about teachers exposing pupils to a strategy of planning, doing and reviewing their activities in order to develop and grow. This is summarised in Figure 18.2 below and in Figures 18.3, 18.4, 18.5, 18.6 and 18.7 at the end of the chapter.

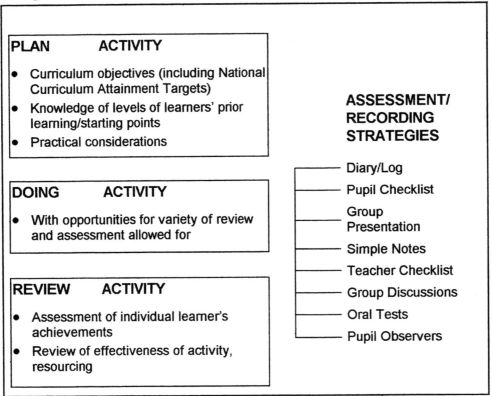

Figure 18.2

The success of experience-based learning is largely dependent upon effective teaching.

The success of experience-based learning is largely dependent upon effective teaching.

Good quality teaching is best achieved by:

♦ Effective planning and preparation which takes into account the needs of pupils in providing challenging, relevant activities for their age and ability.

♦ Clear aims and expectations which are communicated to pupils and where relationships are positive.

♦ Good organisation and management, where lessons have an appropriate pace; where explanations and tasks are clear and where intervention, questioning, encouragement and feedback are given.

♦ Purposeful, differentiated tasks which provide pupils with the opportunities for sustained work and to exercise some independence and take responsibility.

♦ Clear assessment criteria which uses feedback, marking, pupils' self assessment, recording and reporting as an integral element of teaching and learning strategies.

♦ Appropriate use of resources and attention to health and safety issues.

Good learning is evident when pupils demonstrate:

♦ positive attitudes, behaviour and relationships;

♦ high motivation and sustained interest;

♦ good concentration and perseverance;

♦ ability to co-operate and work independently;

♦ ability to respond to challenge, with confidence and initiative;

♦ ability to select and use different methods and resources;

♦ ability to question, find out and think for themselves;

♦ ability to use and apply learning in new contexts;

♦ ability to plan, modify, rework and evaluate tasks;

♦ gains in knowledge, skills and understanding.

Assessment

Assessment can be defined as an estimation of the 'value' of a pupil's achievement. Achievements are seen as gaining mastery of certain skills, knowledge and understanding in a particular aspect of work.

"Assessment is at the heart of the process of promoting children's learning. It can provide a framework in which educational objectives may be set and pupils' progress charted and expressed. It can yield a basis for planning the next educational steps in response to children's needs. By facilitating dialogue between teachers, it can enhance professional skills and help the school as a whole to strengthen learning across the curriculum and throughout the age range." (TGAT Report; paragraph 3)

Assessment assists pupils to:

♦ improve their performance;

♦ diagnose their strengths and weaknesses;

♦ match their individual work with their capabilities;

♦ receive feedback on their achievements;

♦ develop pride in the range of their achievements.

Assessment assists teachers to:

♦ evaluate their teaching programmes;

♦ meet learning objectives and adjust their teaching approaches accordingly so that pupils' learning can be taken forward;

♦ identify the need for further diagnostic assessments for particular pupils where appropriate;

♦ record overall achievements at critical stages (e.g. transfer).

Assessment assists parents to:

♦ have a more comprehensive notion of their child's progress and development;

♦ have opportunities to participate more fully in their child's progress both in and out of school.

Assessment assists employers to:

♦ receive more relevant information about pupils strengths, skills, qualities and experiences.

Summary

♦ Assessment is not something that is completed at the end of a course of study.

♦ Assessment is not a bolt on process.

♦ Testing is not the only method of assessment.

♦ Assessment should not detract from teaching and learning.

♦ Assessment is part of the learning process and the outcomes should be fed back into the programme objectives.

♦ Assessment should include a variety of tasks, tests, practical activities and observations.

Example of the Plan-Do-Review approach

A   Environmental studies

An example of using the plan-do-review model based on a visit to the local environment.

Plan	Link to specific targets in National Curriculum
1. Aims of visit:	
(a) investigate and record evidence of change in Morpeth;	History
(b) identify and provide evidence of the use of different materials in the construction of buildings;	Science AT3
(c) identify and record evidence of architectural patterns in the urban landscape;	Mathematics AT4
(d) identify and map load bearing structures (bridges) in the urban landscape, to lead later into investigations into structures which will support weight.	Science AT3
2. Planning details of visit:	
(a) preparing - work cards, question sheets, guidelines to direct children's investigation, arrange for speakers	
(b) teacher introduction of theme: "Street Study in Morpeth".	

Figure 18.3

Doing

1. Visit to Morpeth

Children use guidelines to direct their investigations

(a) Looking for and record by drawing important or unusual building, e.g. church, school.

(b) Look for evidence of change: facelifts, alterations and change of use in buildings.

(c) Look for evidence of what goes on beneath the road: grids, manhole covers etc.

(d) What building materials have been used - iron, bricks, stone etc.

(e) Investigate the textures on the surface of the building materials.

(f) Look for patterns in the buildings.

(g) Look at the street furniture - what is its purpose, letter box, street lights etc.

(h) Study the railway bridge. How has it been constructed?

Assessment by teacher on how children are carrying out investigations

(a) Observations of group work

(b) Observation of commitment to task

Collecting evidence during the visit by children as individuals or as a group

(a) Diary entries

(b) Completing questions or guidelines

(c) Taking photographs or video recordings

(d) Making sketches

(e) Making tape recordings or interviews or impressions

Figure 18.4

261

Example of the Plan-Do-Review approach

B   Outdoor adventurous activity

An example of using the plan, do, review model based on an activity in the local environment.

Plan	
1. Aims of visit:	
(a) to introduce children to orienteering;	PE AT1
(b) to develop concepts of spatial awareness;	Geography AT1, 2
(c) to develop children's physical skills and stamina;	PE AT1
(d) to develop children's personal, social and environmental awareness.	Geography AT5
2. Planning details of visit:	
(a) preparation of base maps of Plessey Woods Country Park also marker cards and control points;	
(b) teacher to carry out several introductory exercises in basic navigation at school;	
(c) focus of activity 'Plessey Woods'.	

Figure   18.5

Doing

1. Visit to Plessey Woods Country Park (orienteering course)

(a) Children placed into groups of 2 or 3.

(b) Teacher clearly delineates area of orientation; amplification of task.

(c) Children given base maps and begin to work out routes.

Assessment by the teacher

♦ Observations of group work

♦ Observation of commitment to task

(a) Children note down items to look out for en route.

(b) Children embark upon trail, collecting information and artefacts as required.

(c) Children return when task is complete.

Children collecting evidence either as individuals or as a group

(a) Completed marker cards

(b) Completing questionnaire

(c) Requested artefacts collected

Figure   18.6

Examples of active reviewing

Outdoor adventurous activity and outdoor environmental studies

---

Review

1. Assessments back either in classroom or on site:

(a) oral quiz or summary;

(b) written description of visit;

(c) visual or artistic symbolic summary;

(d) graphic summaries;

(e) diary record;

(f) group presentation;

(g) written test;

(h) 3D presentation;

(i) investigation (child initiated);

(j) role play;

(k) debate.

2. Evaluation process:

(a) by teacher to inform:
teacher records;
existing prepared material - changes required?
aims - achieved, realistic?
National Curriculum Attainment Targets achieved.

(b) by pupil to inform:
pupil profile or evidence folder;
provide information on achievement attained.

Figure 18.7

Conclusion

The teaching, learning and assessment strategies outlined in this chapter as they affect children's education through the medium of outdoor education rely mainly upon participants being involved in their own learning. The approach involves young people taking genuine responsibility for their own learning, throughout the planning, execution and reviewing of projects. Teaching and learning cannot be separated from assessment strategies. This is the very essence of the "experiential", active learning approach to education out of doors. Teachers need to recognise that there is so much more to teaching and learning than the mere acquisition of cognitive and physical skills. It is much more to do with teachers facilitating a "holistic" approach, which recognises the distinctive nature of experienced based learning out of doors and its contribution to the "affective domain" of individual growth and development.

Chapter 19

How children learn: an examination of the processes of good learning and how it affects 'learning out of doors'

INTRODUCTION

Most children are spontaneous learners. From an early age they strive to make sense of their world and understand it. They are naturally curious and inquisitive; they possess an innate capacity and appetite for doing and exploring. Talk is central to their learning. It is often initiated and led by them and requires the involvement of interested others. Engaging in a range of first hand experiences and opportunities which have meaning and relevance to them also figures strongly in the learning process.

Educators have a significant role to play in progressing children's learning. They need to ensure that children continue to acquire and develop the necessary disposition to learn and the necessary competencies for learning.

Propositions about learning

In considering the process of learning it is important to recognise that there are a number of propositions about learning which are common to all learners. These need to be taken into account when planning the curriculum for children in general. The propositions outlined are considered by some (NCC 1993) to be the most common.

1.   *Learning is an active process*

Children are constantly working on developing their understanding. In their talk, through first hand experiences and in their interaction with others they are continuously involved in raising questions, listening, imitating behaviours, observing and exploring natural phenomena.

As a consequence of this activity most children's ideas go through a history of development in their minds, some of them changing continuously throughout their lives. Learning therefore is rarely simply a matter of adding pieces of information to an existing store of knowledge. For nearly all children their most important learning involves them in reshaping their existing understanding as a result of new experiences. New learning is very much dependent on what children already know. If the intended cognitive learning is too far removed from what is already known, it will most likely be forgotten. It is therefore important that educators offer children learning experiences which build upon children's prior knowledge and understanding, which invite their interest and active involvement, are enjoyable, and which are mediated through activity, talk and first hand experiences.

2.   Learning is recursive

All learners need to revisit their learning. They need opportunities to repeat experiences, to revisit the same learning in different contexts and to practise and consolidate skills, knowledge and understanding. Revisiting is fundamental and an essential aspect of all learning and growing.

3.   Learning is strongly influenced by its context

For most children every setting is a possible source of learning. Invariably all children need the support of a meaningful context, which as far as possible reflects their social and cultural background and which helps them feel valued, to promote and progress their learning.   Unfamiliar contexts are often a powerful medium for learning. Activity based opportunities, first hand experiences and planned occasions to develop discussion can also provide purposeful contexts for learning.

4.   Learning makes effective use of errors

It is a fact that all children need to be given time and opportunity to work through disappointments and mistakes. They should be encouraged to tolerate difficulties in the course of their learning, to be aware that frustration passes and "things come right at the end". They also need to be encouraged to actively look for and resolve problems and errors in order to help them break through barriers which otherwise hinder their achievement. Educators must therefore ensure that children are given problem solving activities in which they have to identify and work through difficulties as they search for possible solutions. Teachers also need to promote an ethos where mistakes are identified as learning opportunities.

5. *Learning is interactive*

Understanding largely stems from an interaction between children and their experience of the world. They therefore need opportunities and space to explore and discover everything about them including the unexpected. Learning is also a social process. Children will need to interact with their peers and with supportive and well informed adults. They should be encouraged to work collaboratively and co-operatively with them.

6. *Learning should promote increased independence*

For learning to be effective, it is important that children develop as independent and resourceful learners; to be able to talk and ask questions, exercise their curiosity and imagination; to be able to be in control in their immediate surroundings; make choices, enjoy learning and regard themselves as competent and confident enquirers who are ready, willing and able to meet the challenges of new learning. Before children can confidently make choices and decisions about learning they must feel emotionally and socially confident, have high self esteem and a respect for their own powers of thinking. They must feel a sense of personal worth, have opportunities to set tasks, develop strategies to solve problems, be encouraged to explore, experiment, discover, reason, represent their ideas through talking, writing, painting, drawing and modelling, and be able to interpret and evaluate these experiences. If children are able to exercise these competencies they are much more likely to continue to engage in these learning processes and build upon them throughout life.

'The Handbook for the Inspection of Schools' indicates that good quality learning is evidenced by children who are able to respond readily to challenges, can concentrate, stay on task, respond to the demands of working in a variety of contexts, select appropriate methods for working, organise their resources, sustain involvement, are confident, raise questions, evaluate their own work and are prepared to help others". Children need to develop these competencies as they progress through their academic career and move on into adult life. Educators need to ensure that the planned curriculum facilitates these competencies.

The content of learning

It is important that children are active partners in their learning and not passive recipients. The challenge of planning the content is in ensuring that children have ownership of the learning; that the curriculum content supports the children's development as a whole; that they receive a broad, balanced relevant curriculum; that children are able to develop positive attitudes to the learning in order that they may be actively engaged in the whole process of learning throughout their lives.

Promoting good learning out of doors

There is much evidence to support that children often learn more effectively out of doors than in a classroom setting. This is largely due to the profound impact, nature and influence of first hand experiences. Children are often highly motivated to learn out of doors largely because what they experience is seen as relevant to their own lives. The outdoor environment can enhance and reinforce all the propositions of learning as set out in the previous pages.

Conclusion

While the outdoor environment has a huge potential to foster and engender good learning in children, there are major implications for education. Teachers cannot assume that learning will automatically occur. Learning programmes need to be carefully structured to ensure that children develop in their levels of skill, knowledge and understanding. First hand experiences are a very powerful medium to effect good learning, but effective teaching is also a vital and crucial element in the whole equation. In devising programmes of learning teachers need to be very clear about:

♦ establishing specific aims for the session;

♦ identifying particular learning objectives;

♦ selecting appropriate tasks and activities;

♦ effectively managing/facilitating the teaching to ensure learning outcomes are achieved.

Educators will need to develop not only effective teaching strategies which involve children in the planning and the doing of tasks, but also create time, space and opportunities for them to reflect upon their experiences, in order to ensure that they learn and grow.

Chapter 20

Promoting pupils' spiritual, moral, social and cultural development, using first hand experience out of doors

INTRODUCTION

The spiritual, moral, social and cultural development of children comes not only through formal schooling but equally through home and family, a variety of social and recreational groups and organisations and also the wider community. Historically teachers have delivered this element of education in a variety of ways, both formally and informally, largely guided by the aims, ethos and curriculum of their schools.

In recent years the National Curriculum Council's *Spiritual and Moral Development - a discussion paper* (April 1993) and OFSTED's *Framework for the Inspection of Schools* (May 1994) have attempted tighter definitions of the spiritual, moral, social and cultural development of pupils for schools. These are helpful starting points, but they do not absolve schools from the necessity of developing their own ethos and rationale for the spiritual, moral, social and cultural development of their pupils.

First hand experiences out of doors contribute significantly to pupils' spiritual, moral, social and cultural development. This chapter has been written for the sole purpose of helping teachers to have a clearer understanding of the terms, and to provide some examples to support teachers in the planning and delivery of spiritual, moral, social and cultural development when engaging children in first hand experiences out of doors (NCC 1995). Figures 20.1, 20.2 and 20.3 highlight a range of examples.

Spiritual development

A definition of spirituality needs to embrace both the religious and the non-religious if it is to encompass the experience of all individuals within a school community. Spirituality need not be confined to what we call the mystical or other world but is a necessary aspect of human consciousness.

A notion of spirituality viewed in this way concerns the development of an individual's set of beliefs that stem from a sense of personal self worth and a recognition of the uniqueness of every individual.

Although this development is focused on the individual, it carries with it some understanding that a relationship with other people, animals, the Earth and for some, a sense of Deity, is necessary if we are to determine our identity within the world. It is important that the development of an awareness of our world is stimulated through curiosity, reflection and questioning about why the physical world functions as it does and allows answers that move solely beyond an intellectual understanding.

Some examples:

♦ The migratory habits of the swallow may be studied in depth and the actual mechanics explained but this cannot account for the amazement felt when a flight of swallows takes to the air in autumn, in preparation for what seems an impossible journey for such small birds.

♦ The fact of a small blade of grass pushing through concrete, would seem to be beyond logical thinking.

♦ The near impossible task of untangling and accounting for the way human relationships and behaviour can enrich and affect our lives.

Spirituality is about our capacity to value and experience the beauty and wonders of the world in which we live and the response of the human spirit through loving, caring, persevering and coping with adversity. This experience may be heightened by the fact that we may encounter things in our world that leave us with a sense of awe and wonder.

Moral development

Moral development helps pupils distinguish between right and wrong within the parameters of their own developing moral code. This will be informed by knowing where they stand in relation to contemporary values and attitudes and how these values and attitudes have been influenced by history and other cultures.

Morality implies the ability to make decisions about our behaviour based upon a considered judgement of the context in which we find ourselves, the attitudes and likely reactions of others and the consequences of our actions.

The moral development of pupils has two facets:

(a) developing an understanding for the prevailing moral code and the factors which influence it;

(b)   growing towards an understanding of oneself and one's own code of behaviour.

In order for these two facets to be realised, teachers should encourage pupils to consider whether morality is absolute or unchanging and that we should not condemn the actions of others or ourselves without careful consideration. Any pre-determined moral codes may well be questioned by pupils as their personal moral code develops.

Some examples:

♦   The use of casual opportunities to challenge pupils as to the way in which different user groups make use of rivers, lakes, rock faces, woodlands, seashore and cave environments.

♦   The dilemmas facing an expedition group when one or two members decide to do their own thing, split up and go their own way.

♦   Conservation issues as they relate to an open moorland when used by walkers, Ministry of Defence, blood sport groups, mountain bikers and 'quad' users.

Social development

The social development of pupils is concerned with their ability to recognise that individuals are interdependent. It is about their ability to understand the implications and consequences of their actions, both short term and long term for themselves, for other individuals, for the whole group and for society.

Through positive socialisation pupils gain self esteem, confidence and assertiveness which equips them to take on responsibilities as individuals, within groups and within the context of wider societies. These pupils can take the initiative and play their part in decision making in a variety of contexts; they can co-operate and contribute to the work of small groups, take on responsibility in large groups such as the whole class or whole school and they can play a positive part in their local community and wider society. They can also make a positive decision not to participate or take responsibility within a group. In order to make these decisions rationally pupils need to have an awareness and an understanding of the ways in which different societies function. To play their part within school they need to gradually develop an understanding of its ethos and their role within it. To contribute effectively to a pluralist society they need to be aware of the variety of perspectives it embraces and to be sensitive to the needs of others.

Social development is not simply about forming good relationships and getting along with people. Central to it is the ability of pupils to make informed decisions about their level of participation in groups and societies and the ability to do so effectively whilst developing an awareness of the needs of self and others.

Some examples:

◆ Providing opportunities for young people to take responsibility for themselves; in taking their own actions and in making decisions.

◆ Providing opportunities for individuals to work co-operatively in different age, gender and ability groups.

◆ Creating the right climate/organisational strategies for pupils to plan and evaluate their work in pairs or in groups.

Cultural development

Cultural development permeates the whole curriculum. Its aims should be to:

◆ help pupils understand how their culture(s) have influenced and made them who they are. This implies a notion of culture as a continuum in which present experiences are influenced by past understandings;

◆ enable pupils to enjoy, question, reject, participate in and make informed judgements about the cultural opportunities on offer;

◆ widen and deepen pupils' grasp of world cultures so that pupils have the freedom to make informed choices.

Teachers should provide and facilitate a range and variety of learning experiences:

◆ both on and off the site;

◆ which are school or community driven;

◆ through raising awareness of the wider community;

◆ including opportunities for pupil initiative.

Inherent in the above is the assumption that we do not necessarily accept or reject without question our inherited culture or the culture of others or the handed down definitions of high and low culture.

Some examples:

- Enabling pupils to explore the use of a natural resource in their local area.

- Enabling pupils to compare and contrast their every day life to that of an expedition, or a journey, on foot, bicycle, canoe, sailing boat or horse.

- Compare lifestyles, occupations, quality of life of people living in an area with their own.

Examples of practice

Outlined below and over the page are several examples of how teachers have used a range of experiences to develop pupils spiritual, moral, social and cultural awareness:

Phase	Spiritual	Moral	Social	Cultural
First	*Experience: Day visit to Bolam Lake in the autumn or winter*			
Key Stage 1 and 2	◆ Exploring feelings about the natural world through asking pupils to touch, listen, smell and look at such things as frost patterns, animals, birds, wind, rain/weather	◆ Explore feelings about the environment - what do pupils like about it? What do pupils think might harm it? ◆ Ask pupils to develop their own country code.	◆ Who uses Bolam Lake? (look at gender, age, social class)	◆ Explore the use of pupils' leisure time. ◆ Would they come to the lake in their spare time? ◆ What else would they do?

Figure 20.1

Phase	Spiritual	Moral	Social	Cultural
Middle	**Experience: A journey down the Tyne or Tweed using Canadian canoes**			
Key Stage 3	♦ Give pupils the opportunity to express their feelings in response to the experiences of the day such as: ♦ - dawn and dusk ♦ - reflections on water ♦ - the power of water ♦ - the exhilaration of movement ♦ - individual or group achievements (this can be done through discussion, a private diary, painting, poems, music) ♦ Through team building and shared experiences create opportunities for empathy.	♦ Use casual opportunities as they occur for discussion about the way in which different groups use the river, e.g. anglers, canoers, those who dump waste, the water authority. ♦ Development of behaviour which is responsible and appropriate in the group.	♦ Riverside settlements: ♦ - why do people choose to live by rivers? ♦ - who owns the land and the river bank and the river itself?	♦ How is life on the move different from normal life? ♦ Develop questions about needs, wants and material possessions. ♦ Compare with other cultures - e.g. nomadic.

Phase	Spiritual	Moral	Social	Cultural
High	**Experience: An overnight expedition on foot either in the Lake District or the Cheviots**			
Key Stage 3 and 4	◆ Opportunities to express feelings in response to the experiences of the day such as: ◆ - inversion clouds in a valley bottom ◆ - rare animals encountered. ◆ Reflection on and talk about: ◆ the human spirit of endurance ◆ how a shared experience can heighten spiritual response to it.	◆ Develop questions about land use and access in the Lake District/ Cheviots. ◆ Opportunities to discuss responses to potential situations such as: ◆ - one of the group is 'frozen' on a rock face and cannot move ◆ - one of the group is too tired to keep up with the rest of the group.	◆ What types of group use the Lake District/ Cheviots for leisure time? ◆ What impact does this have on local residents?	◆ Who uses the Lake District/ Cheviots? ◆ What changes have occurred over time? ◆ (refer to social changes/ changes in mobility)

Figure 20.3

Teaching and learning styles

The appropriate teaching and learning styles necessary to promote the spiritual, moral, social and cultural development of pupils are no less important in areas of outdoor experiences than in the more traditional areas of the curriculum. Outlined below are some broad teaching approaches and learning strategies which support the spiritual, moral, social and cultural development of pupils whatever the topic, focus or subject under consideration.

Spiritual, moral, social and cultural development is supported when pupils:

- have time to reflect;
- are encouraged to pose questions;
- have the opportunity to explore and discuss grey areas;
- have the opportunity for individual and group work (see section on group work);
- take the initiative;
- express their feelings and opinions;
- are curious;
- ask questions;

and when teachers:

- plan work so that pupils are allowed choice;
- create a secure and trusting ethos in which pupils feel trusted and valued;
- allow time for the expression of feelings;
- are flexible enough to allow a lesson to follow pupils' interests and respond to pupils' curiosity;
- respond to 'here and now' events which occur in the classroom, in the school, in the locality, nationally and internationally;
- challenge stereotyping and prejudice and encourage pupils to do so.

Group work

Group work can contribute significantly to the social development of pupils and to a lesser degree their spiritual, moral and cultural development. Careful attention to the process of group work is needed if pupils are to develop from their work in groups. Effective group work helps pupils to improve their listening skills, helps them to explain and clarify their ideas, encourages pupil confidence and assertiveness and widens and deepens understanding of the attitudes of others in the group. The checklist outlined gives some suggestions for teachers to help plan and carry out small group and whole class group work effectively.

Pupils should understand that during group work:

♦   all contributions will be valued; everyone has a right to express her or his opinion without fear of being laughed at or shouted down;

♦   everyone will be listened to;

♦   only one person may speak at a time;

♦   no-one has to speak if they do not want to;

♦   everyone helps each other.

Group work should be organised so that:

♦   pupils have the chance to work with a wide range of their peers;

♦   pupils have the chance to lead the group.

Teacher interventions in group work should:

♦   encourage talk between pupils and not just between pupils and teacher;

♦   encourage quality talk;

♦   check that everyone who wishes to contribute has a chance to do so;

♦   encourage reflection and thinking;

♦   value pupil contributions.

Conclusion

Outlined in this chapter are a number of ways in which the spiritual, moral, social and cultural development of young people can be addressed within the context of first hand learning out of doors. However, while some reference has been given to a clarification of terms with examples of good practice, teachers will need to agree with their colleagues/communities upon their own particular approach and how it reflects the unique ethos and rationale of the school or centre in which they are working.

Chapter 21

Towards a sensitivity and awareness of the natural environment

INTRODUCTION

With the overwhelming evidence of human influence upon the British countryside all around, it is difficult to imagine that much of the landscape was once entirely wild, being largely dominated by forest. The gradual destruction of this wilderness environment originally commenced soon after Bronze Age man began to create settlements and by felling trees in an attempt to cultivate some areas and exploit others for the purposes of extracting natural materials. With the arrival of the Vikings and the introduction of sheep to many parts of Britain, the wholesale decimation of our landscape took place. Progressively through the ages, partly by means of a process of exploitation, human beings have succeeded in changing the face of the natural landscape into the largely unnatural environment, much of which is in evidence today.

The unprecedented use of countryside resources by groups from education, leisure and recreation in recent times has merely accelerated the gradual destruction of large areas of once unspoiled countryside. Large scale pressures are currently being experienced in all of Britain's National Parks, and those designated areas of outstanding natural beauty, country parks, moorland and woodland environments. People's greed for additional land both for agriculture, housing, minerals and industry have caused further despoliation of large tracts of countryside on an alarming scale.

There is a modern tendency for human beings to use the natural environment entirely for their own ends and by so doing be insensitive to the consequences of their actions. The continuous destruction of the natural resources for material and economic gain may eventually lead to the complete deterioration of all areas of wilderness and natural beauty if positive steps are not taken to ensure that the balance of nature is maintained.

Rhythms of the Natural World

The natural world is a living, flowing complexity of natural forms and systems, of which we are all part. All living things, whether plant or animal, belong in a delicate ecosystem of inter-relationships. Each has evolved to play an important part in the ecology of the landscape. Historically, all aspects of nature precede the human race. We are a recent event in the cycle of evolution. We are only a small part of the natural stage. Although at one time most of the population worked upon the land, and people had to be in tune with nature or they would not be able to reap a living, this is no longer so. As people have become more urbanised much of this dependence has been forgotten. People have chosen to ignore their place in the grand plan of nature and have gone their own way.

For too long those using the natural environment, whether for economic or material gain, for leisure, education or recreation have done so with an arrogance and a disdain towards all forms of life, whether plant or animal. They have neglected to consider their place both in the pattern of evolution and their responsibility to the natural world which nurtures them.

Sadly, even some practitioners of outdoor education have been guilty of such arrogance leading to the despoilation of the countryside in order to satisfy their selfish ends. It is high time that reparation was made.

The future of our land, and indeed the world, depends very much upon people leaving behind their arrogance and disdain towards it. If the future of the natural environment is to be assured, we must strive to be at one with the other forms of life around us. Above all, we must learn humility and begin to develop an awareness, respect and concern for that rich natural heritage upon which we so depend. It could be argued that nature holds the key, not only to the many problems of the world, but also to the future of the human race. We therefore despoil our natural heritage at our peril.

Raising Awareness

All learning out of doors and awareness go hand in hand. One enhances and enriches the other. Anyone who has enjoyed journeying through, over or under an environment must have known that at its best it is accompanied by a greater awareness of nature. For example, a climber finishes his route on Troutdale Pinnacle with an indescribable feeling of liberation, of accomplishment and enlightened consciousness - that view bursts upon you - and you enjoy it ten times more than if you had been lifted to that summit by helicopter!

Underlying all approaches to learning out of doors should be the notion that teachers and leaders should strive to develop a holistic approach to teaching and learning. The task, be it a climb, a ski run or grade III river, instead of being the most important aspect of the experience should take on less prominence than the group, the individuals and indeed the natural environment in which the experience takes place. Such an approach relies very largely upon leaders distilling from the experience all learning which relates both to developing sensitivity and awareness at the person to person level, the group to person level and the effect of both the individuals and the group upon the environment and vice versa.

Responsibility

All those involved in introducing young people to the great outdoors should aim to inculcate within them a deep personal satisfaction for being in touch with different environments, their natural rhythms, the changing seasons, beauty and mystery.

Leaders should strive to teach pupils' a love of nature and a realisation that there is a life force that is far greater than the affairs of the human race. Young people are part of the natural world and in so are able to learn more about themselves and the inter-relationships of that system. Out of this awareness should develop a care and concern of the natural world to include a commitment to a conservation ethic, leading ultimately to political understanding of environmental issues locally, nationally and globally.

The natural world is a very special place. It is the nearest thing we have to a wilderness where people can escape from the hurly-burly of life to find contentment and recreation. We need to minimise the evidence of human wear and tear on the landscape and stem all development of human impact and intrusion. We must learn to see once more that the lakes, the crags, the moors, hills and forests are living, vibrant ecosystems of interdependent life of which we are a part.

The human race is not a trespasser in the natural world, we are part of it. Any damage or neglect which occurs we do to ourselves. That implies freedom with responsibility.

Bibliography

Chapter 1

Board of Education 1927	*The Haddow Report: Education and the Adolescent* London HMSO 199:210
Board of Education 1933	*A Syllabus for Physical Training in Schools* London HMSO 3.4
Board of Education 1943	*The Norwood Report: The Curriculum in Secondary Schools* London HMSO 89
Board of Education 1944	*The Education Act 1944 Section 52 s/s A Section 53 s/s 2* London HMSO 82, 85
DES (Department of Education and Science) 1966	*The Plowden Report: Children in the Primary School* London HMSO 697
DES 1972	*A Report of PE in Primary Schools* HMSO 12
DES 1975 (A)	*The Aims and Content of Outdoor Education* DES Conference Report NOM 496 Darlington Hall
DES 1975 (B)	*The Aims of Outdoor Education* Appendix C17 DES Conference Report NOM 496
DES 1979	*Curriculum 11-16* HMI Report on Outdoor Education DES Report 1979 3-7
DES 1983	*Learning Out of Doors* HMI Survey of OE Centres DES Report 1983 1-27
SC (Sports Council) 1994	*A Review of LEA Outdoor Centre Provision* Sports Council Publication

DFE (Department for
Education)
1989

The Education Act 1989
The National Curriculum
Section 22 p.41

DES
1985

Better Schools: Policies for Schools in England and Wales
Cmnd 9469
DES Publication 1985

MoE (Ministry of
Education)
1961

Camping and Education
London HMSO 41:2, 3

MoE
1963

The Newsom Report: Half Our Future
London HMSO 73, 138:7

Mortlock, C
1973

Adventure Education
Middleton Publishers
Ambleside 22

Kraft, R and Sakofs, M
1977/8

The Theory of Experiential Education
Association of Experiential Education
University of Colorado Publications

Chapter 2

YOP (Youth Opportunities
Programme)
1979

OE and Residential Education
DES Publication 7, 8

William, G.
1976

A Definition of Outdoor Education
DES Report
Course no. 650: Brathay

SED (Scottish Education
Department)
1974

Environmental Education
HMSO Edinburgh 14

NAOE (National Association
for Outdoor Education)
1970

Statement of Aims and Objectives of OE
NAOE Journal Vol. 1 no. 1.2

NAOE
1976

OE and Curriculum Development
A Private Paper
NAOE 2

NPA (Northern Panel of
Advisers)
1978

A Statement of Outdoor Education
NAOE Bulletin 78 Vol. 7:10

Hopkins, K and
Putnam, R
1993

Personal Growth Through Adventure
Fulton Publications

NCC (Northumberland
County Council)
1992

Outdoor Education in the National Curriculum
Advisory/Inspection Unit

CCC (Cumbria County
Council)
1986

Outdoor Education in the Curriculum
Paper No. 3
Advisory/Inspection Unit

DFE
1995

The National Curriculum
HMSO London

AHOEC (Association of
Heads of Outdoor
Education Centres)
1990

*Outdoor Education and the Delivery of the
National Curriculum*
Unpublished paper 1990

Chapter 3

NCC (Northumberland
County Council)
1992

Outdoor Education in the National Curriculum
Advisory/Inspection Unit1992

Chapter 4

DFE
1995

The National Curriculum
HMSO London

McNeil, C
1992

Orienteering and the National Curriculum
Harvey's Publication

NCC
1994

Outdoor and Adventurous Activities in the National Curriculum
Advisory/Inspection Unit

Chapter 5

DFE
1995

The National Curriculum
HMSO London

CMC (Charlotte Mason College)
1984

Problem Solving Activities
College Publication 1984

Rohnke, C
1985

Silver Bullets
Project Adventure Ltd.
Wilkscraft Publishers
USA Massachusetts

Rohnke, C
1977

Cowstails and Cobras
Project Adventure Ltd.
Wilkscraft Publishers
USA Massachusetts

Glover, D and Midura, D
1992

Team Building Through Physical Challenge
Human Kinetics Publishers

Chapter 6

Orgill, R
1984

"Outdoor Education"
Journal of Adventure Education
Vol. 5, p. 22

The Editor
1981

"Manifesto for Change"
Times Educational Supplement

Smith, J
1981

"Outdoor Education in the 80's"
International Congress of Health, PE and Recreation
Bulletin
Congress Report, New York, USA

CCC
1985

Outdoor Education in the Curriculum
Curriculum Paper No. 3
CCC Print Out, Kendal

Greenaway, R and
Crowther, S
1983

Active Reviewing: A Background Paper
National Conference of Education and
Development in Organisations
University of Lancaster

Spragg, D
1982

Learning to Learn
Unpublished paper
Brathay Hall Trust, Cumbria

Watson, RC
1979

Outdoor Education and the Local Environment
Unpublished MA Thesis, University of Keele

Drasdo, H
1973

Education and Mountain Centres
Tyddyn Cabrael, Denbighshire

Hopkins, D
1976

Self Concept and Adventure
Unpublished MEd Thesis, University of Sheffield

DES
1985

Better Schools
DES, London

Pinder, J
1984

Integrated Learning in the Outdoors
An occasional paper
Cumbria Education Department

Chapter 7

Longstaff, T
1950

This My Voyage
John Murray Publication

Mortlock, C
1984

The Adventure Alternative
Cicerone Press Publications

DES
1988

The National Curriculum: Science for Ages 5-16
DES Publication

Keighley, PWS
1987

Current Trends in Education and Training Affecting Outdoor Education
An occasional paper
Cumbria LEA

Kay, D
1986

TVEI Land Based Industries - Adventurous Journeys
An occasional paper
Cumbria LEA

Smythe, F
1935

The Spirit of the Hills
Hodder and Stoughton

Chapter 8

NCC   (Northumberland County Council) 1992

Outdoor Education in the Curriculum
Advisory/Inspection Unit 1992

Cooper G.
1991

The role of Outdoor and Field Study Centres in Educating for the Environment

JAEOL: 1991

SC (Schools Council)
1980

Outdoor Education in Secondary Education

SC Publications 7027 48

Chapter 9

DFE
1995

NICC (Northern Ireland Curriculum Council)

Environmental Education in the Curriculum

NICC Publication

NCC (National Curriculum Council)
1990

Environmental Education

Paper No. 7

NCC

Palmer, J
1992

Blueprints: Environmental Education Key Stages 1 & 2

Stanley Thornes Publishers

Chapter 10

DFE
1971

The Outdoor Classroom

DES Bulletin

LTL (Learning Through Landscapes)
1991

Learning Through Landscapes

LTL Publication

EN (English Nature)
1994

Schools Grants Schemes

English Nature Publication

LTL
1992

Play, Playtime, Playgrounds

LTL Publication

NCC
1990

A Northumberland Nature Diary

Advisory/Inspection Division

DFEE (Department for Education and Employment)
1995

The Revised National Curriculum

HMSO London

NCC   *Environmental Education in the National Curriculum*
1993   Advisory/Inspection Division

NCC   *Nature From Nothing*
1993   Advisory/Inspection Division

NCC   *Creating Opportunities for Developing School Grounds in the NC*
1996   Advisory/Inspection Division

Keighley, PWS   *Outdoor Studies as a Vehicle for Enrichment*
1991   *in the Primary National Curriculum*
                                  Unpublished paper, Carlisle

Chapter 11

DFE   *The Revised National Curriculum: Post-Dearing*
1995   DFE Publication

Cornell, J   *Sharing Nature with Children*
1974   Exley Publications

Cornell, J   *Listening to Nature*
1987   Dawn Publications
                                        USA, CA 95959

Cornell, J   *Sharing the Joy of Nature*

1990   Dawn Publications
                                          USA, 14618

Van Matre, S   *Sunship Earth*
1989   Institute for Earth Education
                              American Camp Association

Chapter 12

NCC   *Inspirations: Guidelines for Teachers of*
1994   *Environmental Education*
                                  Advisory/Inspection Unit

DFE   *The National Curriculum*
1995   DFE Publications

Chapter 13

NCC
1992

Outdoor Education in the Curriculum
Advisory/Inspection Unit

MOE
1963

The Newson Report
Half our future
London HMSO 73. 138.7

Hichlin P and Hunt J
1986

A Residential Course Planning Pack
Ground Work Press

Chapter 14

CCC
1986

Outdoor Education in the Curriculum
Advisory/Inspection Unit
Paper No. 3

YOP
1979

OE and Residential Experiences
DES Publication 7:8

Hitchin, P and Hunt, J
1986

A Residential Course Planning Pack
Groundwork Press

Chapter 15

HMSO
1963

Half Our Future
A Report of the Central Advisory Council for
Education

DES
1983

Records of Achievement for School Leavers:
A draft policy

Hunt, J and Hitchin, P
1986

Creative Reviewing
Groundwork Press
Meathop Fell, Cumbria

Everard, KB
1987

Developing Training Progress and Prospects
DTAG Publication

Belshaw, PE
1984
Pupil Profiles and Records of Achievement: The contribution made by outdoor and residential education
An occasional paper
DES Publication

Dulton, P and
Nichols, P
1984
All Change
A National Extension College Publication

Keighley, PWS
1983
The Role of Residential Outdoor Education in State Education
MA Thesis, Keele University

Spragg, D
1983
Learning to Learn
Unpublished paper
Brathay Hall Trust, Cumbria

DES
1975
The aims of outdoor education
DES conference Report

NOM 496

DART (Darlington Amenity
Research Trust)
1980
Groups in the Countryside
Countryside Commission Publication

SED
1980
Outdoor Education and Outdoor Centres
HMSO London

Kolb D A
1981
Towards an Applied Theory of Experimental Learning
Cooper CL Publications

Curriculum 11-16
DES
1979
A DES Report

Cheesmond, J and
Yates, J
1980
OE in the Lothian Secondary Schools
Dunfermline College of PE Publications

Sakofs, M
1978
"Proposition 13 and OE"
Journal of PE and Recreation

Strutt, B
1966
"The Influence of OB on the Personality of Girls"
PE Journal No. 58

Tosswill, R
1964
Outward Bound Students: A follow up study
University of Bristol Publications 26

Fletcher, BA
1970

Students of OB Schools in Britain
University of Bristol Publications 140

Clifford, E and
Clifford, M
1967

"Self Concept Analysis Before and After
Survival Training"
Journal of Clinical Psychiatry No. 6

Jickling, R
1977

"The Effects of an OB Course"
*Journal of Physical Health Education and
Recreation* No. 40

Payne, J, Drummond, A
and Lunghi, M
1970

*"Changes in Self Concept of Participants of
an Antarctic Expedition"*
Journal of Ed. Phy. No. 40

Heaps, R and
Thorstenson, C
1973

"Self Concept Changes in Survival Training"
Journal of Therapeutic Rea. No. 7

Becker, J
1960

"The Influence of Residential Camping on Participants"
Journal of Ed. Phy. No. 51

Kaplan, R
1974

*"Psychological Benefits from Outdoor
Challenge Programme"*
Journal of Environmental Behaviour No. 6

Wood, D and
Cheffers, A
1978

"Analysing Adventure Education Through
Interaction Testing"
FEIP Bulletin No. 38

Jones, G and
Carswell, R
1975

"An Affective Evaluation of the Outdoor
Education Experience"
Journal of Education and Recreation No. 46

Chapter 16

HMSO
1963

Half Our Future
A Report of the Central Advisory Council for Education

DES
1983

Records of Achievement for School Leavers
A draft policy

Balogh, J
1983

Profile Reports for School Leavers
Longman: Schools' Council Publication

Keighley, PWS
1985
Using the Potential of Outdoor Education as a Vehicle for Integrated Learning
An occasional paper
Cumbria County Council Education Department

Belshaw, PE
1984
Pupil Profiles and Records of Achievement: The contribution made by outdoor and residential education
An occasional paper
DES Publication

Dulton, P and Nichols, P
1984
All Change
A National Extension College Publication

Keighley, PWS
1983
The Role of Residential Outdoor Education in State Education
MA Thesis, Keele University

Spragg, D
1983
Learning to Learn
Unpublished paper
Brathay Hall Trust, Cumbria

Gregory R
1988
Pupil Profile and records of achievement in outdoor education
Unpublished paper
Sedburgh, Cumbria

Chapter 17

NCC
1994
Using a Residential Centre for Geographical Investigations
Advisory/Inspection Unit

NCC
1992
Outdoor Education in the Curriculum
Advisory/Inspection Unit

CCC
1985
Outdoor Education in the Curriculum
Paper No. 3
Advisory/Inspection Unit

Angus P & Jackson D
1994
Primary Geographical investigations in a Residential Situation
Unpublished paper 1994

Chapter 18

Mortlock, C
1984
The Adventure Alternative
Cicerone Press, Cumbria

Priest, S
1989
"Teaching Outdoor Adventure Skills"
Journal of Adventure Education

Vol. 6, No. 4

Bunyan, P
1991
"Making the Most of our Teaching"
Journal of Adventure Education Vol. 8, No. 1

Hammerman, D
1989
"The Enquiry Discovery Approach to Learning in Adventure Education"
Journal of Adventure Education

Vol. 6, No. 2

Keighley, PWS
1986
"Using Outdoor Education as a Medium for Experiential Learning"
Journal of Adventure Education

Vol. 2, No. 6

Brandes, D and Ginnis, P
1986
A Guide to Student Centred Learning
Basil Blackwell Publications

HMI
1992
Outdoor and Residential Education in the National Curriculum
HMI Conference Paper (Charlotte Mason College)

NCC
1993
Outdoor Education in the Curriculum
Advisor/Inspection Unit

DES
1989
T.G.A.T Report on "Assessment"
Paragraph 5 page 10
HMSO London

Chapter 19

NCC
1993
Maintaining the Balance: Early Years Education
Advisory/Inspection Division

Keighley, PWS
1992
A Consideration of Teaching, Learning and Assessment Styles in the National Curriculum
Unpublished paper

OFSTED (Office for Standards in Education)
1994
A Framework for the Inspection of Schools
HMSO, London

Chapter 20

NCC
1995

Spiritual, Moral, Social and Cultural Development
Advisory/Inspection Unit

OFSTED
1994

A Framework for the Inspection of Schools
HMSO, London

NCC
1993

Spiritual, Moral, Social and Cultural Development
A discussion paper
Advisory/Inspection Unit

Chapter 21

Cornell, J
1987

Listening to Nature
Dawn Publications
USA, CA 95959

Carson, R
1962

Silent Spring
London: Paladin Press

Schumacher, EF
1974

Small is Beautiful
Abacus Publications

Watch
1984

A New Way of Exploring Nature
Watch Publication
Nettleham, Lincoln

About the Author

Pat Keighley grew up exploring the natural environments surrounding his home and village in North Yorkshire from a very early age. He was brought up through a tradition of journeying out of doors, by his parents and developed a love of nature and of the natural world largely through his father's encouragement. By the age of 20 he had built his own canoe and sailing dinghy and undertaken many ventures both in the Lake District and in Scotland. Since then he has participated in several mountaineering expeditions in Europe, particularly the Pyrenees and the Alps, in East Africa and in Scandinavia.

After a period working for Outward Bound and for VSO in Nigeria in the late 60's, he returned to this country to commence a teacher training course where he specialised in physical education and geography. Upon appointment to his first teaching post at a large High School in South Yorkshire, he quickly set about developing a programme of outdoor education for ROSLA pupils and was instrumental in establishing the school's own outdoor education centre in the Craven Dales.

Seeking promotion and the opportunity to embark upon further studies, he was appointed to Stanley Head Outdoor Centre in Staffordshire in 1976. During this time he undertook to develop the Centre's curriculum and was successful in qualifying for a master's degree through a research project. The focus of his study was to examine the role of outdoor education in state education.

After seven years of teaching in Staffordshire, Pat was appointed to the post of Advisory Teacher of Outdoor Education in Cumbria. During this time he initiated several innovations in the areas of curriculum development, safety, in-service training and in the exploration section of the Duke of Edinburgh Award Scheme. In 1989 Pat was appointed as Inspector/Adviser of Outdoor and Environmental Education for Northumberland County Council.

Although the whole area of outdoor education nationally has come under enormous pressures in recent years, largely due to the inadequate arrangements of government funding for local education authorities, Pat remains committed to and optimistic about the value and purpose of exposing young people to the great outdoors. In his private life he remains active in hill walking, sailing and canoeing. He enjoys the challenge of solo journeying and of alpine and Nordic skiing. He has a passionate commitment to the preservation of the natural environment and in particular the conservation of ancient native woodland. He lives with his wife and two children on the flanks of the Simonside Hills.